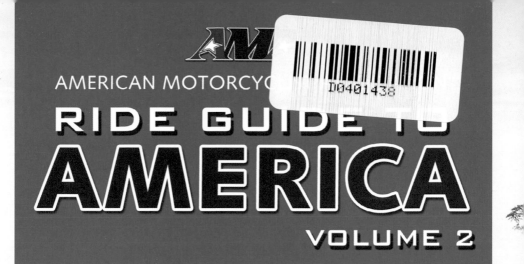

AMA
AMERICAN MOTORCYCLIST
RIDE GUIDE TO
AMERICA
VOLUME 2

Whitehorse Press
Center Conway, NH

Between the Mountains, The Killer Ride, To Da Yoop, Ohio's Twisty Roads, The Great River Road, The Other Ozarks, The Dead Zone, and Oregon's Coast Highway; Copyright © 2003-2008 by The American Motorcyclist Association/American Motorcyclist. Reprinted from *American Motorcyclist* with permission.

Mt. Desert Island Loop, Edge of Wilderness Loop, Western Notches Loop, Northeast Kingdom Loop, and Lake Placid Loop; Copyright © 2003 by Martin C. Berke. Reprinted from *Motorcycle Journeys Through New England* with permission.

Monument Valley, Highlander Loop, New River Gorge, and Them's The Breaks; Copyright © 1995, 2004 by Dale Coyner. Reprinted from *Motorcycle Journeys Through the Appalachians* with permission.

Top of the Rockies, Up the Staircase, Sedona and Mormon Lake Loop, and Lewis and Clark Country; Copyright © 2006 by Toby Ballentine. Reprinted from *Motorcycle Journeys Through the Rocky Mountains* with permission.

Riding the Viper, Riding Florida's Mountains, and Natchez to Windsor Ruins; Copyright © 2007 by Scott Cochran. Reprinted from *Motorcycle Journeys Through the American South* with permission.

The Enchanted Circle, and Organ Pipe to Saguaro Trail; Copyright © 1994, 2008 by Martin C. Berke. Reprinted from *Motorcycle Journeys Through the Southwest* with permission.

Presidio to Marfa, Copyright © 2009 by Edward N. Davis. Reprinted from *Motorcycle Journeys Through Texas and Northern Mexico* with permission.

Joshua Tree National Park, Via Lassen Volcanic National Park, and Sonora and Tioga Passes; Copyright © 2007 by Clement Salvadori. Reprinted from *Motorcycle Journeys Through California & Baja* with permission.

Wilderness Breakthrough, and Lower Columbia Basin Sampler; Copyright © 2005 by Bruce Hansen. Reprinted from *Motorcycle Journeys Through the Pacific Northwest* with permission.

Photo credits: Cover photo by Sylvia Cochran; pg. 62 and 112, photos courtesy of the American Motorcycle Association; pg. 1, 150, 194 and 198, photos by Toby Ballentine; and pg. 222, and back cover photos by Bruce Hansen.

We recognize that some words, model names, and designations mentioned herein are the property of the trademark holder. We use them for identification purposes only.

Whitehorse Press books are also available at discounts in bulk quantity for sales and promotional use. For details about special sales or for a catalog of motorcycling books and videos, write to the publisher.

Whitehorse Press
107 East Conway Road
Center Conway, New Hampshire 03813
Phone: 603-356-6556 or 800-531-1133
E-mail: CustomerService@WhitehorsePress.com
Internet: www.WhitehorsePress.com

ISBN 978-1-884313-79-0

5 4 3 2 1

Printed in China

Books in the Motorcycle Journeys Series
from Whitehorse Press:

Contents

THE SOUTHWEST 151

THE NORTHWEST 223

Foreword

By Rob Dingman

Members of the American Motorcyclist Association (AMA) love to ride. And so do you.

The *American Motorcyclist Association Ride Guide to America, Volume 2,* is for you. It is a collection of riding stories from top *American Motorcyclist* magazine editors and some of the best motojournalists in the country. We hope the stories will not only entertain you, but will inspire you to set off on your own motorcycle journey.

Great rides don't always involve exotic locations. Some of the best riding you'll ever do may be on an obscure road just a few miles from home. Use the tours and stories in the *AMA Ride Guide to America* as a departure point for your own travels, and you're sure to create motorcycling memories for a lifetime. Then, write up your adventures and send them to us, along with high-resolution images, to submissions@ama-cycle.org. Who knows, we may include them in an upcoming issue of the magazine or on the website!

The AMA is synonymous with riding and promoting all things "motorcycle." In *American Motorcyclist* magazine and at www.American-Motorcyclist.com, we shine a spotlight on our members and the motorcycling lifestyle. Whether racing, cross-country touring, trail riding, or riding around the block, we all share a common bond created by the distinct culture of American motorcycling—a culture that we preserve for future generations in the AMA's Motorcycle Hall of Fame Museum.

We are also committed to the growth of amateur racing. Through member clubs, promoters and partners, the AMA sanctions more motorsports competition events than any other organization in the world. We are dedicated to providing amateur competitors and their families, friends, and fans with exciting and enjoyable racing events that reinforce the love of riding.

Our core responsibility at the AMA is protecting your right to ride. Our Government Relations Department—with staff in Washington, D.C., Pickerington, Ohio, and on the West Coast—is on top of the issues that threaten our lifestyle. Motorcycling is constantly under assault from those who would deny us access to publicly funded trails and HOV lanes on Interstates, single us out for selective enforcement of traffic laws and equipment regulations, discriminate against us in health-care regulations, and impose on us unreasonable mandates. Together with the active volunteer support of our 300,000 members, we advocate for our rights in the halls of local, state, and federal government, the committees of international governing organizations, and the court of public opinion.

The AMA is dedicated to all these things, and more. Plus, we provide our members with the best benefits possible to save them time and money.

So read this book, pull out your map, run your finger along a squiggly line that looks like it would be a great road to ride, and then pack up, hop on your bike, and take off. The sights, sounds, and people you come across on your journeys will provide you with experiences that only a motorcyclist can appreciate.

Because we love to ride.

Rob Dingman
President and CEO
American Motorcyclist Association

THE NORTHEAST

Between the Mountains

Text and Photos by Bill Kresnak

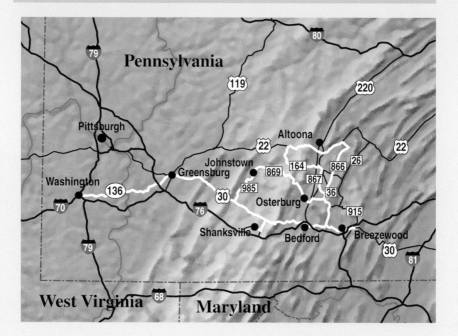

I TAP THE front brake on the Honda Interceptor, click it down a couple gears, then bank left into the Mingo Creek County Park just outside Washington, Pennsylvania. The Ebenezer Church Bridge, one of two covered bridges in this 2,600-acre park, quickly comes into view, its bright red siding harkening back to a time when life was simpler, and slower. It's a past I hope to explore more fully over the next few days.

I stop, put the sidestand down and take some time walking through the bridge, contemplating my ride ahead. I'm headed through the heart of central Pennsylvania. It's hilly country, bordered by some of the most rugged mountains in the East. But it's also home to remnants of history that always seem to hang on in rural landscapes long after they disappear from more populated places.

Like this covered bridge, for example.

Built in the late 1800s over a creek located several miles away, it was moved here 30 years ago by preservationists. Some legends tell of bridges being covered to ward off evil spirits or safeguard livestock driven across them, but the truth is probably far more mundane. After all, what would keep damaging rain and snow off the wooden bridge better than a roof?

The Ebenezer Church Bridge harkens back to simpler times.

The bridge is a reminder of what transportation used to be like in this area. And although I'm aboard a much-more-modern vehicle than the wagons this bridge was built to accommodate, I can appreciate the history that got me to this spot.

I'm in search of relics from various eras, beginning in the time when farmers tilled their fields with horse-drawn plows, through the Age of Steam, when train transportation forced engineers to come up with creative routes through Pennsylvania's mountains, on to the time when the popularity of cars led to the creation of the Pennsylvania Turnpike—and the abandonment of part of it.

But first, I'm headed to one of the best motorcycle rallies in the East.

I hop on the Interceptor and ride east along state Route 136, which swoops and turns in the general direction of Johnstown and the Thunder in the Valley Rally. I pass through a countryside of dairy farms and horse pastures, looking remarkably like they might have 100 years ago. In Greensburg, I pass the gold dome of the Italian-Renaissance-style county courthouse, towering 175 feet in the air. It was built on the location of the original log-cabin courthouse, way back in 1797.

Not far away, at Jacob's Creek, is the spot where local historians claim the world's first suspension bridge was built. County boosters note that the structure, built right at the turn of the 19th century, was an amazing 70 feet long.

The Thunder in the Valley rally in Johnstown is a family friendly affair.

The closer I get to Johnstown, the more motorcycles I see. Soon, there are so many that by the time I reach the city limits, we're not even waving to each other anymore.

I ride straight to the rally site at a park in the center of town to check out the scene at the Thunder in the Valley, which is an AMA Regional Convention, part of the AMA Premier Touring Series, presented by Dunlop.

Bikes are everywhere, with motorcyclists cruising the roads and bikes filling every parking space along the streets. Vendors sell county-fair-style food right next to helmets and chaps. The rally has all the usual attractions: bike shows, bands, demo rides, and more. But its location in the center of town adds a different audience, as quite a few locals—grandparents, parents, and kids—are checking out the activities.

Johnstown, of course, is known for much more than a motorcycle rally. In 1889, heavy rain caused a dam to break 14 miles upstream, sending 20 million tons of water roaring down on the town in a wall that was 60 feet high in places. More than 2,200 people died in what became known nationally as the Johnstown Flood.

Locally, that devastation is known as the great flood, since Johnstown is prone to periodic flooding. In fact, one of the town's main attractions, the Johnstown Inclined Plane, played a major part in a subsequent flood in 1936.

The inclined plane is essentially an 896-foot railway up a 35-degree slope —making it the world's steepest railroad, according to the Guinness Book of World Records. Construction began in 1890 to help supply a hilltop mining community, and the incline ferried more than 4,000 people to high ground during the flood in the '30s. You can still ride it today, and a lot of rally-goers do just that.

Of course, the true riding highlight of the rally consists of the magnificent roads to be found in the area. And if you're looking to sample the best twisty roads between the mountains in central Pennsylvania, you could do a lot worse than Thunder in the Valley.

Looking for good pavement, I point the Honda out of town, and come upon a fun road called, aptly enough, Mile-High Road. It's a twisty roller-coaster ride up and down through dense forest and past horse pastures. I spend miles climbing mountain slopes, traversing valleys, and enjoying some great twisties.

Ahh, nirvana.

Near Osterburg I come across the 90-foot-long, almost-120-year-old Bowser Covered Bridge. Then it's back to the curvy world on Pennsylvania Route 869, a great find of a road, with tight, tree-covered turns.

When the road hits a T-intersection at state Route 36, I look ahead and see the tallest old-style farmhouse I have ever seen. Turns out this five-story stone home has been inspiring awe since it was built in 1812 by John Snider to house his 11 children and their families. It has 25 rooms and 16 fireplaces. For a time, the fourth floor even served as a tavern for passing travelers.

Eventually, I reach the outskirts of Pennsylvania Dutch Country, the nation's most famous Amish Settlement, where life seems slower, and the towns are much closer together.

I know I've arrived when I begin to see farmhouses that have no power lines stretching out to the road, a sure sign of people who live life as it was in an earlier age.

The other obvious sign comes in the form of Amish buggies on the roads. I pull in the clutch and coast past, so I don't scare the horses, then wave to people who also appreciate an alternative style of transportation.

When progress came to this area in the 1800s, it arrived by rail. Steam engines made it possible to transport goods and people farther and faster than ever before. And the center of that industry, then and now, is the bustling town of Altoona.

It's very evident riding into Altoona that I've left the peaceful countryside behind, much like trains left behind the buggy age in the 1800s.

Altoona was home to the Pennsylvania Railroad's locomotive construction operations, maintenance and repair shops, and testing facilities well into the 20th century. In fact, in the

This stone home was built in 1812 by John Snider for his family, including 11 children, and his children's families.

It's easy to get away from it all in Pennsylvania farm country.

1920s, more than 15,000 workers were employed at the company's Altoona works. And over several decades, more than 6,000 steam locomotives were built here.

I thread my way through the streets of Altoona and park the Honda at the Railroaders Memorial Museum. It shows how locomotives were built, how crews maintained the tracks, how they cleaned up wrecks, and more.

It also serves as a showcase for what may be the most opulent railroad car of the era, the Loretto, a private Pullman car owned by Charles M. Schwab, who headed up Carnegie Steel, U.S. Steel and Bethlehem Steel. It was built in 1917 at a cost of $151,000—nearly $2.7 million today.

While the museum is interesting, there's a living, working piece of railroad history halfway up the side of the mountains to the west: the spectacular Horseshoe Curve.

A short ride up steep roads brings me to a park at the curve just in time to hear a long, piercing whistle. There, rounding Horseshoe Curve, is a long freight train, pulling slowly up the curve's steady grade.

Horseshoe Curve and the nearby Gallitzin Tunnels were engineering marvels of the mid-19th century. Engineers faced the challenge of getting trains over the steepest grades of the Allegheny Mountains. And their answer was to route the tracks around the perimeter of a natural bowl in the mountains, allowing trains to gradually gain altitude.

TRAVELOGUE: NORTHEAST

Some 50 trains a day still roll on these tracks, on a route that leads to the Gallitzin Tunnels, the highest and longest tunnels used by the Pennsylvania Railroad. Together, they are 3,605 feet long.

As I watch another train slowly work its way around Horseshoe Curve, I think about how amazing it is that this original route is still in use. It's like a modern interstate that follows the course of an old stagecoach route.

Which leads naturally to my next stop.

America's love affair with the car led to famous roads crossing the nation like Route 66, the National Road, and the Lincoln Highway. But when it comes to the nation's interstate system, none is more famous than the Pennsylvania Turnpike, which opened in 1940.

Based loosely on the German Autobahn, the Pennsylvania Turnpike was the country's first long-distance, limited-access highway.

Of course, when you're creating something brand new, you don't always get it right the first time. And that was true of the Pennsylvania Turnpike, which originally had four fast lanes of traffic feeding into tight, two lane mountain tunnels at several locations. By the late '50s, traffic jams at those locations forced the turnpike authority into action, and several tunnels were "twinned" to create four lanes. But one location near here, a 13-mile stretch of the original turnpike, which included two tunnels, was abandoned. And it's still there.

The road leading to the abandoned stretch of Pennsylvania turnpike is not an easy one.

I point the Interceptor back through farm country toward Breezewood. At the edge of town, I stop to check my notes, and find my way to the Ramada Inn. A short walk down a gravel road takes me to a small, maybe eighth-mile stretch of the abandoned Turnpike.

The congestion of Breezewood makes this seem more like a parking lot than an abandoned stretch of historic highway. So I go off in search of another segment.

An abandoned stretch of the Pennsylvania turnpike.

Heading down U.S. Route 30, I turn onto state Route 915 and then onto a gravel road that passes under the current Turnpike. Once on the

There are twists around every turn.

rugged, narrow road, I'm in dense forest, going down on a steep grade. It's a tricky descent, but the trip is worth it.

I park the machine and gingerly step down an embankment on the side to find myself smack in the middle of a stretch of the abandoned Pennsylvania Turnpike that disappears into trees in either direction.

It's quiet, but as I stand there, I imagine how, at one time, cars would have been speeding by in both directions. Now, the asphalt is crumbling, the dividing lines are gone, and the only traffic consists of the occasional hiker or bicyclist.

It's getting late, but there's one last stop I need to make before I end my Pennsylvania adventure. This one has nothing to do with horse-drawn buggies, trains, or even automobiles.

Instead, it's the location of an airplane tragedy.

I head west on U.S. 30. About 25 miles past Bedford, I make a left on Buckstown Road. I pass open fields that give the area a desolate, lonely feel.

I find Skyline Road, tap the brakes, downshift, and make the turn. There, about a mile down the road, I find it: the temporary Flight 93 National Memorial near Shanksville.

Everyone knows the story of the September 11 hijackers who crashed three commercial passenger jetliners into the twin towers of the World Trade Center in New York City and the Pentagon in Arlington, Virginia.

A fourth plane, United Flight 93, was hijacked while flying from Newark, New Jersey, to San Francisco.

The hijackers took control of the plane over eastern Ohio and diverted it toward Washington, D.C., apparently with plans to plunge it into either the nation's Capitol or the White House.

Passengers aboard Flight 93 learned of the attacks on the World Trade Center and the Pentagon, and decided to risk their lives in an attempt to regain control of Flight 93.

The passengers made their move, and the hijackers plunged the plane into a Pennsylvania field rather than be overpowered. If the plane had stayed in the air, no one knows what additional destruction would have resulted. Even

Tokens of sorrow and gratitude left at the Flight 93 Memorial.

a minute more would have put the crash site right on top of an elementary school in Shanksville.

I stand at the site, which will one day be home to a permanent memorial. I look across the field at the American flag where the plane crashed. At the memorial plaques in the ground donated by motorcycling groups and others. At the patches, pins, and other tokens of sorrow and gratitude left on a chain-link fence.

A message from Shanksville Elementary School students.

And then a little yellow toy plane on the fence catches my eye. It contains a message from Shanksville elementary school students that reads:

"Thank you for giving your lives and for not hitting our school."

It's late, and I should be going. But it seems disrespectful to hurry.

1 Mt. Desert Island Loop

Text and photos by Marty Berke

- **DISTANCE** *61 miles*

- **HIGHLIGHTS** *Open ocean, seawall and coastal riding, harbors, mountains, and lake vistas*

0.0 From Mt. Desert Campground, turn left onto Route 198 north

0.9 At Somesville, turn right onto 102/198 north

3.1 Turn left onto Indian Point Road (first left after Town Hill Store)

4.9 Bear right at fork

8.9 At stop sign, go left

9.2 Bear right at fork onto Pretty Marsh Road/102 south (also called Seal Cove Road)

17.9 Stay straight to join 102A south

18.2 At stop sign go left to continue on 102A south

24.8 At stop sign go right onto 102 north

31.8 Turn right onto 198 south

32.5 (Pass Mt. Desert Campground on right)

34.4 Turn right onto Sargent Drive

38.4 Turn left at stop sign at end of Sargent Drive onto Summit Road

38.5 Turn left onto Harbourside Road/Main Street/Route 198

39.5 Turn right onto Route 3 south

42.5 Turn left to continue on Route 3

50.7 Turn left onto Route 3 (in the center of town)

51.2 Turn right onto Route 3 west

54.0 Turn left onto Crooked Road

58.8 Turn left onto 198/102 south

60.9 Turn left onto 3W/198 south

61.7 Turn left into Mt. Desert Campground

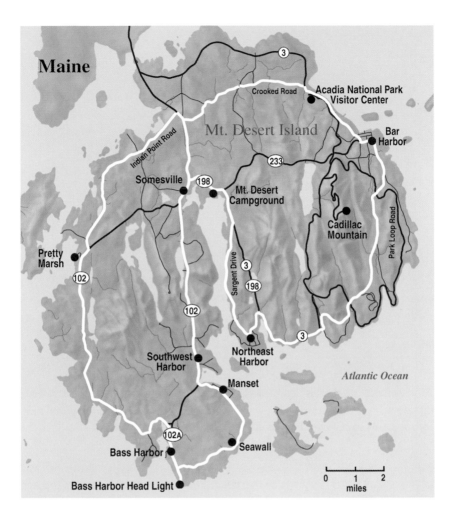

Our home base for the Mt. Desert Island Loop is the **Mt. Desert Campground** (516 Sound Drive/Route 198, Mt. Desert Island, 207-244-3710, www.mountdesertcampground.com; open June through September; 175 sites, water view upon request, reservations recommended; $29-49). Nestled at the top of Somes Sound, most sites have platforms, many sitting high above or directly on the water. The scent of the ocean and the cry of a gull reflect the journey's theme. Note: although the name of this popular area is spelled like an arid place, it is pronounced like the diet-buster.

The first chance you get upon arrival on Mt. Desert Island, pick up a copy of the *Acadia Weekly*. This free weekly publication is a combination almanac and tourist guide. It lists sunrise, sunset, high, and low tides for each day of that week. All of these will come in handy as timing, as we all know, can be of the utmost importance when visiting various island attractions. It includes

Just off Main Street and a stone's throw from Northeast Harbor's marina you'll find the Dockside, a quaint spot to grab some great coastal New England eats.

a dining and entertainment guide, suggested activities, maps, houses of worship, and, of course, advertisements from many of the fine local tourist traps. Also included are listings for the Acadia Park Ranger programs, which are a great way to see and learn more about the local ecology, geology, and history.

The western side of Mt. Desert Island has more quiet harbors and year-round residents and fewer commercial developments and tourists than the eastern side of the island with the town of Bar Harbor and Acadia National Park Visitor Center and activities. It is just this lack of attention that appeals after battling the old tourist shuffle. The road to Pretty Marsh, a local favorite, runs through the pine forest on the way to the lowlands in the west. Pretty Marsh Harbor is a very small boat launch and not much else.

Just after rejoining Route 102, you'll come to the Pretty Marsh picnic area, a serene, wooded spot on the ocean. In fact, all of Route 102 down to Bass Harbor is empty of anything retail. All the roads on the east side of Route 102 are either dirt or turn to dirt soon after you get on them. Route 102 itself has sweeping curves with a couple of hard turns and no interruptions all the way to Bass Harbor.

The only type of establishment that counts when you eat Maine lobster is a lobster pound. You will recognize a lobster pound by the billowing smoke-stacks and steam rising from large washbasins of boiling sea water.

As you enter the wooden shack, you are immediately enveloped by the aroma of chowdah, buttah, steamahs (clams), and, of course, lobstahs. The sharp cracks coming from the long wooden family-style tables tweak your interest about what's going on o' yondah.

As you approach the "order here" counter, you watch the small net bags of red lobsters returning from their fate, being grabbed by . . . number four! The menu is a la carte, written on the blackboard. You buy your soft drinks, corn, butter, and bread individually.

When it's your turn, address the cooler or salt-water trough with your index finger poised, and begin the hunt for your main course. Focus, aim, aannd . . . point. You order and buy the lobster by the pound (make sure it's hard shell because they molt). Two pounds is a good meal, three is glut-tonous, four is a massacre (and a tougher tasting bird).

The wait person will net and bag your choice, give you a number, carry your catch to the salt-water vats you passed on the way in, and drop them in. You'll get a call in about 12 to 15 minutes. You will receive your lob-ster in a baking pan similar to a corn bread pan. This is your dinner plate. Tear off the claws, grab your nut-cracker, and join the cacophony of the dining room. There is meat in the claws, in the knuckles attached to the claws, in the small eight legs, inside the body at the junction of the small legs and body (don't eat the gray fi-brous pieces, they're the lungs), and in the tail. Don't forget the five little fantails. It is a messy, sensual experi-ence, and everybody gets into it. There is usually a communal sink in the dining room to hose yourself down. *Bon appetit!*

The **Bass Harbor Head Light**, the southernmost point on Mt. Desert Is-land, is anticlimactic compared to others but is easy to get in and out to see.

Staying on Route 102A brings us to my favorite spot on this loop. The **Ship Harbor Nature Trail** is a 1.6-mile nature trail that opens up on the sea. The point faces south for sunning and the pink granite rocks are flat. The rocks where you sit seem to be contoured to your body. It's a good spot to nap, especially after breakfast and a stroll, with the sun warming your bones. The loop is short enough that you can take time for these types of digres-sions. The tough part is getting up to explore all the tidal pools. Rocks that are underwater in any part of the tidal flow are very slippery!

Asticou Azalea gardens in Northeast Harbor can be a peaceful, relaxing way to take a break from your ride.

Route 102A continues past the **Seawall Campground,** one of two federal campgrounds in Acadia National Park. The campground gets its name from the natural seawall built up over time just up the road. The picnic area across from the campground is a good place to see this formation.

Just before the village of Southwest Harbor, on the southern shore, is Manset, a one-working-street complex of restaurants, the Hinkley shipyard, and marina. The **Moorings Restaurant** boasts a "billion-dollar view." The pier offers the same view for less money. Watch the ships in dry dock being pulled in and out of the water.

Southwest Harbor is home to shipbuilders and a Coast Guard station. Opposite the Coast Guard station is **Beals Lobster Wharf,** where you can eat a lobster roll right on the pier. Just off Main Street is the **Wendell Gilley Museum of Bird Carving.** The museum houses an impressive display of Gilley's creations along with those of other noted carvers.

Route 102 out of Southwest Harbor passes Echo Lake (good for swimming) and heads straight into Somesville, the oldest village on the island. Built at the headwaters of Somes Sound (the only fjord in the continental United States), the village has a historical society and is home to the Acadia Repertory Theater. Rounding Somes Sound and heading south you pick up Sargent Drive, which parallels the Sound. Trailers and campers are excluded from the road and turnouts make stopping easy.

As you head south on Sargent Drive, getting closer to Northeast Harbor, you can see mailboxes but no houses to go with them. Northeast Harbor is the wealthiest place on Mt. Desert Island. The harbor is the usual turnaround spot for people sailing up the Maine coast.

The Colonel's Restaurant on Main Street offers excellent food at reasonable prices. You have to walk down the alley between two buildings to get to the restaurant. I had the broiled haddock filet, a large piece of *fresh* fish on a homemade roll. The storefront is the Colonels' bakery, with outstanding desserts. The hermit (a raisin gingerbread cookie) was huge, with a strong, almost hot flavor.

Asticou Azalea Gardens, located just north of the intersection of Route 3 and 198 at the head of Northeast Harbor, is a great place to stop, stretch your legs, and enjoy one of the finest botanical collections on the island. Here you can wander along the sand paths through sunny clearings and shaded woods, along flowing streams and lily ponds, or just sit and rest upon the stone benches while taking in the sights and smells. Make sure to check out the ever-changing Japanese sand garden. This is a solemn place where you can easily get away from the rest of the world and its worries, at least for a short while. They do ask for a small $2 donation on the honor system at the entrance.

Route 3 east takes you back to **Bar Harbor** through Acadia. The road has lots of sweeping turns and twists. It is the best sustained bike riding road on the island.

Motorcyclists love the Park Loop Road with it's opportunities to stop and chat with other motorcyclists, while enjoying the scenery.

Bar Harbor is the commercial hub of the island, with many places to eat. In the evening, many establishments have live entertainment.

Geddy's on Main Street, down by the harbor, has an outdoor backyard game room and features live entertainment every night. A gift shop offering "Geddy Gear" fills the basement.

The Casino, on Main Street by the park, offers live music on weekends and a singer/guitarist on weekday nights.

The Lompoc Cafe, off Cottage Street, offers folk/mountain music. In the building next door, the cafe makes Bar Harbor Real Ale in its microbrewery. Tours are offered. The beer is very good, so plan to stay in one of the many inns or motels within walking distance if you decide to try it! The food is excellent, with a spicy hummus worth trying. The espresso and dessert bar make this a favorite late-night spot.

The Unusual Cabaret is just that. They offer fresh pastas each day with a serving of talented waiters and waitresses putting on musical plays after dinner.

And, if you really want to be *bad,* the **Chocolate Emporium,** on Main Street opposite Cottage Street, is unbelievable. The aroma, display, and the actual creation of the delights on the premises prohibit you from leaving without gorging yourself on the light chocolate, dark chocolate, and everything in between. Consider yourself forewarned!

■ For more trips in this region see *Motorcycle Journeys Through New England* by Marty Berke, available from Whitehorse Press.

The views from Precipice Trail on Mt. Desert Island are awe-inspiring. Here you can see a cruise ship docked in the harbor.

ACADIA NATIONAL PARK

Acadia National Park is the second most visited national park in the United States. More than four million people play in the park yearly. The visitor's center located north of Bar Harbor on Route 3 has an excellent topographical model of the park and sells a motorist's guide to the park's loop road that provides descriptions of points of interest along the route and a synopsis of the 13 most popular scenic spots and walking trails. The trails range from a pleasant 0.3 mile shore path along the 90-foot Otter Cliffs (I've seen pilot whales from the cliffs) to the iron rungs and ladders of the Precipice Trail.

Cadillac Mountain is named for Antonine de la Mothe Cadillac, the Frenchman who took possession of this island in the late 1600s under a grant from Louis XIV. Later he founded Detroit, inspiring the name of the prestigious automobile.

The climb to the summit of Cadillac Mountain, besides being a fun road with many switchbacks and cliff hangers, is one of the best ways to greet the sunrise and sunset. From Cadillac Mountain—at 1,530 feet, the highest point on the Atlantic Ocean north of Rio de Janeiro—you can be one of the first people in the United States to see a spectacular sunrise. You can also see a magnificent sunset over the western part of the island. The barren granite summit, open until midnight with very little traffic after sunset, offers a surreal moonscape with vistas of Bar Harbor and the Atlantic.

If your astronomical timing is right, exactly two miles up the mountain, from the entrance to Summit Road, on the left, is a lookout where I saw an orange-crimson sunset to the west and a full moon rising in the east. I didn't know whether to howl or meditate! When I returned to the summit around 11:00 p.m., the wind was rising to 35 or 40 mph. The two other people on the summit were chilled by the wind and sea air and left as soon as they arrived. As I was dressed for a 60-mph wind chill factor anyway, I stayed to enjoy seeing my moon shadow dancing to the cosmic rhythms.

Hint: when the summit is crowded, go just behind the tourist shop to a trail head. Cross over the trail to the outcrop of rocks and you will discover that the crowds are about 300 yards away in the tourist-designated summit area, and you are about five feet higher. Just in front of the radio towers, on the outcrop where you are standing, is a rock formation that looks placed. It is the U.S. Geological Marker for the summit!

2 Edge of Wilderness Loop

Text by Marty Berke and photos by Marty Berke and Ken Aiken

■ **DISTANCE** *229 miles*

■ **HIGHLIGHTS** *One of the most scenic roads in Maine (Route 201) and many miles on remote roads along the edge of the Maine wilderness*

0.0 From downtown Farmington, take Route 43 east (Allens Mills Road)

6.5 Turn left onto Route 148 north

18.2 At Anson, turn left on Routes 148 north/43 west

19.7 At Madison, continue straight on Routes 201A north/8

31.5 Turn right and continue on Route 201A

32.7 At Solon, turn left onto Route 201 north

90.2 At Jackman, turn right onto Routes 6 south/15 east

160.3 At Abbot Village, turn right onto Route 16 west

175.0 At Mayfield Corner, turn left onto Route 151 south

188.2 At Athens, turn right onto Route 43 west

190.0 At Cass Corner, bear right and continue on Route 43 west

195.8 Bear left and proceed diagonally across Route 201

203.0 At Madison, turn right onto Routes 43 west/148 south

203.5 Turn left and continue on routes 43 west/148 south

205.0 Bear left (actually a 90-degree corner) and continue on Route 43 west

212.2 At Anson, where Routes 43 and 134 split, turn left onto Route 134 south

220.3 At New Sharon, turn right onto Routes 2 west/27 north

227.2 At Farmington, bear right and continue on Route 27 north

228.7 End of tour in downtown Farmington

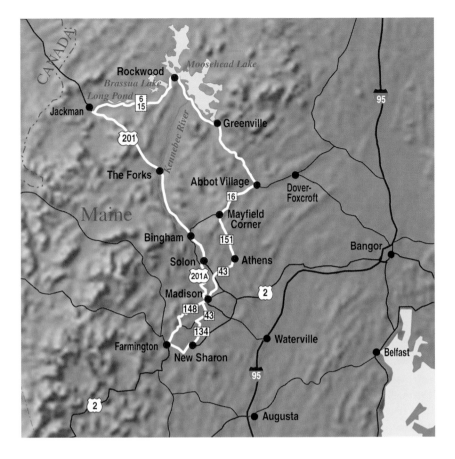

Just the mention of Maine evokes images of lobster boats, lighthouses, and a rocky coastline, but this is just a small portion of the Pine Tree State. Riding inland from the coast you discover beautiful small villages, picturesque lakes, and old mill towns. Still farther north, riders encounter the very edge of civilization and the great northern wilderness.

Farmington, the hub city for central Maine, is also one of the main campuses for the University of Maine. The vitality inherent in all college towns means plenty of good food, specialty shops, and things to do. **Twice Read Books** is one of the finest used book shops in Maine. **Reny's Department Store** is the place to pick up MyCoal heat pads for your boots, heavier socks, or whatever else you need for summer camping or chilly fall weather. All in all, it's a particularly nice place to begin or end a day of touring the countryside of central Maine.

More importantly, it's a crossroads with multiple routes spanning out in four directions. If you're not camping, stay at the **Farmington Motel,** a 1950s vintage establishment that allows your bike to be parked outside the

A view up Main Street in downtown Farmington. Being a college town, there are quite a few hotels, restaurants, and stores to provision your journey.

door. Take a load off fanny, and sit in a chair on the front walkway to enjoy the evening air.

Most of the rural roads in this part of Maine are relatively free of traffic; the scenery, especially during foliage season, is glorious. Early morning rides can be quite chilly in Maine during foliage season, and sometimes even in August. In some ways it's the best time to camp in the Maine woods, since the arrival of frost eliminates the mosquitos and black flies, which can turn an otherwise enjoyable tour into hell on earth. Two additional cautions about traveling in northern Maine: top the fuel tank often, and take the signs warning of moose very, very seriously. Moose are not mice.

Traveling on Route 43 east of Farmington the landscape seems more appropriate for Vermont. Many of the local roads in northern Maine are crowned by logging trucks much like old wagon trails. Also, shoulders of most highways are of soft gravel which, if ridden on, give you those front-wheel wobblies.

Fog, a reality in New England river valleys during the first cold autumn mornings, creates an ethereal quality to the landscape. This was certainly true for my ride along the **Kennebec River** from Anson to Solon. Electrically heated gear and heavy gloves are necessities for fall foliage riding—especially in Maine!

Route 201 is designated a National Scenic Byway and riding it will feel like a national holiday. Stop in Bingham to top off the fuel tank. The many miles of solitude also means few opportunities to gas up. Besides, on a morning when the temperature hovers just above freezing, a cup of java is almost as essential for the rider as gasoline is for the bike.

Wyman Lake is a reservoir on the Kennebec River created by the dam at Moscow. It's a beautiful stretch of highway with curves and scenic pulloffs that overlook the reservoir. The northern stretch of this river above the lake is famous for its white water rafting, and many tour operators offer a wild ride down Class IV rapids. It's also a mountain region with a multitude of hiking

There was a moose here just a couple of minutes ago. It's amazing how quickly an animal weighing up to 1,800 pounds and supporting antlers spanning five feet can just melt into the dense scrub woods. They can appear just as quickly.

trails leading off into the remote wilderness. Route 201 in conjunction with combined Routes 6 and 15 forms the demarcation line between civilization and the remote wilderness heaven of northern Maine.

When Route 201 leaves the river just above The Forks, the road begins a long climb into the mountains. Here, signs of moose (mud wallows) and signs warning of moose (big yellow signs with flashing yellow lights) become more frequent alongside the highway. Since the average adult moose outweighs a rider and heavily laden motorcycle by about five hundred pounds, pay attention to the signs and constantly scan left and right ready for an ambush.

Jackman is a small village, but a major outpost for those venturing into the backcountry. The turn onto combined Routes 6 and 15 is about a half-mile south of the village, but if you didn't top your fuel tank in Bingham, you had better consider riding into Jackman before continuing because there are only two or three small one-pump gas stations for the next fifty miles.

The vast lands of northern Maine are primarily owned by the paper companies, and the softwoods logged here are hauled south to the pulp mills in towns like Livermore and Rumford. Despite the meager "beauty strip" left along the road, the effects of clear cutting are evident and the height of the

Another beautiful spot alongside the road. Western Maine abounds with photographic opportunities.

scrub brush is an indication of how long ago the logging took place. Signs for guide services are frequent as you ride down the southern sides of Long Pond and Brassua Lake. **Moosehead Lake** is one of the largest in New England and one of the least populated. I tried to find a vantage point from which to photograph the dramatic cliff face on Mt. Kineo, an island in Moosehead Lake just north of the small village of Rockwood. This far north, trees form an important barrier that prevents drifting snow from blocking the roads during the winter and the highway department isn't about to remove them simply to provide a view for tourists.

Greenville is located at the southern end of Moosehead Lake, and besides being the region's service provider, it's a thriving summer tourist town. I stopped and enjoyed my picnic lunch at the public park and boat dock,

Maine's rural roads twist through woods, around spectacular lakes, alongside rivers, and over mountains.

In the wilderness of northern Maine the pontoon plane becomes a preferred mode of travel. Here in Greenville you can charter one of the planes to take you to your backcountry campsite.

but there are numerous restaurants, cafes, and a couple of grocery stores in the village. If you're up for a different type of touring, stop at the **Moosehead Marine Museum** and take a look at the *Katahdin,* a former steamship now converted to diesel-powered engines. Several tours of Moosehead Lake are offered, but even the shortest of them would take up the remainder of the day, so you decide.

In Abbot Village, turn right onto Route 16 west and enjoy a pleasant ride through shaded woods. Mayfield Corners is simply a name on a map where Route 151 junctions with Route 16. Not a building is to be seen, but in the middle of the nineteenth century, places like this were thriving small communities that dwindled in population and finally were abandoned as New Englanders heeded Horace Greeley's admonishment to "go west young man."

Pick up Route 43 west by the Athens General Store. It leads you into Madison and across the bridge into Anson. For 1.5 miles you'll be back on pavement covered during the morning. Route 43 west takes you directly back to Farmington.

The return to Farmington on combined Routes 2 west and 27 north is smooth as silk, and a rider can look around and enjoy the views of rolling farmland as the late afternoon sun throws long shadows across the landscape.

■ For more trips in this region see *Motorcycle Journeys Through New England* by Marty Berke, available from Whitehorse Press.

3 Western Notches Loop

Text by Marty Berke and photos by Marty Berke and Ken Aiken

■ **DISTANCE** *217 miles*

■ **HIGHLIGHTS** *Enjoy rural highways and ascents to river runs and famed tourist attractions. If you spend lots of time at the latter, the route can be easily shortened by about 40 miles. Notch roads are known for being twisty, up-and-down, scenic runs.*

0.0 From White Lake State Park, turn left onto Route 16 north

14.2 Near Conway, turn left onto Route 112 west (Kancamagus Highway)

26.4 Turn right onto Bear Notch Road

35.4 In Bartlett, turn left onto Route 302 west

66.5 In Bethlehem, turn left onto Route 142 south

71.8 Turn left onto Route 18 south

75.8 Turn right onto I-93/Route 3 south

81.6 At Exit 34A (the Flume), bear right onto Route 3 south

86.8 In North Woodstock, turn right onto Route 112 west

89.3 Turn left onto Route 118 south (Sawyer Highway)

102.2 At Warren, turn right onto Route 25C west (Moosilauke Highway)

115.8 At Piermont, turn right onto Route 10 north

124.0 Proceed straight ahead onto Route 10 north/Route 302 east

135.7 A mile or so beyond Lisbon, turn right onto Route 117 east

143.9 In Franconia, turn right onto Route 116 south

144.4 Turn right to stay on 116 south

155.6 At the junction with Route 112, turn left onto Route 112 east

202.4 Near Conway, turn right onto Route 16 south

216.6 Turn right into White Lake State Park

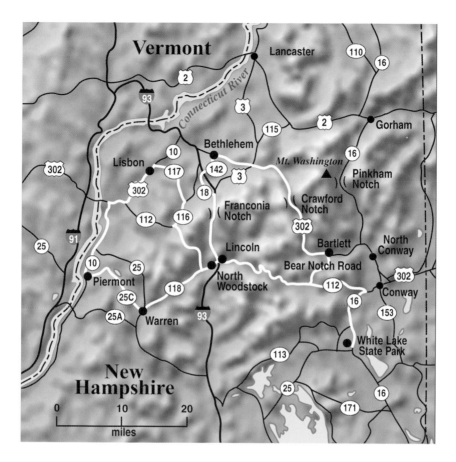

The White Mountains are located in the upper half of New Hampshire, bordering the Connecticut River and Vermont to the west and a small portion of Maine to the east. Here you will find some of the most dramatic mountain scenery in the northeast. New Hampshire is the most mountainous of the New England states. In fact, Mt. Washington is the highest peak in the Northeast (elevation 6,288 feet). There are 12 notches in the White Mountains, 11 in New Hampshire and the twelfth, Grafton Notch, in Maine. In Yankee parlance, a "notch" would be what everyone else refers to as a pass through the mountains. The early New Englanders likened these steep, rugged granite cuts to the sort of notches a woodsman's axe made in the logs he meant to use for building a cabin, and the term has stuck (or is it struck). Breathtaking in their grandeur, dramatic to drive, the notches are blessed with a variety of good roads ranging from two-lane highways to narrow locals with more curves than a snake's back.

Our base for touring the notches is **White Lake State Park** located on Route 16 south of Conway, N.H. There are many lodging places of all

New England is characterized by green fields, mountains, and picturesque white churches.

comfort levels to choose from in the region. The **Conway** area is quite a resort town, catering to both outdoor recreation and outlet shopping. There are many good restaurants, several movie theaters, and every other amenity you might be searching for, including several motorcycle dealerships. It is also home to Whitehorse Gear and **Whitehorse Press,** publisher of books and supplier of apparel and accessories for motorcycle enthusiasts.

A vital safety tip: the moose population in northern New Hampshire and Maine is growing faster than the permits to trim it; there are literally hundreds of collisions each year. You will lose the war running into a moose. These animals can weigh up to a ton! Some sound advice from the local human inhabitants about the moose inhabitants: moose are nocturnal, so limit your night riding or at least lower your speed. Unlike deer, which freeze, moose put their heads down and bolt across the road once they decide to go. Moose also tend to be long-legged, so your headlight barely catches their belly hair. The best way to spot moose is to scan the road side-to-side continuously, because they do blend into their surroundings.

This loop includes some of the best-known natural attractions in the region and quite a few notches. Prepare for a long day if you want to see everything, since the sights are usually crowded, although the facilities seem to manage the flow well. If necessary, you can shorten your ride by cutting off the last portion of the loop, depending on your sightseeing preferences.

If you wish to grab some food to have a picnic along the scenic

Kancamagus Highway, proceed about a half a mile beyond your intended turn onto Route 112 and you will find the **Chinook Café,** known locally for its sustaining and tasty wraps—a portable feast in the making. But any time of the day, you will find wonderful fare and a cozy atmosphere; consider a dinner stop, since you will be returning to the junction of Route 112 and 16 at the end of the day. Note that their Sunday brunch is a worthy occasion.

Route 112 is the **Kancamagus Highway** (locals call it "the Kanc," pronounced like "crank" without the "r"). A nationally renowned scenic highway, the road can carry heavy tourist traffic, especially during foliage season. The route will sweep and twist as it follows the meandering Swift River. On a hot day you will see plenty of ponies parked by the road as motorcyclists stop to claim a spot of their own along the tumbling banks. In about seven miles you will pass Lower Falls, a wonderful multi-level swimming hole with deep pools and cascading waters.

While the Kanc is generally in pretty good shape, you should not expect perfection. Most of these traditional mountain roads will have flaws and bumps in the pavement and you should pay close attention to the road surface. Besides, this ride should be savored, not swilled. You will be returning this way at the end of the day.

About 13 miles up the Kancamagus is **Bear Notch Road,** the first notch of the loop. The nine-mile drive north on Bear Notch Road offers several overlooks with views to Crawford Notch, Mt. Washington, and the Carter Range. This is a lovely, untrafficked stretch of sun-dappled pavement overhung with trees.

Route 302 ascends to **Crawford Notch** with wide passing lanes, so the traffic is not a bother. As the hills rise up abruptly on either side, you can clearly see the trestles of the Conway Scenic Railroad running horizontally along the steep slopes.

As the road begins to crest,

The train station in Crawford has been renovated into the Macomber Information Center.

take a break at the Crawford Notch train station and **Macomber Information Center.** Built in 1891 as an outpost for the Maine Central Railway, the depot is now used by the **Conway Scenic Railroad**, which runs tours through the notch. The newly constructed **Appalachian Mountain Club Highland Center** offers rooms, meals, and other amenities to hikers—the Appalachian Trail intersects with Route 302 here, a junction that brings together people from diverse backgrounds, all sharing in the raw beauty of the area. It makes a great 20-minute people-watching break.

As you approach the summit of Crawford Notch, the road tends to flatten. About four miles up the road, the **Mt. Washington Hotel** comes into view: an elaborate wooden structure built in the tradition of the grand hotels popular in the early 1900s here in the White Mountains. Few others have survived over the years, some falling to fire, others to the economy. Newly refurbished, this particular place was the site of the famous 1944 Bretton Woods Economic Summit, which established the International Monetary Fund and World Bank. Feel free to park your bike and wander about, soaking up the history and luxury from the veranda.

From this spot, you can enjoy a most dramatic view of **Mt. Washington,** as it seems to loom over the hotel. On a clear day, you should be able to see the towers of the Observatory building, as well as the chuffing smoke of the **Cog Railway,** as it works itself up Jacob's Ladder, a stretch of track with a grade in excess of 37 percent! Built in 1869, this mountain-climbing steam locomotive was the pinnacle of engineering technology in its day. If you'd like a closer look, take a right onto Base Road just before **Fabyan's,** the terminus of the modern Scenic Railroad.

Before you've gone too much farther on Route 302, note that the speed limit will abruptly decrease to 30 mph and you should comply: this portion of the road is heavily patrolled, as the state police station is only a few miles away.

The ride from Route 142 to Route 18 to Interstate 93 consists of small roads with little of note. Franconia Notch Parkway holds the main events in the area for tourists. The **Cannon Mountain** tramway will give you unprecedented views of **Franconia State Park** and the rugged granite peaks for which the area is known. Also located at the base of the ski area is the **New England Ski Museum,** with rotating yearly exhibits as well as videos and a permanent display depicting the history of the industry as it evolved from barrel slats and thong bindings to the high-tech equipment used today.

The natural phenomena of the Flume and the Old Man of the Mountain have been enduring tourist magnets, exploited to the hilt. They are worth going through and to; I just want to set your expectations for the six miles (Smokies are everywhere).

The **Old Man of the Mountain** is the state symbol of New Hampshire

Out of the rugged New Hampshire wilderness, the fabulous Mount Washington Hotel emerges.

and his likeness graces many things, including the highway signs you have been following. The granite visage was formed of five separate ledges that totaled more than 40 feet in height. However, in early May, 2003, the fog lifted after several days of cold, damp weather that obscured the Old Man, and National Forest personnel were aghast to find that the Old Man was gone! Millennia of hard weather had finally taken their toll and the face literally fell from the mountain. To get a good view of where it once was, you must park and walk about 1,800 feet along a broad footpath that curves around Profile Lake. You'll notice that the remaining section of Route 93/3 is a fairly claustrophobic stretch of high-speed divided highway, one lane in either direction, but it doesn't last too long.

The **Flume Gorge,** a geologic wonder, offers a spectacular walk through a natural chasm of cascading waterfalls. From this point onward, Route 3 is chockful of family attractions, resorts, cottages, and campgrounds pandering to the summer trade.

Whew! Once you make it through the Franconia Notch gauntlet, open up the throttle, accelerate out of the attractions, and head straight into the curves of our original objective. All the "100" routes (Routes 112, 116, 117, and 118) are joys to ride—twisting and turning like Chubby Checker on a cheap vibrator bed, no quarters needed! You can add two more notches to your belt

The road into Franconia Notch State Park with Cannon Mountain ski area in the distance provides you with loads of sweepers.

along the way, too. The **Oliverian Notch** can be seen from Route 25C just over Lake Tarleton. Route 112 west to Route 118 south will get you there.

If you'd like to maximize your sightseeing time, shorten the trip by 38 miles by staying on Route 112 west to 302 east. Skip the 118-to-25C-to-10 loop.

Route 10, like most major north-south roads, follows a river (the Connecticut). Unlike most river roads, which travel the floor of the valley, Route 10 sits high up, with gentle farmland fields flowing down to the river banks. This reminds me more of Vermont terrain than of New Hampshire; in fact, the opposite shore line is Vermont. Where Route 10 north joins Route 302 east, you start to veer away from the river.

About four miles up Route 10/302, you will run into the wide-spot-in-the-road that is the town of **Bath,** N.H., the Covered Bridge Capitol of New Hampshire and home of the **Brick Store,** the oldest operating general store in America, and it still manages to retain a cracker-barrel authenticity that Hollywood can't quite imitate. Original counters and glass cases display groceries and sundries, as well as their very own smoked meats and homemade fudge (free samples). A quick left behind the store has you at the threshold of the **Bath Village Bridge,** the longest covered bridge in N.H. and one of the oldest in America. Note that the weight limit for the structure is six tons, so go easy on the fudge . . .

Route 117 is a lazy road of forest and hills. When you reach the town of Sugar Hill, slow down and look for Sunset Hill Road. It doesn't matter what time of day it is; the 1,500-foot elevation atop Sugar Hill makes the view one of the sweetest. If you want to blow your budget, make reservations for the **Sunset Hill House.** Its rooms overlooking the Presidential Range and its country French cuisine will provide a lifelong memory.

Just after Sunset Hill on Route 117 is **Polly's Pancake Parlor.** If, like me, you're a firm believer that breakfast is the most important meal of the day, regardless of the hour, Polly's Pancake Parlor is a must on your list if you arrive before they close. The "parlor" was built in 1830 as the carriage shed and later woodshed to the Hildex Maple Sugar Farm. During the Depression, Polly and Wilfred (Sugar Bill) Dexter began serving "all you can eat" pancakes and waffles for fifty cents. Sixty years later, the family still lives at and manages the farm and Parlor. All the mixes are made from scratch and include whole wheat, buckwheat, oatmeal, buttermilk, and cornmeal pancakes. The grains are organically grown and are stone ground by the proprietors. Their forte though are maple products, which are toppings for the fare. (Did I mention the cob-smoked bacon?)

Upon rejoining Route 117, you will merge with Route 116 south. These roads bring you straight (figuratively, not literally) back to Route 112. Route 112, west of Interstate 93, parallels the wild Ammonoosuc River and is a much less traveled road than the Kancamagus Highway, which is the east side of Route 112. The **Kinsman Notch** is on Route 112 heading east, just before North Woodstock, N.H.

If you need to top off your human tank, you will find ample refreshment in the town of **Lincoln.** For a taste of homemade pastry and Italian treats, check out the **Wise Guy's Café** in the Mill Front Marketplace. On the left side of the plaza you'll find the **Chatroom,** a nicely appointed internet café where you can sip a fruit smoothie or a cappucino while checking your email.

When you cross Interstate 93 in the town of Lincoln, the Kancamagus begins. There are many scenic vista parking areas overlooking the Pemigewasset Wilderness, and **Kancamagus Pass** could be your sixth notch of the loop except for the nomenclature. Kancamagus, the grandson of Passaconoway and the nephew of Wonalancet, was the third and final sagamore of the Pennacook Confederacy. As you crest the height of land, you will be crossing from the Merrimack to the Saco River valley. A right turn onto Route 16 south will have you back at home base in less than 15 miles.

▪ For more trips in this region see *Motorcycle Journeys Through New England* by Marty Berke, available from Whitehorse Press.

4 Northeast Kingdom Loop

Text by Marty Berke and photos by Marty Berke and Ken Aiken

DISTANCE *206 miles without side trips*

HIGHLIGHTS *St. Johnsbury is an interesting stop on this loop, but mostly it's riding through extremely rural areas that range from cultivated land to the deep Northern Boreal Forest. The lakes, especially the ride along the shore of Lake Willoughby, are a special treat.*

0.0 Turn left onto Route 12 north leaving Elmore State Park

3.6 Turn right onto Route 15A east (Park Street)

5.4 Turn right onto Route 15 east

17.5 At the stop light in Hardwick, turn left and go one short block on Route 15 east

17.6 Turn left onto Main Street, proceed over the railroad track, then to the police station and library

17.7 Turn right onto Church Street; as you proceed, it becomes Maple Street, then Center Road

24.0 In Greensboro, turn right around Willey's Store onto East Street

24.1 Turn right onto The Bend Road

26.8 At Greensboro Bend, turn left onto Route 16 north

42.4 At Barton, turn right onto Routes 16 north/5 south

42.6 Turn left and continue on Route 16 north

49.7 Near Westmore, turn right onto Route 5A south

60.1 At West Burke, bear left onto Route 5 south

76.9 In St. Johnsbury, turn left onto Concord Avenue

77.5 Turn left onto Route 2 east

103.6 Near Lancaster, proceed straight onto Route 102 north

126.3 At Bloomfield, turn left onto Route 105 west

142.3 At Island Pond, proceed straight onto Route 114 north

145.0 Where Route 111 joins Route 114, turn left onto Route 111 north

159.5 At Derby Center, turn right onto Routes 5A north/105 west

160.0 Turn left onto Routes 5 south/105 west

164.8 In Newport, turn left onto Third Street

164.9 Turn right onto Pleasant Street

165.7 Bear left onto Route 5 south

170.9 At Coventry, where Routes 5 and 14 split, bear right onto Route 14 south

188.5 Turn right onto Branch Road, which changes to North Wolcott Road, following signs to North Wolcott

197.0 Turn right onto Route 15 west

200.7 Turn left onto Route 15A east

202.5 Turn left onto Route 12 south

206.1 Turn right into Elmore State Park

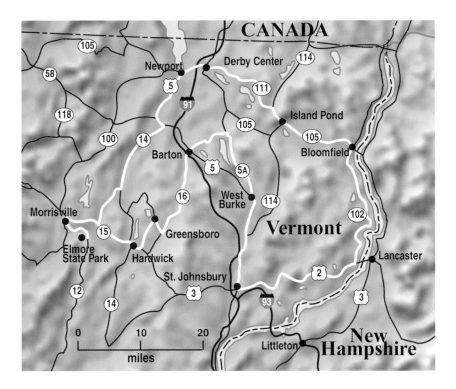

The day begins with the beautiful vistas of the northern Green Mountain Range directly ahead and the expanse of the Northeast Kingdom stretching to the horizon on your left. Route 15A is a shortcut to Route 15 east, but if your fuel tank isn't topped off, you might want to take the loop through **Morrisville** on Route 100 and attend to it now. While you're at it, get some breakfast to fortify yourself for the long ride ahead.

Soon you'll reach poor Hardwick, often the butt of crude Vermont jokes, but we're not going to stop long enough to hear any of them. After making the left turn at the blinking red traffic light, the next left turn comes up as soon as you shift into second, and you're no more over the little bridge than you're making the right turn around the library.

Greensboro is situated on Lake Caspian and this beautiful gem of clear water is visible throughout the descent into the village. Laura H. Wild, Ann Stoddard, and Silas Mason were born here and there are more than a few famous names who reside here during the summers. **Willey's Store** is a rare establishment, the true general store where you can purchase car batteries, fishing equipment, groceries, appliances, and clothing. Make a right around Willey's Store and then a right by the post office to get to Route 16.

About six miles north on Route 16, and just past Horse Pond, there is an expanse of cattails and a granite historic site marker. This used to be the site of Long Pond, but in 1810 a group of local residents decided to direct the outflow of water to run into the Barton River to help power the local mill. The trench for the new stream had been dug, but when the men tried to breech the bank of the pond they hit quicksand and Long Pond began to move. In fifteen minutes, two square miles of water rushed north with a sixty-foot-high wave front racing through the towns of Glover and Barton and continuing all the way to Lake Memphremagog. The surface water has never returned and this expanse of cattails and quicksand is now known as Runaway Pond.

Glover is best known for Peter Schumann's radical religious-political **Bread and Puppet Theater.** The theater troupe moved here in 1974 and a museum has now been established in a converted barn where their giant neo-medieval puppets are on display.

Panoramic views can be enjoyed from many of Vermont's backroads.

They may look docile and slow, but don't be deceived. Moose can move very quickly, and they do not back down if they feel they are threatened.

In Barton, Route 16 north makes a hard right turn and briefly combines with Route 5 south before breaking away crossing the railroad tracks and climbing the hill. **Crystal Lake** can be seen to the left.

Coming down to the north end of **Lake Willoughby** is an experience and you might wish to pull into the parking lot for North Beach to appreciate its beauty. Like the Finger Lakes of New York, Lake Willoughby and Crystal Lake were carved by the advancing mile-and-a-half wall of glacial ice during the last Ice Age, but only here is the cutting of the scarp plainly visible. It's also a deep and cold body of water where lake trout grow to trophy size. Stop into any of the small convenience stores along Route 5A and you'll see photos posted on the bulletin boards that define the fish that didn't get away.

Route 5A goes south along the very edge of the lake; in places it's even cut into the very sides of Mt. Pisgah. It's such a scenic stretch of highway that you'll probably want to stop three or four times just to take pictures; with

THE NORTHEAST

Looking south from North Beach on Lake Willoughby.

each turn of the road the vista seems to get more breathtaking.

The run down Route 5 will naturally feel anticlimactic after this, especially as traffic thickens close to **St. Johnsbury.** The quickest way through this city is to take a left at the second traffic light, cross over the Passumpsic River on Concord Street, and then continue east on Route 2. There are even picnic tables along the river in Fred Mold Memorial Park for a delightful break.

In 1830 Thaddeus Fairbanks invented the platform scale to weigh hemp (in those days it was used to make rope) and the Fairbanks family became very wealthy. Part of their legacy was the establishment of the (Franklin) **Fairbanks Museum,** one of the finest classic natural history museums still in existence. The public library, the **Athenaeum,** was built as a present to the city from Horace Fairbanks; the oldest unaltered art gallery in the United States is attached to it. *The Domes of Yosemite* by Albert Bierstadt, *The Views from South Mountain in The Catskills* by Sanford Gifford, and works by Thomas Waterman Wood and Asher Durand are some of the great pieces of American art to be discovered there. A rare E. Howard Street clock, which was once located in Grand Central Station, a Civil War memorial designed by Larkin Mead, stained-glass windows in the South Methodist Church by Lewis Comfort Tiffany, classic Victorian homes built by noted architect Lambert Packard, and much more are to be found along Main Street. The easiest way to reach Main Street is to bear right at the first traffic light and climb

Mt. Pisgah and Lake Willoughby seen from the South Beach along Route 5A.

Hastings Hill or to take a right turn at the second set of lights and go up Sand Hill. At the southern end of Main Street, Eastern Avenue (Route 2 east) goes down the hill, through the downtown area, and past Concord Avenue. On the way out of the city you'll notice **Maple Grove Farms of Vermont,** the oldest and largest maple sugar candy factory in the world, and a place to learn about Vermont's maple sugar industry.

The next 26 miles is a fast run to the Connecticut River. Route 2 is the main thoroughfare from Vermont to Bangor, Maine, and the traffic can be heavy at times. Continue straight, following the river north on Route 102. You'll encounter very little traffic on this road and you can have a great time on the sweepers or just enjoying the scenery. As soon as you turn onto Route 105 and leave the river, you're into the Northern Boreal Forest, a land of conifers, bogs, almost no people, and lots and lots of moose (or is it meese?). These lands are owned by various paper companies who manage and log hundreds of square miles of forest land.

The village of **Island Pond** is named after the lake on the edge of town and its 11-acre wooded island. There's a public beach and picnic tables with barbecue pits should you choose to take a break. This was once the headquarters of the Grand Trunk Railway, but the exquisite stone depot and vast rail yards are all that remain of that famous line.

Route 114 goes north into the remote woods, but turning onto Route 111 leads you around the gorgeous Seymour Lake and some of the prettiest country in the Northeast Kingdom. Touring this deserted, winding road with gorgeous views will make your day.

Newport, once a famous port on the south end of **Lake Memphremagog,** is the commercial hub of the region. Riding through the bustling downtown is like going back in time to the early 1960s. This is a downtown of owner-operated businesses and not the series of chain stores that have so frequently taken over small town commercial centers. The signs for Route 5 south are clearly posted as you ride through a residential section, but almost before you know it you're back on open highway.

A farm shrouded in morning fog east of St. Johnsbury.

Route 14 briefly merges with Route 5 in Coventry. Bear right to continue south on Route 14 along the edge of the Lowell Mountains. Slightly less than two miles south of North Craftsbury Road, turn right. This road is one known only to locals, but like most of these small town roads, it's officially known as Branch Road when heading south and North Wolcott Road when

Route 111 skirts beautiful Lake Seymour in Morgan.

going north. In local conversations it is simply called Wolcott Road. It's an enjoyable ride as the pavement follows the Wild Branch River. Finally it runs between two silos in a farmer's backyard and junctions at Route 15.

Route 15 east to Route 15A and Route 12 retrace the first few miles taken this morning, but riding in the opposite direction provides very different scenic views. Once again, the choice is yours whether to ride into Morrisville and enjoy supper or to head directly back to the campsite and cook your own.

■ For more trips in this region see *Motorcycle Journeys Through New England* by Marty Berke, available from Whitehorse Press.

5 Lake Placid Loop

Text by Marty Berke and photos by Marty Berke and Ken Aiken

■ **DISTANCE** *193 miles without sidetrips or alternate routes*

■ **HIGHLIGHTS** *Mountains and lake views, twisty roads, and an optional ferry crossing. Also, sidetrips up Whiteface Mountain and to Ausable Chasm*

0.0 Turn left exiting the Crown Point Campground

3.6 Turn right onto Routes 9N north/22 north

17.6 At Westport, bear left proceeding on Route 9N north

26.0 In Elizabethtown, turn left on combined Routes 9 south/9N north

26.5 Turn right on Route 9N north

36.5 Turn right on Routes 9N north/73 north

38.4 At Keene, bear left on Route 73 north

52.4 In Lake Placid, turn left onto Route 86 west

62.0 In Saranac Lake, where Route 86 bears right, keep left on River Street, which becomes Route 3 west after two blocks; follow Route 3 west

77.4 Turn right onto Route 30 north

91.6 At Lake Clear Junction, proceed straight onto Route 186 east

95.5 Near Harrietstown, turn right onto Route 86 east

100.1 In Saranac Lake, turn left onto Routes 3 east/86 east for one block

100.2 Turn right on Route 86 east

100.6 Bear left (River Street is on your right) on Route 86 east

110.2 In Lake Placid, proceed straight on Route 86 at the junction of Route 73

122.2 At Wilmington, turn right to continue this tour on Route 86 east, or turn left onto Route 431 for the side trip up Whiteface Mountain

127.2 At Jay, turn left onto Route 9N north

144.7 At Keeseville, turn right onto Routes 22 south/9 south, or bear left onto 9 north to Ausable Chasm sidetrip

149.2 Turn left to stay on Route 22 south

162.2 In Essex, stop at the ferry dock to take the alternate route back to Crown Point

175.2 In Westport, turn left on Routes 22 south/9N south

189.2 Turn left onto Route 8 east toward the Champlain Bridge

192.8 Turn right into the campground

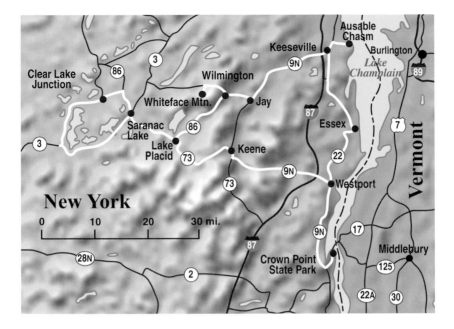

This loop is high drama from the beginning run along the shore of Lake Champlain on through the climb into the Adirondacks, an outstanding loop around Saranac Lake, the piercing of Wilmington Notch, and the conquering of Whiteface Mountain. Once on combined Routes 22 north and 9N, the highway hugs the shoreline affording great views of Vermont on the opposite shore. Just north of the village of Port Henry, you can look over your shoulder and see the arched silver bridge and the old ruins on the Crown Point peninsula. However, in the spring and fall the difference in temperature between the air and the lake water frequently creates heavy fog, obscuring these beautiful views.

At the northern end of the downtown district in Westport the routes divide, with 9N bearing to the left. Four miles farther, the highway passes under Interstate 87 and the views of the mountains to the west promise exciting riding to come. With the Adirondacks rising directly ahead, the view becomes ever more teasing as you approach Elizabethtown, where Route 9N briefly merges with Route 9 before turning west and winding its way through the mountains for the next ten miles.

On the long descent to Keene, the view of Lake Placid is obstructed by a formidable barrier of the next range of mountains, but Route 73 loops around Owl's Head Mountain and begins to climb a narrow passage through them. For several miles, the highway offers a very necessary truck-passing lane so you can get by the long lines of recreational vehicles that crawl through this pass on summer weekends. The road skims along the edge of the long, narrow Cascade Lake and the numerous pulloff areas are the most pleasant you'll find for many miles. Just beyond these small lakes are parking areas for the numerous trailheads that lead into the Mt. Van Hoevenburg State Recreational Area and to Round Lake; be alert for turning traffic and hikers.

The first indication that you're approaching **Lake Placid** will be the towers of the Olympic ski jump rising above the tree line. This small village is an international destination and the center of tourism in the Adirondack region. If you've been on the road too long and need a little culture, Lake Placid is a place to recharge your civilization batteries. There are plenty of places to eat and shop in the busy downtown area, which is designed to resemble a quaint alpine European village. There are plenty of commercial American-style offerings along Route 86 as you leave the village en route to Saranac Lake.

The loop around **Saranac Lake** is fun, with Route 3 offering long straights with some dipsy-doodles in the road. Route 30 is challenging—especially around **Fish Creek Pond**—with its 90-degree turns and twists providing excitement to contrast with the scenic beauty. The degree of difficulty, as always, is determined by your speed. The state parks on this loop (for example, Fish Creek Pond) offer swimming and camping facilities on the lake

Rainbow Falls at Ausable Chasm can be seen from the Route 9 bridge over the Ausable River.

and are great places for a picnic or to rest and savor your experience. Route 186 and Route 86 bring you back into the village of Saranac Lake where, in the middle of town, the park and picnic tables along the shore of Flower Lake offer another option for an idyllic break after hours on the road.

Following Route 86 east you once again go through the village of Lake Placid and soon are following the West Branch Ausable River into the mountains on a very twisty road. The valley keeps getting narrower mile after mile until finally there's barely enough room for both the river and the road as you ride along **High Falls Gorge** in the middle of Wilmington Notch. After passing the Wilmington Campground and the entrance to the **Whiteface Mountain Ski Area,** the valley widens a little and you'll reach the four-way intersection of Routes 86, 19, and 431.

SIDE TRIP TO WHITEFACE MOUNTAIN

If it's a clear day, you'll want to take the 15-mile side trip to the top of Whiteface Mountain. Route 431 is also called the Veterans Memorial Highway and will take you to 4,460 feet above sea level. The tollhouse is only three miles from the intersection and you'll want to check the weather conditions at the top of the mountain before plunking down your five bucks per person.

The next five miles of pavement are twisty and filled with frost heaves and dips as it climbs more than 2,300 feet in elevation. There are numerous places to turn off and park along the way, including the stunning overlook of Lake Placid and the Wilmington Turn, which at 4,300 feet affords an incredible view of Lake Champlain and Vermont. From the upper parking area an elevator transports visitors to the summit at 4,867 feet for unparalleled views of the Adirondack region. On the way back down the mountain you can practice your swerving techniques against the mogul-like frost heaves. If you're economizing, the road just

below the tollhouse to the Atmospheric Sciences Research Center (State University of New York at Albany) provides similar views, but at lower elevations. Be nice, though, since the road to the testing center is not a public right-of-way.

Several separate groups of riders have chosen to take the elevator to the summit of Whiteface Mountain.

Route 86 junctions at Route 9N in the upper Ausable Valley. Taking a left turn, follow the East Branch Ausable River to where it is joined by the West Branch in Au Sable Forks (Note: the town is spelled as two words; the river as one), then farther downstream to Keeseville. When you pass under Interstate 87, only a mile and a half remains of Route 9N and a decision whether or not to take a short side trip to visit Ausable Chasm. To ontinue south on combined Routes 22 and 9 requires a hard right turn and crossing the bridge over the Ausable River; bearing left on Route 9 leads to Ausable Chasm.

AUSABLE CHASM

Ausable Chasm is a box canyon cut through sandstone by the Ausable River. Located only a mile north on Route 9, this scenic wonder has been a popular tourist destination for decades. The canyon is privately owned property and a fee is charged for access to the maintained walkways within it, but the lofty view of Rainbow Falls from the bridge over the Ausable River (Route 9) is free.

The best find was **Harold's Bar**. Just follow the walkway out behind the tourist center, across the old bridge by the dam. Harold will provide a nonstop history since the thirties, a few times over, in the space of a cold drink. It's less expensive than the tourist center, the entertainment by Harold is free, and the horseshoe pits are beside the dam.

Two ferry crossings offer alternate modes and roads back to Crown Point. The first, just five miles down Route 373 from Ausable Chasm, crosses from Port Kent to Burlington ($5 for bike and rider and $3.50 for a passenger) and the forty-five-minute crossing is the most scenic ferry ride in New England. From Burlington, take Route 7 south to Route 22A at Vergennes to Route 17 west. The second—and, I think, better if Burlington is not your destination— is the ferry from Essex, N.Y. to Charlotte, Vermont.

Following Route 9 back to Route 22 in Keeseville, you'll ride parallel to I-87 for a few miles until, at one of the interstate highway exits, Route 22 makes an abrupt left turn and runs southeast towards the lakeshore. Vistas of the Green Mountains are plainly visible while riding down the hill, and the V-shaped notch in those mountains marks the location of the village of Bristol. After going through the beautiful village of Willsboro and following the lakeshore, you'll arrive at Essex and the Champlain Transportation Company's ferry dock for the crossing to Charlotte. The **Champlain Transportation Company** is the oldest continuous operating shipping company in the world, beginning service on the lake with their first steamship, the Vermont, in 1809. This was the second commercial steamship in existence (Fulton's North River of Clermont was first in 1807), built and operated by the original pilot of the North River. Essex is a charming little town in which to eat. The Old Dock Restaurant is surrounded on three sides by water, just within view of the ferry. Don't bother to count the number of ferries you missed.

■ For more trips in this region see *Motorcycle Journeys Through New England* by Marty Berke, available from Whitehorse Press.

The ferry, which runs every half-hour, is a pretty 30-minute ride with the Adirondacks and the Green Mountains as opposing backdrops. It's inexpensive—$4.25 for the bike and rider; $2.50 for a passenger—and it provides a break from two-wheeled transportation. (Be sure to put the bike in first gear on the centerstand and don't take it off until the ferry bumps the dock for the last time.) When you disembark, proceed on Route F-4 to Route 7 south, then Route 22A south to Route 17 east and back to Crown Point.

From Essex, the highway turns away from the lake and runs inland before turning and meandering across the agricultural landscape back to Westport. Here joining Route 9N south, it's just an 18-mile run back to the Crown Point campsite. The views of Vermont are just as spectacular when traveling south as when riding north, and if your morning ride began in the fog, this late afternoon return will reward you with previously unseen panoramic views. The view of the Champlain Bridge and the old fortifications of Crown Point are clearly visible just across Bulwagga Bay, but it's another 13-miles before pulling into the campground and the end of today's ride.

Sweeping curves and panoramic views make the climb up Whiteface Mountain a worthwhile side trip.

6 Monument Valley

Text and photographs by Dale Coyner

- **DISTANCE** *132 miles*
- **HIGHLIGHTS** *Twisty roads over and around small hills, Cunningham Falls, The Cozy, Catoctin Mountain Park, Washington Monument State Park, Antietam National Battlefield, Harpers Ferry National Historic Park*

0 Begin at town square in Gettysburg, US 15 Business South	**67.7** Left onto Keep Tryst Road
7.0 Join US 15 south toward Emmitsburg	**68.1** Left onto US 340 South
18.0 Right onto MD 77 West at Thurmont	**71.6** Arrive Harpers Ferry Battlefield Visitor's Center, then turn around
28.0 Left onto MD 64 at Smithsburg	**75.4** Right onto ramp for MD 67 North
29.1 Left onto MD 66	**80.9** Right onto Gapland Road
39.4 Left onto US 40 Alt in Boonsboro	**82.4** Arrive Gathland State Park, then continue on Gapland Road
42.3 Left onto Washington Monument Road	**82.9** Left on MD 17 in Burkittsville
43.5 Arrive Washington Monument State Park, then turn around	**103.8** Right onto MD 77 in Smithsburg
44.7 Right onto US 40 Alt toward Boonsboro	**114.0** Left onto MD 550 in Thurmont
47.0 Left onto MD 34 (Potomac Street)	**114.3** Right onto Emmitsburg Road
53.3 Right onto MD 65	**115.0** Right onto US 15 North toward Gettysburg
54.2 Arrive Antietam National Battlefield, then turn around	**125.3** Follow US 15 Business North, first Gettysburg exit
55.2 Left onto Mechanic Street (becomes Harpers Ferry Road)	**132.3** Return town square in Gettysburg

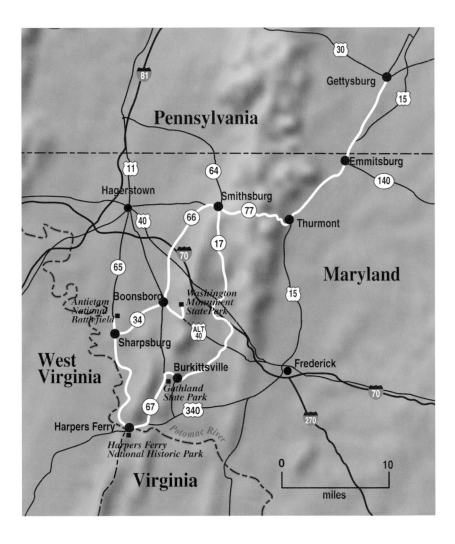

I call this loop "Monument Valley" in honor of the real Monument Valley on the Arizona/Utah border. In this case, the monuments aren't towering rock formations, but rather the memorials raised to those who served in the Civil War. This loop is relatively short in mileage because you'll want an opportunity to get off the bike and browse the museums, walk the trails, or meander the battlefields at a leisurely pace.

A good way to start is by following West Confederate Avenue out of town. You are behind Confederate lines, looking over the meadow that separated the western ridge from the town of **Gettysburg**. On the third day of the Battle of Gettysburg, in a last-ditch attempt to take the town and shift the momentum of the war to the South, General Lee hesitantly approved a bold plan to allow George Pickett, one of his field generals, to lead the Army of Northern

"Guys, follow me. I looked it up on MapQuest. Boca is definitely this way."

Virginia across the wide open expanse directly into the strongest point of the Union line. Pickett's Charge, as it came to be known, was a disaster. As the rebels marched toward the entrenched Union position on the other side of the field, a barrage of Union musket and artillery fire raked the Confederate lines. In a matter of minutes, the Rebel advance was shattered. The Union army held off the strongest offensive the Confederate states could mount. This would be the last significant invasion the Rebel army would make into Union territory, prompting historians in later years to label this battle "the high water mark of the Confederacy."

West Confederate Avenue intersects with Route 15. Take Route 15 south and stop in **Thurmont,** Maryland for breakfast at the **Cozy Restaurant** (cozyvillage.com). The Cozy is a favorite of local motorcyclists. You'll often find a group of bikes in the parking lot, especially on the weekends. On Sundays the Cozy puts out a tremendous brunch buffet that stretches 20 or 30 feet. Not only is it a huge spread, everything is freshly prepared and tastes great.

After tanking yourself and your bike up, the journey begins straight out of Thurmont into the Catoctin Mountains. Follow Route 806 north into town, make a left on Water Street, then turn left on Main Street, MD 77 west. Close at hand are **Catoctin Mountain Park** (nps.gov/cato) on the right side of the road and **Cunningham Falls State Park** (dnr.state.md.us) on the left. Route

77 threads through the middle, an inviting strip of pavement that will whet your appetite for the curves that follow. The short hiking path to Cunningham Falls is perfectly suited to working off a dozen or so of those 10,000 calories you just ate for breakfast. Don't forget to stop by the visitor center at Catoctin Mountain to get your National Parks Passport stamp.

Once Route 77 reaches the summit of Catoctin Mountain, the pace picks up as the road straightens out. It ends on the outskirts of Smithsburg. Make a left on MD 64 for a couple of miles, then another left on MD 66, then slip under the roar of Interstate 70 and pass into the rolling rural countryside of western Maryland. At **Boonsboro**, make the left turn onto Alternate 40 and follow the signs for **Washington Monument State Park** (dnr.state.md.us). Just outside of town you'll begin climbing again, this time ascending South Mountain. There are countless monuments to George Washington scattered all over the country, but the large stone tower erected on this site by local patriots in 1827 was probably the first. Enter at the base of the tower and ascend the narrow circular stairs to reach the platform at the top. From here you can see well into West Virginia across the upper Shenandoah Valley, known here as the "Great Valley." Members of local conservation groups are often present, observing the movements of migrating hawks that follow the thermals created by the mountains. You can also impress your friends by telling them that while you were at it, you hiked a portion of the Appalachian Trail on your vacation. You don't need to tell them it was only from the parking lot to the monument and back.

Return to Boonsboro on Alt 40 and make the left turn onto MD 34 toward **Sharpsburg** and the **Antietam National Battlefield** (nps.gov/anti). The Battle of Antietam marked an earlier attempt by General Lee to take the offensive in the Civil War. His goal was to capture the Union capital, Washington, D.C., which, if attained, might generate European support for and recognition of the Confederate States. Fighting between the opposing forces was ferocious. A field of corn which stood between the two armies was cut to the ground by the exchange of fire. So many soldiers from both armies

What this first monument to George Washington near Boonsboro, Maryland, lacks in design is made up for in sincerity.

fell at Antietam Creek that for a while during and after the battle, the creek ran red with blood.

The battlefield is preserved in a state much as it was when the war raged, and a series of drives allows you to tour the battlefield on your bike to see how the engagement was played out. A reenactor buddy of mine says that to this day it isn't unusual to find artifacts lying around. Once during a reenactment of the battle in the cornfield, he said that as the soldiers advanced, they could be seen stooping over. They weren't pretending they'd just been shot. They were picking up spent miniballs lying all over the ground. Of course, pocketing any artifact is a violation of federal law, so if you do see anything, I'm sure you'll just leave it alone. Before you leave, stop by the visitor center and add another stamp to your passport.

In the town of Sharpsburg, follow MD 34 into town and turn left on Mechanic Street. This becomes Harpers Ferry Road. If you've been looking for a little more riding excitement to go with your scenery, this road delivers. It's a favorite route of area riders and you're apt to meet up with a few along the way. The ride gets even twistier as you near the Potomac River at Harpers Ferry and parallel the C&O Canal Park Towpath (nps.gov/choh) for a mile or two. The towpath is great for a leisurely stroll alongside the river. Just ahead, the Potomac and Shenandoah rivers meet before turning southeast toward Washington, D.C.

A bike can always find a parking spot along the narrow strip of road that parallels the towpath. You can stop here, hike the towpath along the Potomac for a stretch, then cross the bridge at the confluence of the Potomac and Shenandoah rivers to arrive in **Harpers Ferry National Historic Park** (nps.gov/hafe). You can get yet another passport stamp here. If you'd prefer not to walk, it's also just a short ride from this point on the route.

Indisputable evidence that BMW riders do, in fact, wave.

Follow Harpers Ferry Road underneath the railroad bridge and make the left turn onto Keep Tryst Road. Before Harpers Ferry, first a lunch note. **Cindy Dee's Restaurant** (301-695-8181) is at the intersection of Keep Tryst and US 340. It's a good stop for lunch if you've been holding out.

At US 340, turn left to head south across the Potomac River crossing and into Harpers Ferry. On a nice weekend, this brief stretch will be crowded.

Pennsylvania has more covered bridges than any other state.

Once over the Shenandoah bridge you have a couple of options. For the official Harpers Ferry tour, head south on 340 to the visitor's center on the left. Plenty of parking can be had there and a shuttle bus will escort you to the historic district. Your other option is to turn right on Shenandoah Street and drive down into the historic district yourself. Parking is always an issue here, but riders enjoy a distinct advantage since you can often find a place to stash a bike.

Make the return trip by following US 340 north across the Shenandoah and Potomac River bridges into Maryland. Make the turn onto MD 67 north toward Boonsboro. Just a few miles up the road, hang a right onto Gapland Road. The ride up the mountain will bring you to **Gathland State Park** and a wealth of stories. Pull into the parking lot and hop off for a tour.

The first thing you will notice is the large stone monument. This arch, know as the War Correspondents Memorial (dnr.state.md.us), was built in 1896 by George Alfred Townsend to honor journalists of that conflict. Townsend himself was the youngest correspondent of the Civil War and later he was considered an important writer of the Reconstruction Era. Townsend

The War Correspondents Memorial Arch near Burkittsville, Maryland, brings the word "Eclectic" to mind.

designed and constructed many buildings at this retreat. Some have fallen into ruin while a few structures, including the memorial arch, are maintained by the state.

The arch is unusual, but there's something even stranger about this area I'll bet you didn't know. Head down the hill on Gapland Road and you're entering **Blair Witch** country (blairwitch.com). If you're not familiar with the film, the premise is that in 1994, three students went into the woods to shoot a documentary near **Burkittsville, Maryland.** Their film was found one year later. The characters and events depicted in the movie are entirely fictional but the village is real.

Pity then the residents of Burkittsville, especially on Halloween. So many people have made the pilgrimage to Burkittsville in search of the fictional places depicted in the movie that both village officials and residents continually attempt to explain it wasn't real (burkittsville.com). But read some of the letters they've received and you'll soon agree with P. T. Barnum that there really are suckers born every minute.

At Burkittsville, turn left onto MD 17 to make the return trip to Gettysburg. Route 17 is wide and smooth, a great touring road. As it makes its way north, the ride entertains you with several series of tight curves that will have you swaying your bike from side to side to stay with it.

A nice diversion is to follow Harp Hill Road north over higher ground. You'll have to drop down a gear or two as some portions of the road rise and fall like the streets of San Francisco. Harp Hill Road rejoins MD 17 at Wolfsville. In Wolfsville, a right turn on Stottlemeyer Road will bring you back to MD 77 just outside Catoctin Mountain Park. Follow MD 77 east to Thurmont, then US 15 north to retrace your path to Gettysburg.

But please, do check your saddlebags for stowaway witches on your return. The good folks in Gettysburg have all the supernatural manifestations they care to handle, thank you.

Before the War Between the States Gettysburg was a sleepy little town in the rolling piedmont of southern Pennsylvania. Three days in early July of 1863 ensured that it would never sleep again. The worst battle since the war's inception two years earlier left Gettysburg littered with the devastating legacy of bloodshed.

In the end, the Battle of Gettysburg claimed 51,000 casualties. Five thousand horses, broken cannons, shelled and burned homes, trees felled by heavy fire, and soldiers, some still barely alive, were scattered across the fields. The wise and considered words of Abraham Lincoln's Gettysburg Address some months later helped people understand what had happened there.

Little by little, as the nation pieced itself together after the end of the war, monuments were erected to commemorate the dead. Together with cannon placements, they total over 1,000 (gettysburgguide.com/mondx.html).

The battlefield has been preserved in its original state. But most of all, the shadows and spirits of those who were here still roam the fields and woods, at times so tangible you can feel them walk through you as you look across the battlefield. Place your hand on a cannon and it still feels warm. If you don't believe in ghosts or spirits when you come here, you will when you leave.

Today the town rests a bit easier, though it still does not sleep. People from around the world are drawn to this town, some for the glory, some to learn, others to remember. Fortunately for the motorcyclist, there is ample opportunity to experience all three from the seat of your motorcycle. The best time of year to visit Gettysburg is either side of the summer vacation season; April, May, September, and October offer fine riding weather with less competition for travel resources from the masses.

In town, you'll want to visit several places associated with **Gettysburg National Military Park** (nps.gov/gett/). The first is the visitor center, which houses the museum and electric

Two Harleys pose in Gettysburg square.

map room where a 30-minute orientation to the battle and the battlefield is presented. Get your National Parks Passport stamped here. Just across the road from the visitor center is the Gettysburg National Cemetery where Lincoln made his Gettysburg Address on November 19, 1863.

Almost overshadowed by the military park is the farm and home of Dwight D. Eisenhower at the **Eisenhower National Historic Site** (nps.gov/eise/). Ike purchased the farm in 1950 and retired there with his wife Mamie after serving as commander of NATO forces in Europe and 34th President of the United States. They intended to remodel and live in the farmhouse already on the property, but found that it was nearly ready to collapse. Instead, the Eisenhowers built a new home on the site, salvaging as much of the original structure as possible.

Gettysburg is also home to a plethora of private museums, gift shops, and diversions to entertain you during your evenings. The **Farnsworth House Inn** (farnsworthhousedining.com) features an attraction perfectly suited to the Gettysburg area—ghost stories. After descending a narrow set of stairs into the basement, guests are seated on benches. It takes a few minutes for your eyes to adjust to the candlelight, but you can feel the cool damp walls and sense the low overhead beams before you can see them. In the front of the room, a black mound of cloth rises to reveal a seated woman. She puts on a spine-tingling performance, telling grisly stories about the things that took place around the time of the Battle of Gettysburg. The show will have you seeing more than shadows on your way back home.

Gettysburg offers an annual reenactment of the famous three-day battle (gettysburgreenactment.com). Sure, there are other reenactments to be found throughout the Civil War's theatre, but few are held on a consistent basis and fewer still on the grand scale of this one. In 2003, the 140th such restaging, over 13,000 reenactors participated.

With that number of period actors and 1860s era equipment and provisioning, you get a much greater sense of what the era was like and what the real soldiers experienced.

Lodging and food in every price range are easy to find. On the south end of town, right on the battlefield, you will pay an average of $50 per night for a room. I hung out at the **Colton Motel** (232 Steinwehr Avenue, 717-334-5514). It is within walking distance of the major National Park facilities, and is clean and comfortable. **Gettysburg Motor Lodge** (380 Steinwehr Avenue, 717-334-1106) is also close by and offers a good value.

If you prefer the added luxury of a bed-and-breakfast, the **Old Appleford Inn** (218 Carlisle St., 717-337-1711) on the north end of town has a dozen nicely decorated rooms. And if the coin is really weighing down your pocket, you could unload some of it at the restored **James Gettys Hotel** (jamesgettyshotel.com). Once again appearing as it did in the 1920s, the

The Gettysburg Hotel offers accommodations for the discriminating rider.

James Gettys offers suites, so you can really stretch out and relax. The hotel is just west of the town square, making it the perfect spot from which to launch a reconnaisance mission for hand scooped ice cream on a balmy evening. Personally, I just like sitting on one of the benches around the square to watch cars negotiate the busy traffic circle.

Many local restaurants are in the immediate vicinity of the battlefield. My favorite is the **Avenue Restaurant,** (21 Steinwehr Avenue, 717-334-3235) located at the corner of Baltimore and Steinwehr Avenues. Inside, the fifties-era Formica and chrome decor is sparkling. If you're in the mood for pizza, **Tommy's Pizza** (105 Steinwehr Avenue, 717-334-8966) is the answer. On the other end of town, the Lincoln Diner (32 Carlisle Street, 717-334-3900) offers standard American diner fare. If you want to really do it up in style, the **Farnsworth House Inn** offers fine dining, featuring dishes from the Civil War era, including game pie, peanut soup, spoon bread, and pumpkin fritters. Reservations are a must.

For more trips in this region see *Motorcycle Journeys Through the Appalachians* by Dale Coyner, available from Whitehorse Press.

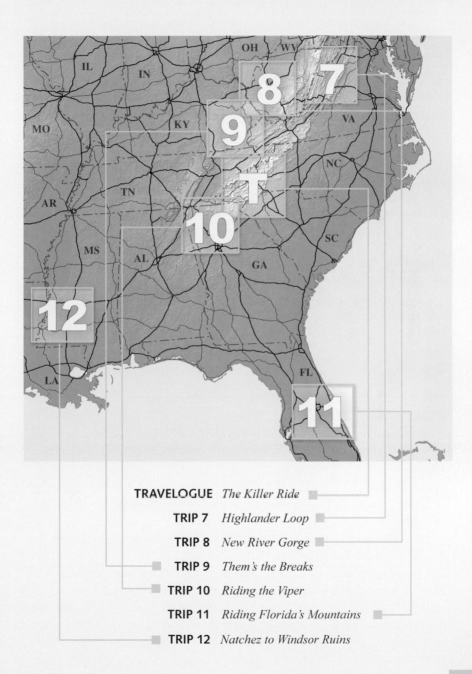

The Killer Ride

Text by Grant Parsons and photos by AMA staff

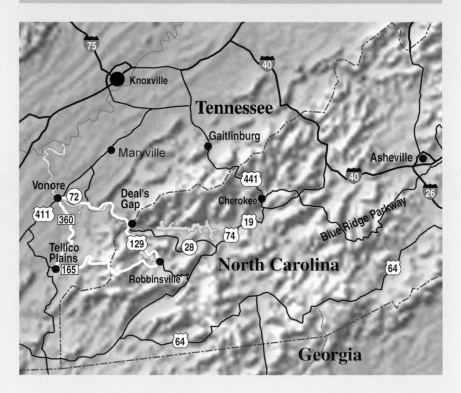

It's a busy day in Deals Gap.

It's Saturday morning. The early fog has lifted. U.S. Route 129 leading across the Tennessee/North Carolina border is clean and dry after last night's shower.

And it seems as if every motorcyclist within 100 miles is here to strafe the 318 curves in 11 miles that have made this road nationally famous as the "Dragon."

We pick up the road on the North Carolina side, just up the hill from the intersection with North Carolina Route 28. The four of us—James, Krez, BA and I—join an endless stream of motorcyclists (with a few members of a Mini Cooper car club mixed in) heading into and out of the gap.

It makes for a lot of traffic on this twisted stretch of two-lane. But the funny thing is, that doesn't hurt the experience. Elsewhere, the combination of traffic and tight curves would make for a slow-moving Winnebago parade. Here, the bikes and cars keep moving at a smooth, brisk pace.

You don't need to be a sportbike rider to enjoy The Dragon.

The road etiquette here feels more European than American. The Dragon offers plenty of pullouts, and people actually use them to let faster traffic go by with a friendly wave.

It's as though everyone here feels privileged to ride one of America's great motorcycle roads. And they want to make sure they don't harm anyone else's enjoyment of this national treasure.

For us, riding the Dragon requires a serious change of gears. We spent yesterday mindlessly slabbing down the interstate from Harley-Davidson's York, Pennsylvania, plant to an area that is rapidly turning into a full-on motorcycle theme park.

By late afternoon, we'd climbed to our first overlook in the Great Smoky Mountains, offering a view of forested ridges stretching to the horizon in pastel shades of pink and blue. Rising up between the ridges was the humid mist that gives the Smokies their name.

Now we're in the heart of those mountains, winding through the woods on perfect, black asphalt.

The heart of the Gap is the stretch that starts on the east at the intersection with North Carolina Route 28, and ends a little past the overlook of Calderwood Lake on the Tennessee side. It's this section of pavement, running along the southwest edge of the Great Smoky Mountains National Park, that riders are referring to when they talk about the Dragon.

Coming from the east, as we are, you hit the tightest, nastiest curves first,

The Killer Ride

The "Tree of Shame" offers proof that the Dragon sometimes bites.

eventually leading to more open sweepers. How tight? The speed limit on the road is 30 mph, and you can have plenty of fun without even risking a ticket.

I'm aboard the new Buell Ulysses, which is a screamin' good time as I bob and weave around what seems like every tree in the forest. I bank hard right, then rotate past vertical into a short, sweeping left leading into a tight bus stop where the road goes 120 degrees right in about a single bike-length.

On the tiny straight that follows, I get a chance to glance in the mirror. I see James, on another Ulysses, right behind, and Krez, on a Harley Super Glide, just emerging from the turn. Before BA appears on the Street Glide, I'm already well into the next lefthander.

The curves just keep coming. I had planned to keep count so I could verify the mythical 318 number that's become the trademark of the Gap, but by 30 I've lost track. They come in endless combinations: left-right, right-left-right, left-left-right-left. The only thing you can do is strain to look ahead far enough that you have some idea what's coming.

Adding to the theme-park feel is the canopy of trees over the road. At times it feels like you're gliding effortlessly down a water-slide tube ride, just wondering where, and when, it will end.

We burst out into the sunlight at the Calderwood Lake overlook, where a couple dozen bikes and riders have gathered. Some have ridden the Gap for years; some are seeing it for the first time. All of them are smiling.

For me, riding the Gap is a bit of a homecoming. I lived in North Carolina for a number of years before moving north. And I made several trips each year to ride the great roads in these mountains. In the decade I've been gone, the region's reputation has grown significantly, and so have the services available to visiting motorcyclists.

Take the motel at the east end of the Gap, the Deals Gap Motorcycle Resort, located right on the Dragon's tail at the junction of North Carolina 28 and U.S. 129. Back in the day, this place had the odd name of the Crossroads of Time, and it was run by a colorful old guy named Pete. Given its location at the entrance to the Gap, it was only natural that the Crossroads catered to motorcyclists, but it definitely had its own brand of run-down backwoods chic. I can still remember the pair of Vise Grips that served as the hot water faucet handle in my bathroom.

These days, that same facility is called the Deals Gap Motorcycle Resort, run by new owners who have fixed the place up significantly, remodeling rooms, adding a restaurant and expanding the on-site store. But one thing hasn't changed. Long after dark, riders still hang out in the parking lot talking bikes, riders, roads, and good times. Riders come from

Brad and Beth Talbot run the Deals Gap Motorcycle Resort.

Bench racing at Deals Gap Motorcycle Resort.

The Killer Ride

Kentucky, Indiana, North Carolina, South Carolina, Iowa—and even one guy from Romania.

"I've been here four of the last five weekends," says Doug McCoy of Burnside, Kentucky, one of the many riders we meet at the overlook. "It's just too much fun."

But that's just the start. Throughout the region, there are plenty of campgrounds, restaurants, and shops that have recognized the value of attracting motorcyclists. The result is a thriving motorcycle-tourist industry that often leaves people who arrive by car feeling as though they're the minority.

After the thrill of riding the Dragon, it's time for a scenery break.

We hang out at the overlook for a while, just enjoying the views of sparkling Calderwood Lake set amid forested mountains. This is one of a series of manmade lakes along the Little Tennessee River created by the famed Tennessee Valley Authority, which dammed the river four times in about 50 miles. Two of the dams are famous—the one near Fontana, North Carolina, is the highest east of the Rockies at 480 feet, while Cheolah Dam, just down from Deals Gap, is the one Harrison Ford's character jumped off in "The Fugitive."

We've hit here at the beginning of fall-color season, which adds to the visual interest. At the peak of the season, fall here is as impressive as anyplace on Earth. The Dragon is definitely the highlight of the Smoky Mountains motorcycling scene, but it's hardly the only standout road in the area.

The pace changes a bit as we leave the Gap behind and cruise along the shores of Chillowee Lake and Tellico Lake to the town of Tallahassee. The roads are sweepy with long straights, giving you time to enjoy the views of blue water and green forest. It's a relaxing contrast to the frenetic Gap.

The shops are very motorcycle friendly around The Gap.

Arriving at the intersection with Tennessee Route 72, we find a motorcycle repair shop/convenience store/diner—a combination that would be highly unlikely anywhere else. We stop in not because we need anything, but because we want to make sure it's real.

From there, we follow Route 72 through the Little Tennessee River valley, pick up U.S. Route 411 and cross the river at Vonore, then turn onto Tennessee Route 360 heading back toward the North Carolina line. The road offers a nice mix of tight

The Wheels Through Time Museum in Maggie Valley, North Carolina, is known as "The Museum that Runs." More than 90 percent of the 260 bikes in the collection are started regularly, both to keep them in running shape and to impress visitors.

turns, wide sweepers, and short straights as it flows through Monroe County on the way to the small town of Tellico Plains.

Somewhere in this county, according to the history books, Tennessee got its name. Early settlers found a Native American village along the river called Tanasi, and the name stuck. The word meant "winding river," but around here, "winding road" would be more appropriate.

There's a restaurant along a creek in Tellico Plains that would make a great lunch stop even if we had no other reason to visit the town. But we do—it's the starting point for another world-class road.

If Deals Gap is Jeremy McGrath—the established legend—then the Cherohala Skyway is Ricky Carmichael. It came along later, but it's earning an equally impressive reputation.

Not bad for a road that was completed only nine years ago.

Named for the two National Forests it passes through, Cherokee and Nantahala, the scenic Skyway rises to 5,390 feet, more than a mile high. The curves are sweepier than the ultra-tight Dragon, and the landscape is more open, meaning that on clear days, the views are exceptional.

We pick up the Skyway just east of Tellico Plains and immediately start climbing. Ahead of us is 36 miles of curves, wide, grassy shoulders, and almost no traffic. In other words, it has all the ingredients for a magazine photo

The Killer Ride

Just below the frost line in the Smokies.

shoot. Normally, picture sessions are the "work" portion of our Ride Guide trips, where we interrupt a great day of riding to make endless runs back and forth past our long-suffering photog, BA.

But not here. On the Cherohala, a photo shoot means riding a perfect set of curves, finding a safe turnaround spot, then re-riding them, over and over. By the third pass, we know every inch of the turns, and we're just playing. I'm actually bummed when BA signals that he has what he needs.

The Skyway is said to have cost $100 million to build, and as we approach the high point, right on the Tennessee/North Carolina border, that's easy to believe. The higher we climb, the more impressive the cuts through the rock are. At the top, the Skyway lives up to its name, and we ride right into the clouds. Visibility is reduced to only a few yards, and the temperature drops a good 20 degrees. Thankfully, the soup lasts only a few miles until we lose altitude on the North Carolina side. Soon we're in sunshine again, and when we stop at an overlook with a view back toward the summit, we realize the clouds are confined to the area right around the mountain. Apparently, it's so tall that it makes its own weather. Impressive.

Of course, all the photo opportunities mean that our progress across the Skyway isn't rapid. In fact, we end up spending more than two hours covering a mere 36 miles of road. Yet as we near the east end of the highway, all of us still have smiles on our faces (with the notable exception, of course, of BA, who did the actual work while we whooped it up).

It's getting late as we pick up Kilmer Road, which skirts Santeetlah Lake on the way into Robbinsville, North Carolina. It's a great roller-coaster road in its own right.

As we roll into town, we're just few dozen road miles away from our starting point on the east end of the Gap. We've completed what may be the number-one riding loop in the East, and one of the top five you'll find anywhere.

BLUE RIDGE PARKWAY

The Blue Ridge Parkway is 469 miles of smooth blacktop that meanders from the Shenandoah National Park in Virginia to Great Smoky Mountains National Park near Cherokee, North Carolina. You can cruise for miles along high-mountain meadows, lonely peaks, wide valleys, and thick forests. The turns are more sweepy than tight, and the dropoffs can be huge—sometimes hundreds of feet straight down.

This recreational and engineering marvel was started in the 1930s as a Depression era public works project and was completed over several decades. What makes it really special, though, is that commercial traffic is banned along its entire length, and development is prohibited within 1,000 feet of the pavement.

The road's highest elevation is 6,053 feet on Richland Balsam Mountain. Then it's all downhill through the high-mountain entrance to Great Smoky Mountains National Park, which has been designated an International Biosphere Reserve.

Because of its altitude and remoteness, the park boasts more than 1,500 species of flowering plants, dozens of native fish, more than 200 species of birds, and about 60 species of animals. Most of the 800-square-mile park is managed as Wilderness, meaning allowed activities are strictly limited.

—*Bill Kresnak*

Cruising the Blue Ridge Parkway.

7 Highlander Loop

Text and photos by Dale Coyner

- **DISTANCE** *197 miles*
- **HIGHLIGHTS** *Mountain passes, narrow river valleys. A wide variety of high speed sweepers and tight switchbacks. Luscious green farm country, Green Bank Observatory, Goshen Pass, Monterey, Warm Springs*

0 Begin on VA 39 West at US 11 in Lexington	**158.3** Left on VA 254
62.5 Right on WV 92	**161.0** Right on VA 876 (Swoope Road/Mish Barn Road)
79.9 Continue straight on WV 28/WV92	**172.3** Right on VA 252 (Middlebrook Road)
94.8 Right on US 250/WV 28	**190.1** Left on VA 39
152.7 Right on VA 42 in Churchville	**197.4** Arrive Lexington via VA 3

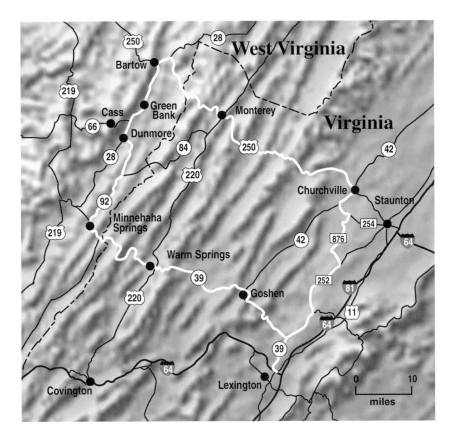

There is no finer road for motorcycling in Virginia than Route 39, which opens this trip. I make this bold statement at the risk of being proved wrong someday, but I don't look for that to happen any time soon. Route 39 threads its way through a series of small hills and valleys, passing through the peaceful burg of Rockbridge Baths before entering Goshen Pass. The road is cut into the side of the mountain high above the Goshen River. Near the summit of the pass there is a wayside where you can relax by the river and enjoy a picnic lunch.

The Boy Scouts of America have a large camp near Goshen which you will pass en route. I'm told that the only problem with having the camp in a remote location like this is finding enough old ladies for these spirited young lads to help across the street. There are fewer than 5,000 residents in all of Bath County, and what few candidates there are for street-crossing are likely to be worn out by the time each budding Eagle Scout fills his dance card.

When Route 39 runs into Route 220, turn left and head south for a short distance. Just to your right you will find the **Warm Springs Pools** (bathcountyva.org). The pools here, and in Hot Springs, have long drawn

Lee Chapel in Lexington, Virginia, is considered the Shrine of the Confederacy.

visitors who wish to relax in the perfect 98.6-degree springs. The Warm Springs pool has separate facilities for men and women. Bring a towel and your swimming trunks.

Follow Route 39 west out of Virginia and into Pocahontas County, West Virginia. The route number does not change. Shortly after entering West Virginia, Route 92 joins Route 39 for a short distance. When the two separate, turn right and follow Route 92 north. This follows a narrow valley bounded by Lockridge Mountain to the east and Brown's Mountain to the west. It's hard to imagine that even in a remote area like this you are still within one day's journey of half the population of the country. Route 28 joins Route 92. After passing the dot on the map called Dunmore, W.Va., you have an opportunity to visit the **Cass Scenic Railroad.** It's about eight to ten miles west on Route 66 in West Virginia (see Cass Scenic Railroad State Park sidebar).

This remote area is good for more than just raising cows and making moonshine, it's also good for star gazing. That's why Green Bank was chosen as the site for the **National Radio Astronomy Observatory** (gb.nrao.edu) in the mid-fifties. Radio astronomy is different from the traditional optical astronomy in that it examines the many different kinds of particles and phenomena that generate radio waves, a portion of which strike earth. It didn't become a serious science until radio technology developed significantly in the 1940s.

The telescopes require an area free of any sources of electromagnetic interference. One look around Green Bank will tell you why they located here. In fact, this area has been designated something of a radio-free zone and special permission is required before anyone can build a facility that might have an effect on the observatory.

Green Bank features a half dozen big scopes trolling the universe for interesting signals. The largest is a 100-meter telescope called the Green Bank Telescope (GBT). The GBT was built a few years ago after the main scope collapsed under the weight of a heavy snow. Operators tried moving the dish back and forth to clear it, but it gave way. Can you imagine the telephone call that took place when the operator had to call his manager to say that the scope had, er, tipped over?

The new scope looks something like a clamshell rising above the treeline. Each of the 2,204 panels which comprise the dish are independently computer-controlled and adjustable so the accuracy of the surface can be maintained to the smallest fraction.

Visitors are welcome at the facility, so be sure to stop by. The observatory opened an expansive new visitor facility in 2003 featuring interactive exhibits that highlight the science of radio astronomy. Tours are offered year round, giving you a chance to see the telescopes up close. Best of all, it's all free.

When you get back on the road, follow Route 28 until it intersects with Route 250 at Bartow. It's time to head

Goshen Pass overlook offers picnic facilities and access to the Maury River.

The people operating the 300-meter dish at the Green Bank Observatory must be serious about receiving ESPN.

The Bluegrass Valley in Highland County, Virginia, is picture perfect. I wish I was there right now.

east, so make the right turn and follow Route 250 back into Virginia. Route 250 is widely known among area riders for its twists and turns. Things start off pretty gently, but as you approach the Virginia state line the frequency of turns quickens, as will your pulse. As you top Lantz Mountain, one of the most beautiful valleys I have seen anywhere opens before you. This is **Blue Grass Valley,** Va. To the north and south lies a picture postcard valley with big white farm houses and manicured grounds so perfect they resemble scale models. These are the real thing. All this beauty is framed against a backdrop of Monterey Mountain, a few miles distant. It is a sight I promise will not disappoint. Highland County, Va. lays claim to the highest average elevation east of the Mississippi. The town of Monterey is 3,000 feet above sea level. That kind of elevation means cool summer nights even when the rest of the eastern seaboard is sweltering. It would be pretty darn easy to put the kickstand down in Monterey and set up housekeeping there on a full-time basis. You can really stretch out in these parts—the 2000 census indicated that only a handful over 2,500 people call Highland County home.

Monterey is home to a group of riders who know they're living in the middle of a rider's paradise and appreciate every minute of it. Be sure to stop by the **Gallery of Mountain Secrets** on Main Street and introduce yourself to Rich and Linda Holman. Rich and Linda are avid riders and they really embody the laid-back, people-friendly Monterey lifestyle. If you happen by

THE SOUTHEAST

the gallery at the same time as local rider Brian Richardson, ask Brian and Rich to recount some of their riding stories, they have a good supply! The gallery is a showcase of items produced by local artisans, but they also have a special bike room featuring items of interest to riders. Rich and Linda also operate the **Cherry Hill Bed and Breakfast** (cherryhillbandb.com, 540-468-2020) located up on the hillside behind Main Street. I can't think of a better place to recommend to you.

If you're of a mind to stop for a bite, you can't go wrong with **High's Restaurant** (540-468-1600) on Main Street in Monterey. If you're staying for the evening, be sure you arrive before 8 p.m. There aren't any all-night joints in this part of the country. Right across the street is the **Highland Inn** (highland-inn.com, 540-468-2143), a frequent retreat for the region's BMW motorcycle clubs.

There aren't many stretches of road on the east coast that cross as many ridges head-on as the section of Route 250 between Monterey and Staunton. The next 30 miles have a generous mix of tight 10 mph switchbacks and double-nickel sweepers. There are three or four main passes interspersed with small valleys, so just as you get tired working the bike from one side to the other, you get a short break, and then another workout. Your trip through George Washington National Forest is like riding an avenue for a king, lined with stately old trees and a brook running on either side. Beautiful!

All too soon you arrive at Churchville. Make the turn south on Route 42 and follow it to Buffalo Gap, Va. Follow Route 254 east to the left at the

The Highland Inn is a favorite destination of riders throughout the mid-Atlantic region.

The 1827 manor house at Col Alto, formerly the social center of Lexington, has been tastefully renovated into the Hampton Inn.

intersection and after a couple of miles, look for county route 876 on your right. This is a neat little road that at times threatens to turn to gravel but never does. It is so deserted and open, it almost feels like you're riding along a farmer's private driveway or through the field. You'll need to exercise all your navigational skills on this route because it takes unexpected turns at some intersections with other roads. It is clearly marked, though, so at worst you'll simply have to make a U-turn and pick up where you left off.

This area is so quiet and unhurried your pace automatically slows. You'll feel a real connection with it—a sense of continuity and stability. Cows march slowly across the field in the evening, keeping their appointment with the farmer as they have day after day, year after year. Folks amble down a back lane, returning from a day at the shop or the office as they have done for the last 30 or 40 years. You could easily fall into the habit of living here yourself.

Eventually Route 876 finds Route 252. Route 252, another well-paved country road, meanders gently through towns with innocent names like Brownsburg, Bustleburg, and Middlebrook. When Route 252 ends on Route 39, turn left to make your way back to Lexington.

▓ For more trips in this region see *Motorcycle Journeys Through the Appalachians* by Dale Coyner, available from Whitehorse Press.

THE SOUTHEAST

CASS SCENIC RAILROAD STATE PARK

Though Cass is a quiet town today, things were different at the turn of the century when the timber operation was in full swing. It was by most accounts a den of sin and iniquity which thrived on the appetites of hard-living lumberjacks. After working from dawn to dusk seven days a week for months on end, these fellas would get their pay and then head into town for some worldly diversions. The town teemed with saloons, women of ill repute, games of chance, and frequent gunplay. By the mid-1900s, the timber gave out and the town was on its way to becoming extinct like so many other small lumber towns. However, fate intervened when the state bought the railroad and most of the town and set it aside as Cass Scenic Railroad State Park in 1963.

The highlight of the park is a ride up the mountain in converted flatbed cars pulled by Shay locomotives. The Shay engine is a wonderfully complex machine and a triumph of engineering. It was designed to reach timber in the higher elevations that couldn't be reached by ordinary engines. It had to handle heavy loads and negotiate frail tracks laid on steep ground, as much as an 11 percent grade.

Runs of different lengths are available. One train runs to an intermediate point at Whittaker Station for a ride that lasts about an hour and a half. For a longer ride and even more tremendous views, the ride to Bald Knob requires four and a half hours. Fall color runs are nothing short of spectacular.

The train ticket includes admission to the wildlife and historical museums. You can also walk along a footpath that passes by the old sawmill site and eventually leads to the machine shop where you are invited to visit the engineers who keep these remarkable engines running. Restored company homes are available for vacation rentals and, like at other West Virginia state parks, come with everything you need.

Visit www.cassrailroad.com for a rate schedule and current calendar, with many special runs and events. Of the many attractions I have visited in West Virginia, Cass has the greatest entertainment value for the dollar.

The first thing that strikes you when you enter Cass, West Virginia, is that all the houses look alike.

8 New River Gorge

Text and photos by Dale Coyner

- **DISTANCE** *154 miles*
- **HIGHLIGHTS** *Mostly river valleys and gorges with a small mountain run. Summersville Dam, Carnifex Ferry, Hawk's Nest State Park, Mystery Hole, New River Gorge and Bridge, Thurmond ghost town*

Mile	Directions
0	Depart downtown Summersville on WV 39
12.0	Left on WV 129
20.5	Arrive Summersville Dam, then turn around
23	Left on CR 23 (Carnifex Ferry Road)
23.9	Arrive Carnifex Ferry Battlefield, then turn around
24.8	Left on WV 129
30.8	Left on WV 39
44.6	Left on WV 16 at Belva
50.2	Left on US 60/WV 16 at Gauley Bridge
54.8	Left on US 60 at Chimney Corner
57.9	Arrive Hawk's Nest State Park, then turn around
61.0	Left on WV 16 South at Chimney Corner
69.4	Left on US 19 North
71.7	Right into New River Gorge Visitor's Center on CR-5
71.7	Right out of NRG parking lot onto CR 5
71.9	Right onto CR-82 (Fayette Station Road) Some portions one-way
78.9	Right onto US 19 South
89.7	Left at Glen Jean exit. Signs for Thurmond National Historic Site present at this exit
89.8	Left onto WV 16 North
90.3	Right onto CR-25 (Thurmond signs should be present)
96.7	Arrive Thurmond, then turn around
103.1	Left on WV 16/WV 61
106.3	Left on WV 61 at 16/61 split
110.7	Left on WV 41
136.5	Left on US 60/WV 41
139.1	Right onto WV 41
153.6	Arrive Summersville via WV 41

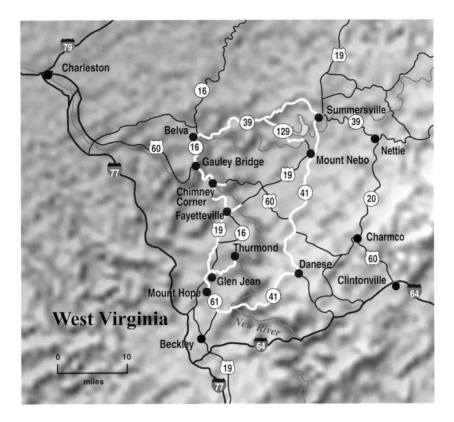

The New River Gorge is the perfect place to gain an understanding of both the old and new West Virginia. Once completely dominated by coal and timber harvesting concerns, the Gorge is now an up-and-coming travel destination. We'll have a chance to see both sides on this loop route.

The route begins in **Summersville** and follows Route 39 west out of town. Route 39 is fairly typical of most roads in the area: where the valley narrows it follows a creek bed and begins to twist and sway; where the valley widens, it stretches out and flies straight. You will see the good and the bad of West Virginia along Route 39.

Some communities look clean and prosperous, others as though they've been bombed. Hang a left on Route 129 to go out to the **Summersville Dam** and the battlefield at **Carnifex Ferry.** This road isn't heavily traveled. It runs over the hills and along the ridges just south of town near the Summersville Dam.

Summersville Dam holds back the waters of the Gauley River, creating a 4,000-acre lake. Route 129 passes over the top of the dam. Pull off to one side and you can gaze upon the boulder strewn back side. Near the bottom of the dam are two pipes, each about 20 feet in diameter, that allow water to pass

At Mystery Hole, near Hawks Nest State Park, the only mystery is what happens to your money.

through the dam and continue down the river. The pressure exerted is so great the water blows horizontally out of the pipes and about 30 feet downstream before landing in the riverbed. At the put-in point near the base of the dam there's a sign warning kayakers that if they hear three short blasts, they can expect a sudden rise in the water level. No kidding. When you leave the dam, turn back toward Route 39. You will have to look carefully for the hidden turn to **Carnifex Ferry Battlefield.** It isn't well marked. About two miles west of the dam, Route 129 makes a sharp right. A smaller, unmarked road to the battlefield branches off to the left at the curve. (Watch for a large billboard advertising the Mountain Lake Campground—it's located along Route 129 at the curve in question.) Make the left turn along this pleasant country lane to reach the battlefield.

The battle at Carnifex Ferry was one of dozens of moves and counter moves conducted by both sides during the War Between the States. According to accounts of the battle which took place in September 1861, a contingent of about 6,000 Union soldiers swept through Summersville to re-establish a supply line broken by the rebels in earlier action. The Confederates, outmanned three to one, had time to dig in. They riddled the Union ranks with fire and suffered only 20 casualties themselves.

Despite suffering a rout, the outlook was undimmed for some Union soldiers like Rutherford B. Hayes. According to him, "[West Virginia] is the land of blackberries. We are a great grown-up armed blackberry party and we gather untold quantities." I'm guessing Hayes, who went on to become the nineteenth U.S. president, didn't see much trench warfare.

Exiting the battlefield, return to WV 129 and head west to WV 39. Turn left and continue south on WV 39, passing through a dozen small villages until you reach Gauley Bridge. Make the left turn on Route 16/60 and head east. You are now following the course the ancient New River has traveled for thousands of years. Follow US 60 East at Chimney Corner where 60 and WV 16 split. This spot is marked by the **Country Store Craft Shop and Gallery,** home to Appalachian crafts including jewelry and crafts made from coal. I don't care much for today's modern tourist traps. Places like Pigeon Forge, Tennessee are just too crowded and overdone for me. However, I do favor those small, independent attractions that catch the eye along the road. Case in point is the **Mystery Hole** (mysteryhole.com), located along US 60 a couple of miles up the road from Chimney Corner. I'm more likely to patronize a place like this to chat with the folks who run and reward their entrepreneurial spirit as I am to "explore the mystery."

Follow Route 60 east from the Hole to **Hawk's Nest State Park.** You'll enjoy this section of road as you climb out of the gorge. Rising higher you can see the gorge below and a thin glittering ribbon that is the New River. The best views are from the park. Hawk's Nest has two sections, upper and lower. The upper portion of the park overlooks the New River Gorge at a point where it forms a lake. Down by the lake, there are the usual water diversions such as row boats and paddle boats. You can also arrange a pontoon boat ride upriver to the New River Gorge Bridge. To navigate the rough terrain between the lake and the lodge above, there is an aerial tramway which is an attraction in itself. At the lodge, ask for a room with a view. There's no extra charge.

The lower area features a hilltop museum constructed by the **Civilian Conservation Corps** (cccalumni.org) in the early '30s. What looks like a chalet is perched on top of the hill over the gorge. Massive stonework and tremendous wooden beams inside display the craftsmanship of the CCC workers who assembled it. The chalet is filled with a collection of Indian, pioneer, and Civil War artifacts. If you feel in the mood for a hike there are trails which lead to views of the gorge and range from 100 yards to about two miles.

When you leave the park, your best bet for a better ride is to simply retrace your steps to the café at Chimney Corner, W. Va. and hang a left, continuing to follow WV 16 and the river into Fayetteville. In Fayetteville, they still talk about "Five Dollar Frank," a name Frank Thomas earned for the five-dollar airplane rides he offered over the New River Gorge. I once took a ride with Frank over the gorge, and after that experience, I decided motorcycling was pretty safe by comparison. Sadly, Five Dollar Frank no longer flies over the gorge in his battered old Cessna; he's taken on a new set of wings. Frank offered a rare view of the gorge, but there is still a way to see the gorge and the New River Bridge from a vantage point that few folks know about.

When Route 16 intersects US 19, turn left and head over the New River Bridge to the **New River Gorge National River Visitor Center** (nps.gov/neri) on the right.

The New River Gorge Bridge is the world's largest steel arch bridge, completed in 1977 at a cost of nearly $37 million. It is the highest bridge in the East, standing 876 feet tall. Before the bridge was completed, the trip from one side of the gorge to the other took nearly an hour; now it takes about 30 seconds. You have to see it to believe it—it is impressive. In fact, if you've seen the television commercial where Chevrolet drops a truck over a bridge on a bungee cord, then you've seen it. On the third Saturday in October, the bridge is closed to traffic and a festival is held on the bridge complete with parachutists, bungee jumping (no, no, after you, I insist), and rappelling.

If you carry a National Parks passport, don't forget to get yours stamped at the visitor center. There are several trails from the visitor center, including one which will take you down to the river for great photo opportunities. Just remember, every step you walk down, you have to walk back up!

The other popular diversion here is river running. The New River Gorge is widely recognized as one of the best white water rides anywhere. In many areas, the river is about a mile wide, but it squeezes down to a few hundred feet through the gorge and the result is a ride that promises to be bumpier than even Frank's ten-minute flying tour.

In season, the traffic down the river is nearly bumper to bumper. There are a dozen or more companies that organize raft trips on the New. Two of the more established companies are **Class VI River Runners** (800classvi.com) and **Wildwater Expeditions Unlimited** (www.wvaraft.com).

Out of the parking lot of the visitor center, hang a right and continue down CR 5 for just a couple of tenths, then make the right turn onto CR-82 also labeled in some parts as Fayette Station Road. Route 82 makes some crazy twists and turns as it travels underneath the bridge and picks its way carefully down the gorge to the very bottom. Here you can hop off the bike and take some great pictures of the bridge from your new vantage point. This is the former route of US 19 which now whizzes by overhead. Can you imagine what travel must have been like when this was a major route? Route 82 is a one-way route at this point, so continue across the bridge at the bottom and up the other side. This returns you to the west side of US 19 just a few tenths up the road from Route 16 where you appeared earlier. Head south on US 19 then turn left at Glen Jean, following signs for the Thurmond National Historic Site. You'll make a quick left onto WV 16 heading north, then you'll see another sign at CR-25. Follow CR-25 all the way to the train depot in Thurmond. You'll cross an open grate bridge across the New River to reach it. The bridge looks dicey for bikes, but just maintain a slow, steady speed across and you'll be fine. My Wing didn't complain, and I didn't look down. Piece of cake.

The New River Gorge is home to dozens of towns that once flourished during the coal boom of the early 20th century. The richest of them was **Thurmond.** Mines from this area generated the greatest revenue and Thurmond's banks held the largest deposits in the state. When the coal played out, so did Thurmond. The National Park Service restored the train depot and is working to preserve some of the buildings that remain along the tracks. I think you'll enjoy time spent here. It's an interesting exercise to walk along

People actually jump off this perfectly good bridge on "Bridge Day" in October.

the row of abandoned buildings and imagine what life was like here during the heady days of the Roaring Twenties.

There are dozens of other sites scattered throughout the gorge though none are preserved like Thurmond. Riding buddies of mine have told me harrowing tales of seeking out these places on their street bikes. I think a dual-purpose bike would be well-suited to an adventure like that, but I wouldn't even think about it on the Wing.

From Thurmond, head back on CR-25 and turn left on Route 16. Follow this down to Mount Hope and make the left on WV 61, then make a left on Route 41 and follow it north all the way to Summersville. This route also crosses the gorge many miles upstream from the main bridge. It plunges down one side of the gorge, crossing the river on a dilapidated steel bridge near the river, then dutifully climbs the other side of the ridge. The scenery is spectacular on both sides and is a pleasant ride to end the day.

For more trips in this region see *Motorcycle Journeys Through the Appalachians* by Dale Coyner, available from Whitehorse Press.

9 Them's The Breaks

Text and photos by Dale Coyner

■ **DISTANCE** *255 miles*

■ **HIGHLIGHTS** *Hills and hollows of Coal Country; Breaks Interstate Park, Natural Tunnel, Trail of the Lonesome Pine, Kentucky Coal Mining Museum*

0 Depart Hazard on KY 550 at junction with KY 476	**146.9** Right on VA 65 at Ft. Blackmore
18.4 Right on KY 160 in Hindman	**161.5** Right on US 23 North at Clinchport
26.7 Left on SR 1410 at Littcarr	**162.7** Right on VA 871 (Follow signs for Natural Tunnel)
32.8 Left on KY 7 at Colson	**164.2** Arrive Natural Tunnel State Park
38.4 Right on KY 317 at Deane	**165.7** Right on US 23 North
47.0 Left on KY 805	**182.0** Right on exit at Big Stone Gap (US 58A/US 23 Business North)
53.1 KY 805 joins US 119/KY 197	**186.2** Stay on US 23 Business North thru Big Stone Gap, then left on VA 160
58.9 Right on KY 197 at US 119/KY 197 split	
75.4 Right on KY 80 in Elkhorn City	**206.8** Right on KY 160 at KY 160/KY 522 split
89.6 VA 83 joins VA 80 in Haysi	**229.7** Left on KY 15 North
90.0 Right on VA 83 at VA 80/VA 83 split	**255.3** Arrive Hazard via KY 15 North
109.0 Left on VA 72 at Clintwood	

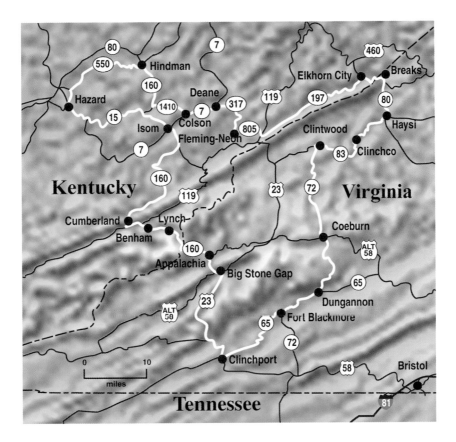

My first touring introduction to coal country was along Route 160, a road that originates in Appalachia, Virginia, and runs the mining region in eastern Kentucky. It is a road of vast contrasts—vistas of beauty and landscapes of destruction, perfectly illustrating the conflicting personalities of the area. Route 160 is featured in this tour along with some other great roads. If you've set out to discover what this mythical region is about and you have time for just one tour, this is it. There's a lot to see and do and tell, so let's get started.

The first few segments of the route move east out of **Hazard** and deep into the center of the active mining region. The first section along Route 550 is not an unpleasant motoring experience. Most of the route cuts through small valleys and is a decent little road. The right turn onto the northern end of Route 160 takes you through Hindman which is fairly active, but after a mile or two out of town, you're back to riding alone. In fact, this was very often the case. I'd find that if I did pick up a car or two along a route, they usually turned off soon. After a while it dawned on me that none of these roads are through-routes, so you wouldn't expect to follow someone for more than a mile or two.

Breaks Interstate Park is a basecamp worthy of consideration for riding in the Appalachians.

The left on Route 1410 is an equally nice stretch bordering on the Carr Creek Wildlife Management Area. Route 1410 ends on Route 7 where you'll make the left turn at Colson. At Deane, pick up the right turn on KY 317 and follow that through Fleming-Neon. This section of the route portrays the current state of the economy in the region.

You can tell that at one time, Fleming-Neon boasted an active retail district. But as you ride down Main Street now it looks nearly like a ghost town. Both sides of the street are lined with boarded-up buildings and shuttered businesses. You have to wonder, will prosperity ever return to this region? Will downtown Fleming-Neon flourish as it once did? For now, the answer seems to be no. Route 317 ends on Route 805. Turn left and follow Route 805 as it joins US 23 Business and US 119 along Elkhorn Creek. Eventually, Route 23 splits off to the north and you'll bear right to continue toward Elkhorn City on KY 197. This again is another section of decent road. But things get really exciting just outside of Elkhorn City.

In town, turn right on KY 80. This leads directly east out of town and into Breaks Interstate Park on the Kentucky-Virginia border. This is a great section of road. Fantastic curves on a smooth ribbon of pavement. I stopped along a wide shoulder to take a break and review my route. For the entire fifteen minutes I was stopped, not a single car passed by. Route 80 is some great riding!

Just a few miles over the border, the entrance to **Breaks Interstate Park** (breakspark.com) appears on the right. The canyon here at the park is the deepest gorge east of the Mississippi River with some areas as deep as 1,600 feet. Breaks is well worth considering as a base camp for exploring this region. There are dozens of hiking trails to enjoy, fishing, boating, horseback riding, rafting, and more. Whether you prefer a room at the lodge, a cottage, or a campsite, Breaks offers inexpensive accommodations in a beautiful setting. Even if you're not of a mind to settle in, you'll still want to visit Breaks for the views of the Gorge.

Back on Route 80, continue east by turning right when you leave the Park. VA 83 joins your route in Haysi. When the two routes split, make the right onto VA 83 and follow it through Clinchco. In Clintwood, pick up Route 72 south and follow it through Coeburn down to Dungannon. At this point, VA 65 joins Route 72. When these routes split at Fort Blackmore, follow route 65 west.

Fort Blackmore was a wooden fort erected here on the frontier in the late 1700s. It mostly served as a waystation for folks passing through on the way through Cumberland Gap. For a period of time there was a small town built here along the banks of the Clinch River. That all changed in 1973 when Hurricane Camille caused the Clinch River to take away the town. After that, the area was declared a flood plain and no further building was allowed.

Traffic census #1: I counted 15 minutes between cars along this stretch of KY 80.

Route 65 ends in Clinchport on US 23. This is a good time to crank up the tunes if you're equipped. I recommend Dwight Yoakam's *Hillbilly Deluxe,* featuring the song "Readin', Rightin', Route 23." Yoakam's song showcases the plight of people who left Appalachia along this road, headed for northern cities seeking "the good life they had never seen." But as the story later reveals, their measure of success was misguided and "they didn't know that old highway could lead them to a world of misery."

Just a couple of miles up Route 23, you'll see the sign for **Natural Tunnel State Park** (dcr.state.va.us/parks/naturalt.htm). Make the right on VA 871 and head up the road about two miles. Natural Tunnel evolved as acid-laden ground water dissolved softer rock compounds. Later in its evolution, Stock Creek was diverted and began its process of carving out the tunnel as it is seen today. Railroad track was laid through the tunnel in the late 1800s and this route is still in use today for hauling coal out of the region. For a couple of bucks, a chairlift will carry you to the bottom of the gorge and bring you back to the top.

Returning to Route 23, head north to Big Stone Gap. Route 23 is a four-lane highway, but typically not very busy, at least not by metropolitan standards. When you arrive at Big Stone Gap, take the exit for the downtown area. That's US 23 Business North/US 58A.

Big Stone Gap is home to the outdoor drama depiction of the **Trail of the Lonesome Pine** (trailofthelonesomepine.org). The original novel by John Fox, Jr. from which the play was adapted, tells of the romance between a young Appalachian girl and an engineer from the East who arrives during the coal boom of the early 20s. The story is as much about the effects of the sudden influx of wealth on clannish mountain families and customs as it is about the lovers. Although the book is a fictional account, many of the characters such as Devil Judd Tolliver and Bad Rufe Tolliver bore striking resemblance to some of the better known (or notorious) real-life clansmen who lived on both sides of the Kentucky-Virginia border.

Ready for a seriously hot stretch of road? Follow US 23 Business north out of Big Stone Gap to Appalachia. On the south end of town, you'll see the left turn for VA 160. Route 160 starts out somewhat inauspiciously through an industrial section, but that soon gives way to long straights. A couple of miles later, you'll look up to the side of the mountain and see a couple of clearings. You'll be riding along those clearings in just a few minutes. At the base of the mountain, Route 160 begins to ascend the mountain with an unending series of sweepers and switchbacks. Some of the curves remind me of Deal's Gap, sweep, sweep, sweep, turn! Sweep, sweep, turn! This glorious pattern continues for a good ten miles over Black Mountain and the state border, depositing you in Lynch, Kentucky.

Like a lot of other towns, Lynch was a company town. This means that the

The setting sun closes another day of exciting motorcycling.

mining company literally owned the town. It shipped in all the building materials and supplies and built the town from scratch. The houses were owned by the company and employees were often paid in "scrip" instead of cash. Scrip could only be used at the company store. Tennessee Ernie Ford sang about this system in "Sixteen Tons." "You load sixteen tons, what do you get? Another day older and deeper in debt. St. Peter don't you call me cause I can't go. I owe my soul to the company store."

Lynch and the next town, Benham, have preserved their coal heritage with museums. In Lynch, you can now tour **Portal No. 31** (kingdomcome.org/portal), what was one of the largest coal loading operations in the country. In Benham, the **Kentucky Coal Mining Museum** (kingdomcome.org/museum) provides an in-depth examination of the mining era and its people. The basement features a mock mine exhibit and the third floor is dedicated to Loretta Lynn.

The remaining section of Route 160 passes through Cumberland then makes a sharp uphill turn right out of town. It's along this section, from Cumberland to Isom where you're likely to run up trucks. If you happen to tour this route on a weekend, you probably won't see any at all. Route 160 intersects with Route 15 at Isom. Turn left on 15 to make the return to Hazard.

◼ For more trips in this region see *Motorcycle Journeys Through the Appalachians* by Dale Coyner, available from Whitehorse Press.

10 Riding the Viper

Text and photos by Scott Cochran

■ **DISTANCE** *118 miles*

■ **HIGHLIGHTS** *Wide, sweeping curves on well-maintained asphalt highway; tight, tortured, hairpin curves on the Viper with several elevation changes; Georgia's highest lake, Wolf Pen Gap, Two Wheels Only motorcycle resort, 1928 vintage restaurant; long two-lane roads through rural north Georgia with light traffic; twisty four lane highways that were made for motorcycle journeys!*

0 Start in downtown Helen, Georgia, Hwy 17 at Chattahoochee River Bridge	**65.6** Turn right on US 76/515/2
1.4 Turn left on SR 75	**86.5** Turn right on US 129 SR 11 (Cleveland Street)
9.5 Turn right on US 129/SR 11	**92.0** Stop at Pappy's Trading Post
16.5 Go straight on SR 11/129	**94.5** Turn left on SR 180
27.1 Turn left on SR 180 (Wolf Pen Gap Road)	**107.0** Turn right on SR 17/SR 75
38.1 Turn right on SR 60	**118.0** Arrive in downtown Helen

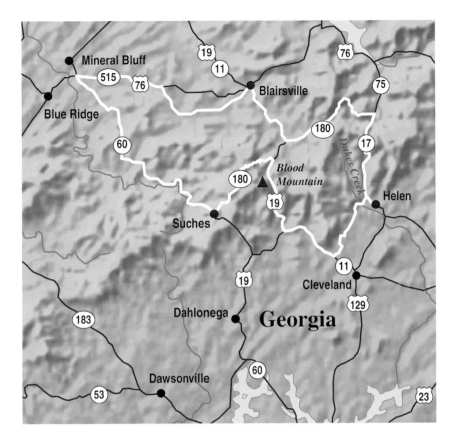

Start your trip in downtown **Helen** where Hwy 17 crosses the river and head north out of town. At Mile 1.4, turn left on SR 75 and ride to Mile 9.5 and turn right on US 129/SR 11.

At 16.5 miles, you'll pass **Turner's Corner Cafe,** a 1928 vintage restaurant and popular motorcycle gathering place. Once operated as a gas station and rural country store, Turner's no longer pumps gas or sells grocery items. It's still a favorite meeting place for the local motorcyclists, however, and the food is quite good. You can sit inside, or outside on the balcony overlooking the **Chestatee River.** Try any of the homemade pies (pronounced paaahz) for dessert. As you leave Turner's Corner continue north on 19/129 up **Blood Mountain.** Local folklore has it that the mountain got its name long before white men came to the area. After a great battle between the Cherokee and the Creek Nations, so many braves were killed that their blood ran down the mountain turning it red. This seems to be a true tale as Indian names were also given to nearby Slaughter Creek and Slaughter Gap. To the Cherokee, Blood Mountain was sacred because it was the home of the Nunnehi, the spirit people who watched over hunters and hikers in the area.

HELEN, GEORGIA

Helen, Georgia, located just a few quick hours north of Atlanta, is an unabashed tourist town, although at certain times of the year it can be quiet and almost deserted. If you're the type of rider who is comfortable using electric gear and will ride year-round, then visit Helen after the Oktoberfest crowds have disappeared, usually around Thanksgiving and before Christmas. Now before you have me committed to an institution for suggesting you ride the mountains in the winter, understand that it snows infrequently in North Georgia and when it does, it's usually gone in a couple of days, as the temperatures rarely stay below freezing for any extended length of time. Having said that, there are spots along these rides where ice can and does accumulate in the shadows of the mountainside, so it's wise to always ride as if there is black ice around the next curve, because you never know.

For accommodations I usually stay at the **Best Western** in Helen. The rates are reasonable, the rooms are clean, and they have wireless for my laptop that I'm forced to lug along. For the most part, Helen is a motorcycle friendly town; however, the biggest complaint I hear is the lack of parking. Admittedly, this is a problem and the poliz'e are inflexible when it comes to parking in loading zones or on yellow curbs. Yet the town isn't very large and you can easily walk to most of the shops from the hotels. Our favorite biker-friendly bar in Helen is the **Southside Bar and Grill** (7934 South Main Street, 706-878-2291). If you find yourself in need of some leathers or some boots, visit **Chattahoochee Biker Gear** and **Das It Leathers** located at 8610 Helen Highway (706-878-0076). You'll find the prices reasonable and the owners helpful.

On my last trip in this area, the Nunnehi must have been watching over me because I was enjoying a spirited ride up SR 129 in the mid-morning hours. The traffic was light and I had become one with my motorcycle, leaning into the curves, and using both northbound lanes to carve this road as I never had before. I was feeling quite good about the trip when something unusual caught my eye and I immediately slowed down and tried to see what it was in my rear view mirror. As I rounded the next curve at about half speed, I rode headlong into a patch of sand covered with diesel fuel! I knew it was diesel by the smell. I almost couldn't believe my dumb luck because there was no reason to suspect any hazard on this highway and I've never seen anything like it before or since. As it turned out, there were three similar patches on this road a mile or so apart. I never discovered the true source of my initial distraction, but there's no doubt that I would've gone down on that first patch had I not slowed to see what it was.

At Mile 27.1, you'll turn left onto SR 180 also known as Wolf Pen Gap Road. I remember "discovering" Wolf Pen Gap Road quite by accident a few years ago. I was scouting a route for a poker run, came upon this road, and decided to see where it would lead me. When I arrived at SR 60 almost 12 miles later I'm sure I shouted something like "YES!" I'd ridden Deals Gap (The Dragon) in North Carolina, and immediately decided that my new find was worthy of being named "The Viper." There are two man-made lakes, constructed by the **CCC (Civilian Conservation Corp)** on this stretch of premium motorcycle blacktop. At Mile 27.5 is the entrance to **Vogel State Park** and **Lake Trahlyta** (www.ngeorgia.com/parks/vogel.html). This 20-acre lake was named for the Cherokee maiden that is buried at Stonepile Gap at the intersection of US 19 and SR 60. At Mile 33.7, you'll pass the entrance to **Lake Winfield Scott** (www. georgiatrails.com/places/winfieldscott.html), the highest lake in Georgia.

At Mile 38, CR 180 deadends at SR 60 in the town of **Suches.** Just south of this intersection is the well-known motorcycle destination, **TWO (Two Wheels Only) motorcycle resort** (3580 State Hwy 60, 706-747-5151). Operated by GT and Britt Turner, TWO offers camping, a four-bedroom lodge, and a fully furnished two-bedroom mobile home. They also boast of having

TWO, Two Wheels Only, is a popular motorcycle destination in North Georgia with overnight accommodations and lunch served daily during the riding season.

For advertising to be successful it must first attract the attention of the public. This advertisement for boiled peanuts is a textbook case. If you didn't know that the name of this establishment is Poor Boyz, you might be left wondering what poor had to do with anything.

the only Wi-Fi internet connection for miles around. Closed during the winter months, TWO usually opens around the end of March for the season. If you're coming to TWO, heed their firm policy that all guests must either be riding a motorcycle or towing one. If you're hungry, ask about the Big Ass Sirloin Burger. Lunch is available on Saturday and Sunday 11 to 2 p.m., Dinner on Friday and Saturday 5:30 to 8:30 p.m. Check the resort's website (www.twowheelsonly.com) for a listing of weekend events. If you're there in the fall, try to time your visit to the 50 cc rally in October, called the **True Grits Fun Run.** This event, started in 1982, raises money for the local volunteer fire department. Watching or joining grown men and women speeding (well almost speeding) for 60 miles around the North Georgia mountains is worth the trip. Browse their website for photos from past rallies and you'll see what I mean.

In addition to TWO, **Copperhead Lodge** (www.copperheadlodge.com, 404-683-6654) is located in nearby Blairsville. Built by motorcycle enthusiasts for motorcycle enthusiasts, this resort features concerts and events during the riding season as well as short and long term rentals. Call ahead for pricing and availability.

When you leave TWO, head north on SR 60 toward the town of **Mineral**

THE SOUTHEAST

Bluff. Stay on 60 through a couple of turns until you reach US 76/SR 2/515 and turn right.

At Mile 87, you'll turn right onto US 129/SR 11, and at Mile 92, you'll pass **Pappy's Trading Post,** an eclectic blend of different businesses with that certain feel of roadside kitsch. The parking lot is gravel and sometimes soft gravel as the proprietor of Pappy's Trading Post informed me one fine day. "The EPA won't let us pave the lot because of the river that runs directly behind the lot, so all we can do is keep putting gravel in every year. I estimate we have about 20 feet of compacted gravel by now beneath your motorcycle, but every year the clay rises to the top and we have to add more gravel." If you're uncomfortable on gravel you can park at the south entrance on the few feet of asphalt there and walk to the different stores. At one time, Pappy, a retired firefighter from Florida, built and owned all the buildings at the Trading Post, but as he approached the time for his second retirement, he began to sell off individual parts of the complex. Now almost each business is individually owned. There's a restaurant on site but I haven't tried it so I can't say

Pappy's Trading Post is a favorite pit stop of mine when traveling this north Georgia route. Just be careful of the gravel parking lot.

In winter , Pappy's Trading Post has an open fireplace and the cider mull really hits the spot.

much about it. In the winter, the Trading Post keeps a fire burning in the outside fireplace and the homemade cider mull is welcome, warm refreshment while you sit on the back porch and watch the **Nottely River** flowing by.

Return to US 129 and head south to Mile 94.5 where you'll turn left on SR 180. At Mile 107 turn right on 75/17 and enjoy the last few miles of this journey on the twisty section of the Unicoi Turnpike. It's a nice ending to a ride you won't soon forget.

■ For more trips in this region see *Motorcycle Journeys Through the American South* by Scott Cochran, available from Whitehorse Press.

11 Riding Florida's Mountains

Text and photos by Scott Cochran

- **DISTANCE** *107 miles*
- **HIGHLIGHTS** *An honest to goodness elevation change in Florida! A few miles of twisty two lanes and quaint and charming Florida towns with fresh oranges (in season).*

0 SR 44 at I-95, head west	**56.4** Bear right on Lake Shore Boulevard
4.6 Left on CR 415	**56.6** Left on SR 19
22.1 Right to stay on CR 415	**58.3** Left on CR 561
25.9 Right on US 17	**67.0** Left on CR 455 (Green Mountain Scenic Byway)
26.7 Right on 1st Street and retrace route to US 17/SR 46	
	78.6 Left on SR 50
27.2 Straight on SR 46	**80.5** Left on SR 438
49.2 Straight on 1st Avenue	**87.3** Left on CR 437 (Ocoee Apopka Road)
49.8 Right on North Highlands	**95.2** Left on CR 435 South Park Avenue
50.4 Left on East 11th Street	**95.5** Left on US 441
51.6 Straight onto Helm Street/Old US 441	**107.0** Right onto CR 46
55.0 Straight onto Alfred Street	

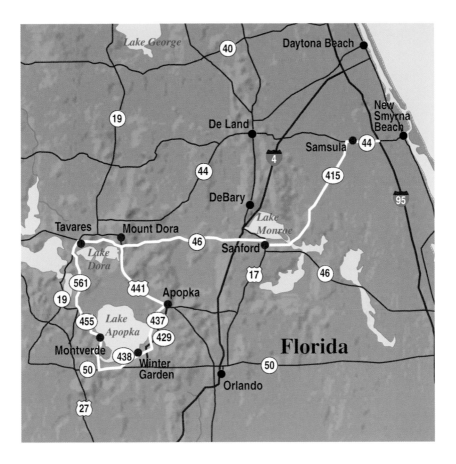

I'd be willing to bet you a dollar to a donut that you thought Florida was completely flat, and admittedly so did I. In fact, I once commented in an editorial that the State is flatter than my Grandma's lacy cornbread. For the most part that's true, yet I can take you on a journey that will give you a "one up" on even some of the locals!

Sometimes you ride for the great roads, other times you ride for a memorable destination, and then sometimes you ride a road or to a destination just because you want to be able to say you did it.

This is one of those times. In any other state in these United States, this ride wouldn't rate an honorable mention, but the look on people's faces when you tell them you rode the only mountain in Florida is—well, almost priceless.

I remember being in a party in Daytona during Bike Week and a real windbag was going on and on about riding his bike through the mountains of some Third World country. Someone asked me if I'd ever ridden anywhere exciting like that and I made the statement, "I've ridden the only mountain in

You'll find yourself wishing you could slow down the hands of time in Sanford, Florida, as you stroll this beautiful town square.

Florida!" The look of disbelief on Mr. Bag-O-Wind was a "Kodak moment." "What mountain?" was the reply and playing the jester I couldn't resist. "You mean you've lived in Florida all your life and you've never ridden Sugarloaf Mountain?" I wasn't sure if his upturned nose and raised eyebrow meant he regarded me as a raving lunatic or a bald-faced liar. I was stretching the truth a bit, because there are actually two high spots that carry the "mountains" designation in Florida. The other is Iron Mountain. Neither is the highest point in the state as that honor goes to Britton Hill near the Alabama line in the Panhandle section of the state; but Sugarloaf Mountain is the highest on the peninsula and the most "motorcycle friendly."

Since many of you visit Florida only once or twice a year and usually during the motorcycle rallies in Daytona, we'll start our journey at the intersection of US 44 and I-95, just south of **Daytona Beach.** Start out heading west on US 44 toward **Samsula.** Bike Week veterans know this area as home to Spotnik's Cabbage Patch, located on Tomoka Farms Road. **Spotnik's Cabbage Patch** hosts the World Famous Coleslaw Wrestling every Bike Week on Wednesday. It's so popular that the roads leading into the campground become jam-packed for several hours before the event starts. While coleslaw wrestling isn't an Olympic sport, I'm proud to say that my town, **Swainsboro,** Georgia, is home to a three-time winner of this event, and no, it's not me!

At SR 415 turn left and head south toward **Sanford.** At Mile 22.6, you have the option to take a short detour and turn right onto Chickasaw Drive. In a couple hundred feet you'll come to an **Indian shell mound** on the righthand side of the road. It isn't much to look at, but I mention it because it's an excellent example of a little known part of Florida's history. Indian shell mounds were the Native American's landfill. These shells, sometimes piled twenty feet high or more, were the leftovers of the shellfish eaten by the natives and piled higher and higher until abandoned. They can be found in

THE SOUTHEAST

other parts of the state as well. There's a sign warning you not to dig around in this historic waste dump!

Returning to Route 415, head west toward town. At the intersection of US 17 turn right for just under a mile until the intersection of SR 46/17 and First Street. If you're hungry, turn right on First Street and head into historic downtown. Sanford is located on the southern shores of **Lake Monroe** and is listed in the **National Register of Historic Places.** Sanford was once the largest vegetable shipping center in the U.S., earning it the nickname of the "Celery City." Today the only celery you'll find is at **Rubyjuice Smoothies** on the corner of West First Street and North Park Avenue (407-322-3779). Rubyjuice was voted "Best Smoothie in Seminole County" according to the plaque on the wall. Since I haven't tried the other smoothie joints in the county I can't dispute that, but I know you can have almost any flavor smoothie you can imagine in this one, plus a few you've probably never even dreamed about. My favorite is the Peachy Keen, but I'm trying to get enough nerve to try the one made from saw grass. Yes, you read that right, grass. It's grown right in the store under grow lamps and it's supposed to cure whatever ails you.

Mt. Dora is a good place to stop and stretch your legs during your "Mountains of Florida" tour.

If you're in need of more sustenance than a fruit (or grass) smoothie, try the **Blue Dahlia** (112 East 1st Street, 407-688-4745, www.bluedahlia-sanford.com). There's a scene from the movie *My Girl* in which Dan Akroyd is seated at the front window of this restaurant. Seating is also available outside. For good German food try the **Willow Tree Cafe** (205 East 1st Street, 407-321-2204, www.willowtreecafe.com).

When you've had your fill of downtown Sanford, head back west on First Street to the intersection of Routes 17 and 46. Continue west on 46 toward the first two "mountains" on this journey, Mount Plymouth and Mount Dora.

For the next 22 miles you'll pass by the **Seminole State Forest,** and you'll see "bear crossing" signs. Now I don't know about you but the prospect of hitting a bear at highway speed is enough to put me on high alert. I can ride through deer country secure in the knowledge that in an encounter with a

WE DIDN'T INVENT MOONSHINE, WE JUST MADE IT FAMOUS

It was around long before Prohibition and known by many names, White Mule, Skat, Stump Juice, Mountain Dew, Fire Water, Rot Gut, and simply Shine. Yes, I have tasted moonshine, and yes, I have made moonshine, and yes, I have a recipe for making it that I can share with you. However, moonshine did not start in the South; that's a Hollywood myth. Actually, **Garrett,** Pennsylvania, had the distinction of being referred to as Moonshine, USA, during the depression. In fact, the first state to threaten to secede from the Union wasn't in the South and it wasn't during the Civil War. It was Pennsylvania, and it happened during the Whiskey Rebellion of 1794 when George Washington instituted a tariff on all homemade whiskey, a/k/a moonshine. This wasn't the only reason for the rebellion, but it was the proverbial straw that broke the camel's back. What moonshine did do for the South was cause the birth of stock car racing, known today as NASCAR. Many of these early stock car legends ran shine on Friday and Saturday nights and raced each other on Sunday. Oh, and about that recipe, you'll have to email me for it: editor@usridernews.com.

deer my odds of survival are left to fate. With a bear it's a little more dicey because what happens if you only graze him and ruin his day! The thought of accidentally hitting a bear and then having him mad at me while I'm laying there with a broken leg is a little disconcerting, so I keep both eyes peeled for Yogi and Smokey.

Soon Route 46 will cross US 441 and dead end at Highland Street. Turn right and travel a couple of blocks to East 5th Street. Then turn left. This will take you through downtown **Mount Dora,** another quaint central Florida town filled with antiques and ambiance. If you're in a mood to try something really different, rent one of the Segways from **Segway of Central Florida** (140 West 5th Avenue, 352-383-9900). At $40 per hour or $10 for 10 minutes, you can see Mount Dora from a whole new perspective.

Fifth Avenue turns into Old US Hwy 441 and continues west along **Lake Dora** toward the town of **Tavares.** About this time the dense traffic will have you questioning my logic, but it's an unavoidable part of the ride. Just watch your Ps and Qs and you'll be fine. Soon old 441 turns into East Alfred Street, which turns into West Alfred Street. At Mile 56.6, you'll need to turn left on SR 19 and at Mile 58, left on CR 561.

It's at this junction where I think the highest point in Florida is. No disrespect to the locals but if you look to your right, you'll spot a very tall hill with a couple of pieces of earth moving equipment on top. This is the county landfill. They wouldn't tell me how tall it is because of a silly Homeland Security restriction, but believe me, it's tall.

Continue on CR 561 south and you may begin to notice a stray cyclist or two. This area is well known to bicyclists who use the area to train. Now I'm not talking about the Schwinn banana-seat-casual Sunday afternoon rider. I'm talking spandex, funny helmet, "I could kick Lance Armstrong's butt if I had the chance" Tour De Wherever cyclist. Since hills are as rare in Florida as moonshiners in Manhattan, the area attracts bicyclists, motorcyclists, and sports car buffs so it hardly qualifies as the "Road Less Traveled."

At Mile 67, turn left onto CR 455, officially designated as the **Green Mountain Scenic Byway.** This road winds and twists among the hills of

With its clean and tidy streets, the quaint town of Winter Garden seems to encourage you to relax and enjoy a slower pace.

The tourists in central Florida are serious shoppers and scarcely notice leather-clad tattooed bikers.

the area geologists call the **Lake Wales Ridge,** and roughly follows the contours of **Lake Apopka** along its western and southern shores. There are a couple of spots where you can catch a good view of the lake and at night you can even see the skyline of nearby **Orlando.**

This twisty section of road is only 12.5 miles long, and ends well before you tire of it. At Mile 73.1, you'll enter the last of our "mountain" towns, **Montverde.** In case you were wondering, Montverde means "green mountain" which is why my friends at Florida's DOT designated CR 455 as the Green Mountain Scenic Byway. The first thing you'll notice when you enter the town is the Mediterranean Revival style buildings of the 125-acre campus of Montverde Academy. CR 455 carries you straight through the campus and just past the southern entrance is Morningside Drive, a nice spot to pull over and stop for a good view of Lake Apopka.

There's something about Live Oak trees dripping with Spanish Moss that carries me back to my childhood and lazy summer days in the rural South. (Photo by Sylvia Cochran)

CR 455 dead ends into Old Hwy 50 at Mile 78.6. Turn left and in 1.9 miles turn left again on CR 438. At Mile 82, you'll know you're approaching the town of **Winter Garden** as you pass under a canopy of moss-draped Live Oaks which completely cover the highway. I love riding the roads that pass under gnarled and twisted outstretched limbs of the great Live Oaks. They impart a mystical and almost foreboding feeling. Yet for all it portends, the feeling is familiar and comforting to this Son of the South who spent his childhood playing and digging in the dirt among the roots and the shadows of Live Oak trees very similar to these.

Soon the asphalt gives way to brick pavers as you enter the downtown area of Winter Garden. Vintage charm is the first phrase that comes to mind. Also, take notice of how clean and tidy this town is. If the renovations are complete and you have time to visit the **Garden Theater** on your right at 160 West Plant Street, stop in and see the crown jewel of this historic central Florida town. Train buffs will want to visit the **Central Florida Train Museum** (101 South Boyd Street, 407-656-0559) open daily from 1 to 5 p.m. with no charge for admission. Inside you'll find an excellent display of railroad china and a restored caboose, my favorite!

Leaving Winter Garden at Mile 86, turn left on CR 437 or Ocoee Apopka Road. If you're in a hurry, jump on SR 429 and head north to Apopka where 429 dead ends into US 441. Turn left and head back to Mt. Dora. If you stay on CR 437 however, turn left at Mile 95.2 on South Park Avenue for .3 mile to US 441. Then make the turn to Mt. Dora.

At Mile 107, our journey ends at the off ramp to CR 46. Turn right to retrace your route to I-4 in Sanford where you can hop on and head straight back toward Daytona and Bike Week madness.

■ For more trips in this region see *Motorcycle Journeys Through the American South* by Scott Cochran, available from Whitehorse Press.

SPANISH MOSS AND LIVE OAK TREES— THE ROMANCE OF THE SOUTH

Native Americans called it "tree hair" and when our country was young it was routinely boiled as tea and used as treatments for rheumatism, abscesses, and birth pains. Legend has it that Henry Ford used it to stuff the seats in his first Model Ts but I can't confirm that.

When I was growing up we always avoided it because we believed it contained chiggers, those nasty little bugs that you can't see but cause a rash of itching and red swollen skin. It is *Tillandsia usneoides,* or Spanish Moss, and it is unique to the South. This grayish silver plant ranges from Virginia to Argentina. Technically, it's not a true moss and is actually in the same family as the pineapple. Don't ask me how botanists arrive at their classifications because I'll never understand.

Contrary to myth, Spanish Moss is not a parasite and does not rob nutrients from its hosts. Instead, it gathers water and nutrients from the air directly through its own stems and leaves. Spanish Moss uses its host tree only for support, and interestingly enough will only grow in trees, not on fences or any other type of support. When I replay scenes from my youth, they always include images of massive 40 foot tall Live Oak trees, their branches heavy with long strands of Spanish Moss casting a 100 foot swath of shade.

The Live Oak tree is another instantly recognized symbol of the region. With a lifespan measured in centuries, the Live Oak has captured the imagination of southern poets and songwriters since this country was formed. When I was a child, I nailed a couple of boards between the branches of a live oak in my parents' backyard for a makeshift tree house and often napped there during hot summer days. Once, I dozed late into the evening and missed supper. This caused a panic in my house and my parents alerted the neighborhood and soon everyone started looking for me. Finally someone thought to ask my older brother where he would look for me and he led them to that oak where I was found, still asleep. Until I became a parent I never fully understood what the fuss was about.

If you've seen the movies *Gone With The Wind* or *Forrest Gump,* you get a sense of how these trees are woven into the very fabric of our lives here in the American South.

12 Natchez to Windsor Ruins

Text and photos by Scott Cochran

■ **DISTANCE** *125 miles*

■ **HIGHLIGHTS** *Pastoral views on the Trace, the oldest mansion in Mississippi, the Ruins of Windsor, a huge hand pointing toward the heavens, and the oldest store in southwestern Mississippi*

0 Start north of Natchez at the US 61/US 84 intersection	**76.8** Turn left on Carroll Street
	77.0 Keep left on Rodney Road
3.8 Enter Natchez Trace Parkway	**87.0** Turn left to Ruins of Windsor. Turn left on Rodney Road as you depart
15.7 Turn right on SR 553 toward Fayette	
23.7 Turn left on Main Street	**89.1** Bear left on SR 552 toward Alcorn
24.0 Turn right on Poindexter Street which becomes Old Hwy 28	**92.1** Stay left on Hwy 552 around Alcorn University
25.9 Turn left on SR 28	**99.0** Turn right to get on US 61/SR 552 and travel south to Lorman
50.9 Turn left on SR 547 to Port Gibson	
76.0 Turn right on US 61 (Church Street)	**125.** End at US 61 at US 84

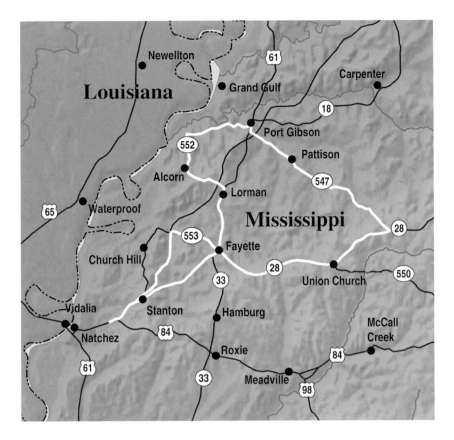

We start today's journey just north of **Natchez** near the entrance to the **Natchez Trace Parkway** at the intersection of US 84 and US 61. Head north on US 61 for 3.8 miles and take the Natchez Trace Parkway heading north. I've included this 12 mile stretch because the Natchez Trace is a favorite road of mine to ride. The reason isn't the throttle-twisting, knee-dragging curves or the roller coaster elevation changes common to other parkways in the South. I love the Trace for its history and link with our past. As you enter this beautiful Parkway here at Natchez, I want you to breathe a "thank you" to Mrs. Roane Fleming Byrnes, who died in 1970, but not before serving for 33 years as the successive president of the Natchez Trace Association. Mrs. Byrnes, more so than any other person, is responsible for keeping the dream of a completed Nashville to Natchez Trace alive. She did not live to see her dream become reality, but we should be grateful for her vision as we ride this beautiful highway.

At Mile 15.7, turn right onto SR 553 and leave the Trace behind. In a few miles you'll come to a faded sign on your left and a gravel drive to **Spring-field Plantation** (1833 River Road, 601-786-3802). In 1791, **Andrew**

Before he became president, Andrew Jackson married his wife here at Springfield Plantation in 1791. At the time, neither one knew that she was still married to her first husband.

Arthur E. LaSalle is the caretaker for Springfield Plantation and he is as interesting as the house itself.

Jackson, before he became our President, married Rachel Donelson Robards in the parlor of the Springfield Plantation. When it was discovered two years later that Rachel was not properly divorced from her first husband, Lewis Robards, the scandal rocked the country.

Built between 1786 and 1791, Springfield Plantation is supposedly the first mansion built in Mississippi. At the time, this area was known as "West Florida" and was under Spanish Rule. After the rebellion of 1810, the region was annexed into the U.S. Springfield Plantation has been preserved as it was when Jackson and Donelson were married with a few exceptions. The longtime caretaker, Arthur E. LaSalle, also exhibits a lot of his personal memorabilia and is a good and interesting tour guide. While Arthur talks fast, mumbles a lot, is hard to hear, and quite cantankerous, there's just something about getting history from the source. Remember the drive is gravel and can be tricky for large bikes or new riders. Admission to the Plantation is $10 per person.

Continue south on Poindexter Street (old Hwy 28) south for approximately one and a half miles and merge with SR 28. At Mile 51.4, turn left on SR 547 toward the town of **Port Gibson.** In about 25 miles, you'll enter town and spot the **First Presbyterian Church of Port Gibson.** The steeple on this Romanesque Revival style building features a hand with a finger pointing the way toward heaven. The first hand was carved from wood by Daniel Foley which time eventually destroyed, and the new hand, cast from over 2000 pounds of silver coins, was erected in 1901. It was refurbished and replated in 1990.

Leaving the church, return one block to Carroll Street, turn right, and in a couple of blocks, Carroll turns into Rodney Road. Ten miles later you'll come to the entrance of **Windsor Ruins** on your left. Down the short two-rut driveway is the commanding presence of the ruins of Windsor Mansion. All that remains of this stately southern mansion are twenty three burned brick columns standing 45 feet tall, stark contrast to

The way to heaven is clearly illustrated by this gold-plated hand on top of the First Presbyterian Church of Port Gibson.

the green grass and blue sky. The story of Windsor Mansion is one of love and loss. **Smith Coffee Daniel II** and his wife Catherine began construction of Windsor in 1859 and it wasn't completed until 1861. Just weeks after its completion, Smith Daniel died at the age of 34. For 29 years the house was the center of culture in the area and was the epitome of the romantic South. Petticoats and silk ascots marked the day and it's not hard to envision the festive gatherings here, just like the ballroom scene in *Gone With The Wind.* Even Mark Twain wrote about Windsor Mansion in his book, *Life on the Mississippi.* In February 1890, a careless house guest dropped a cigarette in some material left by workers who were renovating the third floor and the subsequent fire destroyed everything except the columns. The only rendering of the house as it once stood was done by a Union soldier during the Civil War when it was used as a Union Hospital. During the late afternoon when the air

THE RUINS OF RODNEY

If Arthur Davis, the owner of the Old Country Store is in a good mood you might get him to pencil you a map to the nearby deserted town of Rodney. I've been there but the roads were not in the best of shape back then so I'd recommend asking a local how to get there and the current road conditions. I wouldn't call Rodney a ghost town per se, because that has a Wild West connotation. Rather Rodney simply dried up in the mid 1800s after two fires, an outbreak of yellow fever, and the shifting channel of the Mississippi River took away its main means of commerce. In 1930 the Governor of Mississippi officially declared the town of Rodney "abolished." If you go, look for the cannon ball lodged in the Presbyterian Church façade.

becomes still and the birds quiet down, you can sit in the shadows of the huge columns and allow your imagination to carry you back to the days when cotton was king, the horse and buggy was transportation, and hoop skirts were high fashion.

Leave Windsor and turn left on Rodney Road. At Mile 89.5, bear left on SR 552 toward **Alcorn** and at Mile 92.5 take the Alcorn bypass left. In seven miles, bear right to merge with US 61 and SR 552 and at Mile 100.5, turn right to visit the **Old Country Store** (18801 Hwy 61, South Lorman, 601-831-2568). The doors to this old establishment first opened in 1895 as a hardware and grocery store that provided the surrounding citizenry with the everyday essentials of life. From coffee to caskets, the Old Country Store served its customers from the

Buildings like this old country store used to be the center of the universe for folks living in the rural South. The general store was the place where you bought the things you needed but couldn't grow or build yourself, like nails, candy, coffee, sugar, and flour. Today you won't find hardware, but you will enjoy the best fried chicken within 100 miles.

Natchez, Mississippi, has more than 500 surviving antebellum buildings. A prime example is the octagonal Longwood begun in 1859 by wealthy cotton planter Dr. Haller Nutt. The Civil War interrupted its construction and later caused the destruction of the fortune of its owner, thereby ensuring that it would never be completed. (Photo by Sylvia Cochran)

cradle to the grave. Today they're serving mashed potatoes and gravy and the finest fried chicken in southwestern Mississippi during the lunch hour.

When you're ready, continue south on US 61 toward Natchez where this journey ends at Mile 126.

■ For more trips in this region see *Motorcycle Journeys Through the American South* by Scott Cochran, available from Whitehorse Press.

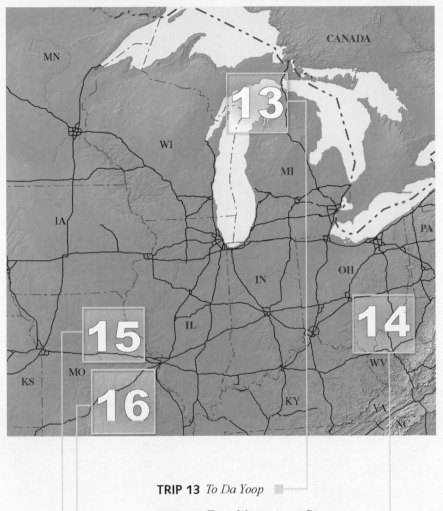

13 To Da Yoop

Text by Grant Parsons and photos by AMA staff

I don't know what it is about ferries, motorcycles, and me. I don't think I've ever been on a boat with a bike when it wasn't raining at one end of the trip or the other.

And today, right on schedule, as I wait for the Lake Express Ferry to arrive at a terminal just south of downtown Milwaukee on the shore of Lake Michigan, a light misting of rain appears.

On this car ferry from Milwaukee, Wisconsin, to Muskegon, Michigan, as on many ferries, motorcycles go to the head of the line.

It's not a big deal—I just put on my raingear—but it does give me pause, wondering how slick the ferry's metal decking will be under the wheels of the $35,000 Harley-Davidson CVO Ultra Glide I'm riding. A mix of wet metal, oil drippings from cars, and rubber tires always gets my attention.

By the time the 200-foot-long, 46-car ferry appears over the horizon, I've envisioned everything from a mild spill to a skid that puts the bike and me straight into the water. Of course, the reality isn't anywhere near that bad.

When the cars making the trip to this side of the lake clear off, I'm the first vehicle aboard—it seems that motorcycles, which can fit in odd places, are almost always first, no matter what ferry you're boarding. I go easy on the brakes on the slick aluminum decking, and in no time, I'm slotted into a narrow corner space and pointed at a set of tie-downs.

By the time I've cinched the CVO Ultra securely to the deck, the ferry is almost loaded. I head up to the passenger deck, find a mostly dry chair, and settle in. The boat's four 3,000-horsepower water-jet engines fire up and propel us away from Wisconsin at an impressive 40 mph. As the Milwaukee skyline shrinks in the background, I have time to ponder the trip ahead.

My plan is to land in Michigan and enjoy a quick trip up to and across Michigan's remote Upper Peninsula—also known as the U.P., or Yoop, to locals. But as time goes by, and I realize it'll take more than two hours to cross Lake Michigan, I find myself smiling—and re-defining my idea of "quick trip."

A little rain never seems to get in the way of having fun.

If ever there was a place that could legitimately be called "Harley Country," the area surrounding Lake Michigan is it. Fittingly, my tour starts a few hours earlier at the Mecca for V-twin fans—Harley-Davidson's Juneau Avenue headquarters in Milwaukee.

It's there that I catch up with H-D's Mike Morgan for a quick tour of the facility before I hit the road on the company's top-of-the-line Ultra. The HQ is impressive, with two six-story buildings that take up nearly a city block. It's a sharp contrast to the company's first "factory," a 10-foot-by-15-foot shed built in 1903, or even the second, a 28-foot-by-80-foot building originally located on this very site.

It didn't take H-D long to outgrow those relatively humble beginnings. The current structure was put in place just a few years later in 1912, testament to how successful the Motor Company was in only its first decade.

With the tour over and the Ultra pointed due east, I head downtown, then south on Sixth Avenue. There are quicker ways to reach the ferry terminal, but I wanted to check out the future site of the Harley-Davidson Museum. By just seeing the nearly complete shell of the 130,000-square-foot building, I can confidently predict that the facility will be impressive when it opens in July, 2008.

As I roll along surface streets, Milwaukee comes across as the quintessential working-class town. In many of the metro neighborhoods, there's literally a bar on every corner. In fact, the locals tell me Milwaukee has more bars per capita than any other large city in the country. I guess that's what long winters can do for you.

By the time I reach the ferry terminal, roll aboard, and head out for Michigan, though, I'm already looking forward to the roads waiting on the other side of the lake. The crossing itself is relatively uneventful, other than the mild swaying of the catamaran's hull in the small swells. The wind is brisk, but the rain is gone. I pass the time watching the gulls and the occasional huge cargo ship go by.

A couple hours later, Michigan comes into view off the port bow. The ferry captain throttles back as we enter a narrow inlet into Muskegon Lake, and the sun comes out for real as we pull up to the terminal.

I go below decks to find the Ultra has stayed put during the crossing—always a good thing. I unlatch, gear up, and am waved off the ferry. After a few feet of slick aluminum decking, I roll back onto dry land in Michigan.

I may be in the Wolverine State, but I don't have to look far to find places that could be a thousand miles away.

Case in point: The Pere Marquette Public Beach near Muskegon. Named for a French Missionary who explored Michigan in the 1600s, the shoreline offers hundreds of yards of blond-sand beach.

I roll up to a parking place and look out at a scene that includes rolling waves, kids playing in the surf, sand volleyball courts, and a weathered snack shack serving up candy bars, hot dogs, and cold sodas.

If I didn't know any better, I'd think I was on the Atlantic, not the shores of Lake Michigan. It's a great place to sit and feel the breeze under a sky that now has more sun than clouds.

An hour later, headed north toward my stop for the night, though, Michigan returns. It's getting toward sunset, and I'm on Michigan Route 22, north of Manistee, a great sweepy strip of asphalt well in from the shore.

Here, the trees close in, and the smell is of humid vegetation. I've killed a few hundred bugs with the windshield of the Ultra. Signs warn of moose, and snowmobile trails occasionally crisscross the road.

By the time I reach Arcadia, I've managed to find Elvis' "Teddy Bear" on the bike's satellite radio, and when I crest a rise that offers a panoramic view of Lake Michigan, life is good.

The Michigan experience intensifies as I near my stop for the night in Glen Arbor. As night closes in, I find myself skirting the shore of Glen Lake on dark, curvy roads, looking for my hotel in a light fog. The Ultra's driving lights are a plus, but my speed slows to a crawl in the curves so I don't override my headlights.

Luckily, I find the hotel with a minimum of fuss, and then discover a great restaurant just down the road. On the waitress' recommendation, I go for the

Picturesque harbors with sailboats on their moorings is a common sight along the Great Lakes in Michigan.

walleye almondine, made with the fish that made the Great Lakes famous. It's pretty darn good, reinforcing why walleye is my favorite freshwater fish.

By mid-morning the next day, I'm huddled under a picnic shelter at a country church in the rolling hills of the Leelanau Peninsula, watching a torrent of rain come down.

Far from being bummed by the rain, I'm enjoying the stop. Besides, if you're riding in Michigan, getting upset about rain isn't the best idea. Storm systems are constantly lifting water off the four Great Lakes surrounding the state and dumping it on the land. In the winter, it means tons of lake-effect snow. In the summer, it produces heavy storms that pass as quickly as they appear.

On the Leelanau Peninsula north of Traverse City, farmers turn that rain into apples and grapes—and then cider and wine. And as I make my way across it in the receding rain, I find plenty of vineyards and groves, along with lazy country roads with little traffic. Nice.

The only downside is that the relative quiet of the peninsula makes Traverse City seem like too big a town, and I'm glad to leave it behind on U.S. Route 31 toward perhaps Michigan's most famous literary landmark: Horton Bay.

A little off the beaten path south of Petoskey, Horton Bay's claim to fame is as the summer boyhood home of author Ernest Hemingway, who vacationed here with his family for years.

I roll into Horton Bay around noon, and pull up to the brightly painted General Store. Before I can even put my kickstand down, there's a guy on the porch of the Red Fox Inn next-door, calling me over for "a little Hemingway history." Like most days here, today must be a slow one.

The guy at the Inn has converted the place into a combo bookstore and shrine to Papa, and he regales me with the area's numerous Hemingway connections.

Young Hemingway shopped frequently at the general store, and even used it as a setting in many of his short stories, including "Up in Michigan." He fished in the creek just west of town. His cabin on Walloon Lake is only a few miles away.

Horton Bay is a great diversion, but I've got miles to make, and after a quick soda break, I point the Ultra toward another of the region's famed landmarks: The Mackinac Bridge. Connecting lower Michigan to the Upper Peninsula, "Big Mac," as the locals call it, is nearly five miles of concrete suspended from steel cables.

Horton Bay was Ernest Hemingway's boyhood summer home.

Several miles north of Traverse City this sign lets you know where you are.

It runs 200 feet off the water and is billed as "the longest suspension bridge between anchorages in the Western Hemisphere."

The wording is important, because it's not the longest between the two spires—the Golden Gate Bridge center section is longer than Big Mac's. And it's not the longest total, because the San Francisco-Oakland Bay Bridge is longer.

Nit-picking aside, the Mac is still mighty impressive.

To Da Yoop

The Mackinac Bridge is impressive from any angle.

I'd heard tales of high winds being a problem for cars and motorcyclists in the high center span. In fact, you can still stop at one end and have someone else drive your car across if you're iffy on the whole thing. I'm good with the Ultra, though, and make it across without incident.

The day has turned beautiful, and the breeze is light. The ride across takes a surprisingly long time, and the views from the span are incredible. The only issue is the open grating in the center two of four lanes. It's there to lessen the effect of wind oscillations and makes the Ultra feel a little nervous. But being able to occasionally sample the view through the grate is worth it.

And at the other end is "the Yoop," also called "the U.P.," or Upper Peninsula. And as remote as northern Michigan had felt, the Yoop seems even more removed from civilization. I log a long 80 miles of lonely interstate before I reach my stop, the small city of Sault Ste. Marie, which, up here, seems like an absolute metropolis.

Luckily, I score a hotel right downtown, opposite the locks between Lake Superior and Lake Huron. I pass the time watching huge container ships float through less than a block from Main Street, right across from Canada.

It's time for breakfast when I arrive in the small town of Paradise on the remote southern edge of Lake Superior. (I had been hoping for a cheeseburger in Paradise, but I showed up far too early.) So I wander into the local diner and order up eggs and bacon instead—and it turns out to be a great choice. Jimmy Buffet, eat your heart out.

Looking over my map, I realize that "remote" is too soft a word to describe the feel of this part of the Yoop. In fact, on the ride up here on Michigan Route 123, I rode more than 5 miles between houses.

The real shame is that I'm not on a dual-sport bike, as I was several years ago when we were riding up here for the AMA Ride Guide to Michigan. We all agreed that the web of sandy forest roads and gravel byways that crisscross Michigan's Upper Peninsula was one of the best dual-sport playgrounds in the country. There's something here to suit any level of adventure-touring bike, from wheel-swallowing sugar sand to fast, graded dirt under canopies of trees.

Imagine five miles of this. That's what you'll get when you cross the Mackinac Bridge.

From Newberry, we had headed due north on H37, a paved road heading for the coast. You could smell Lake Superior long before you could see it. There's a clean, bracing scent over the aroma of evergreens. When I crested a gentle rise I saw the blue of deep water stretching to the horizon where it blurred into the sky.

I parked the bike and wandered down to a narrow, sandy beach that looked more like the tropics than it has any right to. Somewhere, way out there, was the other shore and Canada, but much too far away to see.

I rode for several miles along the shoreline on H58, which soon turned from pavement to hard-packed dirt. Being the week after Labor Day, I had the south shore of Lake Superior to myself, which gave this otherworldly place a decidedly frontier feel.

First charted by fur trappers and scouts in the 1600s, this shoreline quickly became familiar ground to the timber and mining industries. But unlike almost any place else east of the Mississippi, the U.P. has retained a remoteness that you usually only find in the West.

My map showed a finger of land called Lonesome Point extending into the Harbor of Refuge that seems to symbolize that feeling perfectly. After 10 minutes of riding on a dirt road that turned into a rugged two-track, I found

You are so close to the beach and lake that you can smell it when you ride.

that some developer had beaten us to the place. The forest was sectioned off in neat, little plots and posted with "No Trespassing" signs. Apparently, this point wouldn't be lonesome much longer.

Just as I was getting hungry, the outpost town of Grand Marais appeared in front of me. Out by the lighthouse on a narrow spit of land, I found a little restaurant tucked next to the U.S. Coast Guard lifesaving station. A visitors center just outside of town marked the eastern boundary of Pictured Rocks National Lakehore. But a more accurate name would be Dual-Sport National Park.

Set aside by the federal government in 1966, the Lakeshore is 40 miles long and about five miles wide. And within that space, it's hard to find any paved roads. The sign at the entrance read: "Unimproved Roads. Travel at Your Own Risk. Next 20 miles" which sounded good to me.

The first leg takes you past Grand Sable Dunes, huge sand mountains left behind when the glaciers retreated and carved out the Great Lakes. At Log Slide Overlook, a 100-yard hike leads to a breathtaking view of endless sand cliffs standing guard over a deserted beach that really does go on for 12 uninterrupted miles.

After that, H58 heads inland for awhile, eventually leading to the town of Munising. But before that, there's one more treat left: Miners Castle.

A six-mile spur road leads back to Lake Superior and the "castle," which is actually one of the most majestic of the colorful sandstone formations that give Pictured Rocks its name. At the overlook, you can look straight down from a dizzying height into a small bay where waves constantly pound away at the rocks. That day made me a big fan of Superior's south shore.

On this trip though, with the Ultra, I'm sticking to asphalt, which is a good thing as I continue on Michigan 123 toward Newberry. The tight sweepers through Tahquamenon Falls State Park wind through a wildlife refuge with plenty of moose warnings and long views over small foliage. I can see why this region is an outdoorsman's playground.

The road loops me back to Michigan Route 28, a dead-straight east-west road through the middle of the U.P. Mercifully, it only lasts for about an hour or so—it's amazing how spoiled you can get by good roads.

Civilization, of sorts, and the lakeshore return in the small town of Munising. It may only be home to about 3,000 people, but after miles of relatively nothing, it seems huge.

On the way to Marquette, the road parallels the coastline, offering up some great lakeshore views. The sky has cleared and the sun is shining. The only clues I'm not looking out at, say, North Carolina's outer banks, are the chill wind and the deserted beaches.

My final destination in the Yoop is Copper Harbor, way out at the end of the Keweenaw Peninsula. When I get to the town of Hancock, about 70 miles away, though, I realize that much of the peninsula is technically an island.

The map and temperature say 46 degrees north latitude but the view says the tropics.

Down there is Twelvemile Beach in Pictured Rocks National Lakeshore. Other than you, it's probably deserted.

Over lunch at a diner in downtown Hancock, the waitress tells me that the northern part of the peninsula was separated from the lower by a canal built in the 1860s. Turns out the 100-foot-wide Keweenaw Waterway between Portage Lake and Lake Superior created what the locals call Copper Island, the largest island in Lake Superior.

The town itself has some great bits of history. I ride the Ultra past some great Victorian homes and Doctor's Park, once home to some of the richest land barons and doctors in the U.P., before I cross the bridge to the "island."

My last run of the day turns out to be the best. North of Hancock, U.S. Route 41 begins as rather pedestrian, but past the turnoff for Eagle River it gets tight and twisty as it weaves

There's something calming about water, and a motorcycle.

through dense vegetation and sharp hills. After nearly a thousand miles of straighter road, it's a welcome change.

A few dozen miles of fun later, I drop down a steep hill to the water's edge in the town of Copper Harbor, a former copper boomtown that now stakes its fortune on tourism. It'd be a beautiful village under any circumstances, but I arrive late in the day, with the golden light of the approaching sunset, and the view is simply stunning.

Topping off my gas tank and grabbing a snack, I check the height of the sinking sun and jump back on the bike. I've been told of a great overlook just southwest of town that sounds like the perfect place to watch the setting sun.

I ride along Michigan Route 26 to the edge of town, where I turn south on Brockway Mountain Road, which climbs steeply up through several switchbacks. The patched road surface slows my pace, but I soon crest a rise where the trees are cleared away, and a wide pullout is full of cars and people.

Miner's Castle stands up to the constant pounding of the Lake Superior waves.

I guess I'm not the only one who enjoys a good sunset. I park the bike, slide back to the Ultra's passenger seat, pull out some crackers and Gatorade and settle in for the show.

The view is the most impressive I've seen since crossing Big Mac a day and a half ago. There's a panoramic view of Lake Superior, dotted with small boats and the occasional large cargo ship. And way out there, near the horizon, I can see the outline of Isle Royale, the largest natural island on the lake, which is also a protected national park.

The sun nears the horizon, and the dozen or so people gathered on the mountain fall silent. The sinking red sun paints the thin, high clouds in shades of pink, for a spectacular display.

I may have miles to go to get back to civilization tomorrow, but today, I can think of no place I'd rather be.

14 Ohio's Twisty Roads

Text by James Holter and photos by AMA staff

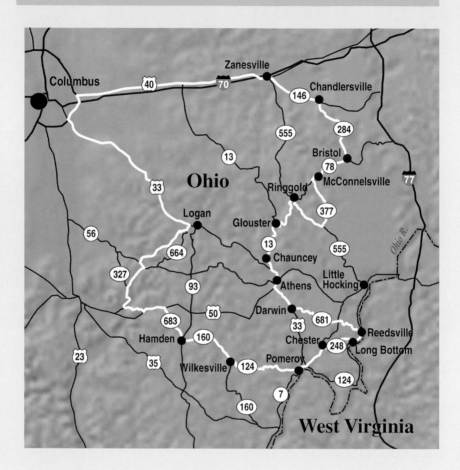

Looking for the best motorcycling that Ohio has to offer? The search is easy. Just get out a state map and draw a wide arc, starting from the upper righthand corner, sloping downward to just south of the center point of the state in Columbus, and finishing up in the lower left near Cincinnati.

Now forget everything to the north and west of that line. That stuff is the mostly flat land that people think of when they hear "Ohio:" arrow-straight roads a mile apart on a grid, dotted with corn, soybeans, and Friday night high school football under the lights.

Instead, look south and east. That way, it's all Appalachian and Allegheny foothills, and some of the best riding you'll find anywhere in the country. And for the best of that, you'll want to point the front wheel of your

The country roads are magical in southeastern Ohio.

motorcycle toward the town of Athens, Ohio, perhaps the epicenter of the best roads in the state.

Which, as it turns out, is exactly what we're doing for the road-riding portion of Ride Guide Ohio. And since the AMA's headquarters is located just north of the good-riding line, on the eastern edge of Columbus, that makes this officially the easiest Ride Guide Launch ever.

All that I, managing editor Grant Parsons and photographer Bill Andrews have to do is ride into work and gather at the AMA garage to load up the stable of bikes offered up by this year's Ride Guide OEM partner, KTM. With Grant laying claim to KTM's Super Duke for the first leg of our ride, B.A. and I each opt for one of two 990 Adventures.

Soon, we're blasting south on State Route 33, the expedient route to Logan, the real jumping-off point for our ride in the heart of the Hocking Hills region. Here, the hills come courtesy of Blackhand Sandstone, which has stood firm over millennia while lesser minerals have eroded, revealing steep cliffs and deep gorges into the tree-covered terrain.

As with anywhere, hills mean grades, grades mean curves, and curves mean great motorcycle roads. And they start quickly with Ohio Route 664, a rolling, curving strip under a canopy of trees. Finally, I can start bending the Adventure into the corners and enjoy satisfying launches on exits that only a torquey V-twin can provide.

Whether you're looking for a spirited ride or a leisurely cruise, you can find what you need in southeastern Ohio.

In no time, the regular world falls away, and we're riding among small farms, barns, and wonderfully tight blind corners. I can tell that this ride, based heavily on a ride that AMA Tours boss and head of the AMA's road-riding department Frank Covucci calls his Magical Twisty Tour, will be a good one. With a few strategic detours, we're heading for a good 350 miles of undulating goodness.

Traffic, however, is still a bit heavy this close to one of the state's primary north-south routes, so we don't waste time looking for a cut-off. We find it in Big Pine Road. This narrow strip of pavement cuts southwest across more of the same topography, but with a lot less of the road traffic—unless you count the occasional bicyclist.

That said, this region can see heavy traffic on summer weekends, with tourists drawn by several nearby state parks. But now, during the week, we seemingly have it to ourselves.

For about 35 miles until we hit U.S. 50—by way of state Route 56, Narrows Road, County Route 17 and state Routes 327 and 671—we're able to relax and focus on the ride. It's a fun route that strikes the right balance between challenging and difficult, with the occasional batch of tight off-cambers and decreasing-radius turns to keep us on our toes.

It's enough of a workout that by the time we reach the intersection of U.S. 50 and state Route 683, we're ready for a snack and fuel break. We find it at the Cross Creek Mart, an eclectic collection of three-quartered-sized, country-themed displays that's as much tourist trap as convenience store. We take our time and wander through some of the backwoods-inspired kitsch.

We continue south on state Route 683, past the Wellston Wildlife Area and 325-acre Lake Rupert, to state Routes 160 and 124. Riding through small towns like Hamden, Wilkesville, and Rutland, the terrain opens up slightly as we approach the Ohio River.

We hit state Route 7 and follow it into Pomeroy, the Meigs County seat. Built along the Ohio river, the main drag is bordered by shops on the north and the waterway on the south. It's a unique layout, one that retains its distinctiveness as the side roads reach into the steep cliffs that start just behind Main Street.

Indeed, Pomeroy's hilly terrain makes it enough of a geographic oddity that Ripley's Believe It or Not! recognizes it twice: first for being the only city in the country that does not have a single four-way intersection, and second for the three-story Meigs County Courthouse, which hugs the steep cliffside and has the convenience of a ground-level entrance on every floor.

Of course, any stop in Pomeroy requires a few minutes to enjoy the view from the parking lot sandwiched between downtown and the Ohio River.

Locals were quick to exploit the 981-mile-long waterway, probably none

What covered bridges lack in visibility, they make up for with atmosphere.

Rivers and river towns are an important facet of Ohio history.

more so than local landholder Samuel Wyllys Pomeroy and his son-in-law Valentine Horton (who would go on to represent Ohio in the 37th U.S. Congress). In the mid-1880s, Pomeroy pioneered the use of coal barges, helping the city that would later adopt his name become a major player in the era's commodity-driven economy.

Today, however, we're interested in the river's impact on the local topography, not so much its century-old contributions to local industry, so we fire up the KTMs and ride out of town on old state Route 7 toward Chester and state Route 248.

After tracking north for a few miles, we head east and hook back up with the river, and state Route 124, at Long Bottom. After another short photo break at the Forked Run State Park's Ohio River boat launch, where we tentatively and carefully back the KTMs out onto the 3-foot-wide concrete walkway jutting into the river, we follow 124 until we hit state Route 681.

Stretching from where we join the road in Reedsville to just north of Albany, state Route 681 is a 40-mile collection of tight twisties, long sweepers, and varied climbs and descents. With B.A. keeping his camera in its case and very little traffic in our way, we're able to navigate the cascading asphalt without interruption until we reach Darwin.

Although state Route 33 has been recently revamped into a two-lane freeway that stretches from here into Athens, we opt for old state Route 33, which roughly parallels the new freeway, but respects the rolling landscape while the new route bulldozes through it. The next 13 miles tack on more hills and twisties, including a few tight 90-degree turns that might have snuck up on me if I weren't so familiar with this area. At the other end of these 13 miles is not just our stop for the night, but the home of my alma mater.

Athens was incorporated seven years after the original Northwest Territory's first college, Ohio University, was established here in 1804. Sitting along the Hocking River on the south and Strouds Run State Park on the north, Athens is every bit as hilly as Pomeroy. What its downtown lacks in

There's a lot to like about rivers, even when they mean you've reached the end of the road.

river views, however, it makes up for in energy. The nightlife is invigorated nine months out of the year by a vibrant population of roughly 15,000 college students.

After parking the bikes at a small motel just outside the city limits, we take a taxi back to Athens' buzzing Court Street. Our first stop is the Red Brick Sports Pub & Grill, where we're primarily interested in the "grill" part of that equation after our long day of riding and photo shoots.

As he often does when it comes to situations that involve consumption, B.A. puts both me and Grant to shame, ordering up the Big Guy, a burger that boasts a full pound of ground beef, and he actually manages to get most of it down after our triple-dog dare before we head out to see just how Athens has changed since I graduated from here 11 years ago.

The answer? I've changed more than Athens, for sure. More important, though, tomorrow calls for more miles—and more curves—so we make it an early night.

Spitting rain greets us the next morning, but it ends as we ride to Chauncey just a few miles north of Athens on state Route 13, and minutes later, we emerge into sunshine on state Route 78 in Glouster. Here, the asphalt is dry and the views are as stunning as any in the state. Autumn is in full bloom, and the hills are dripping with color. We drop our pace, and drink in our fill of the scenery.

We're not getting anywhere fast, but that's fine. Not only do I enjoy the vistas, but I'm happy to get the sightseeing out of my system. Coming up is a road that will demand our full attention at any speed: state Route 555.

Also known as the Triple Nickel, state Route 555 ends at Little Hocking on the south and Zanesville in the north. And we pick it up in the stellar middle of its great 60-mile run near Ringgold.

Other places have their famous A-list motorcycle roads, rides like the Ortega Highway, Deals Gap, and the Angeles Crest Highway. In Ohio, it's the Triple Nickel.

A roller-coaster of a road with blind rises that put your stomach in your throat and devilish curves that replace your stomach with your heart, 555 is not for the squeamish—or those with little cornering clearance. It's a serious challenge even at the speed limit. Luckily for us, B.A.'s shooting photos, so Grant and I get to re-ride the best bits over and over.

The fun ends all too quick, though, and soon we're heading back north on 377, doing our best to stay on schedule. We tie back into state Route 78 in McConnelsville, where we break to shovel a few calories into our mouths before going in search of a much bigger shovel: Big Muskie.

A coal mining dragline as big as an apartment block, Big Muskie was the world's largest earth-moving machine before it was retired in 1991. The humongous crane stood 22 stories tall and weighed nearly 13,000 metric tons. It cost $25 million to build in 1969 and, all told, moved 608 million cubic yards of earth. That's enough dirt to fill in the Panama Canal—twice!

Bend your bike around any tight curves lately? Get your wheels to the Triple Nickle.

Big Muskie was made to do one thing—change the shape of the Earth. It did.

Dismantled in 1999, the last physical reminder of Big Muskie is her scoop, which sits along state Route 78, just west of Bristol. After a hard life, the house-sized bucket rests at a beautiful overlook as a permanent reminder that man can indeed move mountains—well, foothills at least—if he builds a big enough crane.

At Bristol, we turn back north on state Route 284, then west on state Route 146 in Chandlersville. Together, these roads provide a fitting summary of our ride, combining a great deal of curves with some nice views. And just in case we get complacent, the roller-coaster hills are some of the steepest on the trip.

It's not long, though, before the ground flattens out heading into Zanesville, and we merge with another of the region's great historical bits of asphalt, U.S. 40, the National Road.

Long before there was Route 66 to link Chicago to L.A., there was the National Road, linking the Eastern Seaboard to the interior of what was the Northwest Territory. In this part of Ohio, it's mostly straight, arrowing through the small towns that grew up along it, and it's a fitting wind-down to a frenetic 350 miles.

As we head west, on the last 40 miles of the road portion of Ride Guide Ohio, I think back to the sweeping corners, tight twisties, rolling hills, river views, full-cover canopies, and broad country vistas. It's a lot to take in. Luckily, this is one Ride Guide where I can say I'll definitely be back for more.

15 The Great River Road

Text and photos by Bill Kresnak

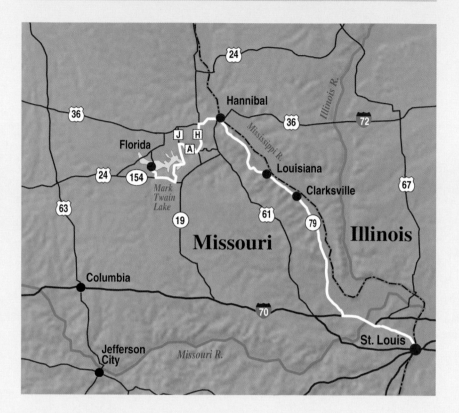

"Twenty years from now, you will be more disappointed by the things that you didn't do than by the ones you did do. So throw off the bowlines. Sail away from the safe harbor. Catch the trade winds in your sails. Explore. Dream. Discover."—Mark Twain

The words of America's most famous 19th century author echo in my mind as I aim the Gold Wing across the Midwest. I'm headed, aptly enough, toward Twain's boyhood home of Hannibal, Missouri, hoping to learn a bit more about the place where Samuel Clemens—the kid who eventually became Mark Twain—grew up.

The stoic flatness of the prairie across Indiana and Illinois gives me plenty of time to contemplate what I'll find along Twain's Mississippi. I know I'm in for some interesting history on the Great River Road, and I've heard there are other scenic routes following the course of this country's most storied

The Missssissippi Queen travels the waters of the Mississippi filled with tourists seeking simpler times.

river. Still, I go into this figuring that it's going to take a little digging to uncover what Twain experienced growing up—which means I'm not quite ready for what I find when I bail off Interstate 72 in western Illinois, and head down U.S. Route 36 toward Hannibal.

At first, I sense it more than see it through the dappled trees—something very large is moving on the river. Then I reach a clearing and come face to face with a modern embodiment of Twain's riverboat dreams. There, making its stately way down the wide river, is the Mississippi Queen, all impossibly long 382 feet of her. That sure didn't take long.

This boat—a modern replica of the sternwheelers of Twain's time—is huge. Floating a full five stories tall in well-maintained white, the Queen is a vision straight from the past. I can only imagine the power needed to drive the boat's massive paddlewheel as it steams for Hannibal.

Can I beat it there? Let's see, I've got the advantage of several decades of mechanical progress. That, along with light traffic and a few lucky guesses, allows me to reach the landing just as the Mississippi Queen approaches. I settle on the dock, recalling Twain's words:

"When I was a boy, there was but one permanent ambition among my comrades in our village on the west bank of the Mississippi River. That was, to be a steam-boatman."

The Great River Road

Tom Sawyer and Huck Finn in search of adventure.

The huge wheel churns the dark water as the boat nudges up to the dock. Deckhands cast giant ropes to shore and secure the big boat. It's even more impressive up close, from the smokestacks on top to the mermaids guiding the boat on its path. Yup. It's pretty easy to see how a young kid could think that something like the Mississippi Queen is pretty neat.

There's plenty to see in Hannibal. And I'll get to that soon enough. But first, I click the Wing into gear and point it toward Florida, Missouri, 35 miles away. It's here that, in 1835, Twain was born. County Route HH winds out of Hannibal and heads for Mark Twain State Park. I don't think the convenience stores were here 170 years ago, but a stately feeling, reminiscent of the Old South, still comes through. The route is bordered by large farms and then forest, while above, the morning heat churns up storm clouds. It soon starts to sprinkle, and just in time, I pull into the Mark Twain Birthplace State Historic Site. I park and sprint to the museum, just as the sprinkle turns into a downpour.

"It's turned a little wet out there," the guide says as I shake the drops off my jacket.

"Just a bit," I reply, thinking again of Twain: *"Everybody talks about the weather, but nobody does anything about it."*

The museum turns out to be the perfect place to wait out a brief shower. There are a few first editions of Mark Twain's works, and a handwritten manuscript of "The Adventures of Tom Sawyer," a reminder that back then, writing literally meant writing.

The museum also houses the small, two-room cabin where Samuel Langhorne Clemens was born on November 30, 1835. The cabin can't be more than 16 feet by 25 feet, with one bedroom. At one time, it was home to Twain, his parents, four siblings, and a teenage slave—all at once. It had to be a tight fit, something Twain realized later in life: *"Recently, someone in Missouri has sent me a picture of the house I was born in. Heretofore, I have always stated that it was a palace, but I shall be more guarded, now."*

I take the quick quarter-mile jaunt to the actual site where Twain was born.

TRAVELOGUE: MIDWEST

It's preserved in a small clearing, marked by a red granite monument, surrounded by trees. Humble beginnings, indeed.

When the weather breaks, I hop back on the Wing and retrace my route. This time, without having to keep eyes on developments in the sky, I can more fully enjoy the road through the 2,775-acre park. I click up a gear, then another, as I cruise through thick forest. The road winds through marsh land alongside Mark Twain Lake.

The trip back to Hannibal takes less than an hour on my modern steed, but it would have taken at least a full day by wagon when Twain was a boy. Back then, the bustling river port must have come as a shock to the 4-year-old Twain when his family moved there. But it quickly became his home:

"Hannibal has had a hard time of it, ever since I can recollect, and I was 'raised' there. First, it had me for a citizen, but I was too young then to really hurt the place."

Just on the edge of downtown, I spot a promising-looking place for lunch. I aim the Honda into a parking place in back of the Mark Twain Family Restaurant, known to the locals as the Mark Twain Dinette, and stroll in

Good eats can be found at the Mark Twain Dinette in Hannibal, Missouri.

A local favorite: Maid-Rites, onion rings and a frosty root beer.

for a bite. I scan the menu, then toss it aside and ask waitress Carla Hamilton for the local specialty: three Maid-Rites, onion rings, and a frosty root beer.

I discover that a Maid-Rite is sort of like a sloppy joe without the sloppy part—a hot sandwich filled with seasoned loose ground beef, served with pickle and onion. They're tasty enough to eat several in a sitting, and I do.

Maid-Rites are, as it turns out, extremely regional.

"They have 'em in Iowa," Hamilton says. "We had a guy from there come in and said theirs are juicier. I told him that's not juice—that's grease. Here, we try to get all the grease out of 'em."

Mark Twain's boyhood home now houses a museum and gift shop.

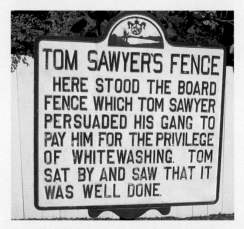
A replica of Tom Sawyer's fence stands next to Twain's boyhood home.

The restaurant is right next to Hannibal's historic district, so I leave the Honda parked and stroll down the block. For a small town, it's pretty packed with literary history. Over there is the J.M. Clemens Law Office, where Twain's father worked. The courtroom in that building was the setting for the trial of Muff Potter in *"The Adventures of Tom Sawyer."* A block down the cobblestone street is the one-time home of the Elijah Hawkins family, where young Laura Hawkins lived. Perhaps you know her better by her alias in *"Tom Sawyer"*: Becky Thatcher.

The Twain look-alike actor greeting tourists in Hannibal, Missouri, was also a motorcyclist.

There, directly across the street, is Twain's two-story boyhood home, and right next to it is a replica of the wooden fence made famous in "Tom Sawyer." Perhaps Twain's recollection of the place, when he saw it in 1902, after being away for 29 years, says it best:

"It all seems so small to me. A boy's home is a big place to him. I suppose if I should come back again 10 years from now, it would be the size of a bird house."

Up the street is a statue of Tom Sawyer and Huckleberry Finn, dedicated in 1926. It is believed to be the first statue in the world dedicated to literary characters.

From the door of Twain's house, I hear a long blast from the Mississippi Queen's steam whistle, indicating that it's time for passengers to board. I fire up the Honda and head back down to the dock to watch. There, I come face to face with Mark Twain himself. He's standing off to the side of the gangway, just chatting up passengers. OK, it's actually actor George Scott, one of several Twain impersonators who make a living in Hannibal.

The Mississippi has plenty of spots to pull over and spend some leisure time.

"I'm the only real Mark Twain," he confides in me. "The rest are all helpers."

It turns out that Scott, a transplant from Waukegan, Illinois, who took up this line of work thanks to an uncanny resemblance to the famed author, is also a motorcyclist. So I spend a few minutes talking bikes with Mark Twain. He tells me he bought a 1958 Harley-Davidson FLH dresser in 1971 and toured the country on it with his wife. He still owns, and rides, that very bike.

Then a tourist walks up for a photo, and Scott the motorcyclist becomes Mark Twain again.

"When I left Hannibal in 1902, I said, 'Don't change a thing,'" he quips. "And they haven't."

Scott walks away to greet more tourists, and I go back to my bench to watch the Mississippi Queen churn down the river. Like me, the big boat will be heading to St. Louis. In fact, I should be shoving off, too. But as I gaze at the lazy Mississippi, I think again of Twain, who once famously said: *"Never put off until tomorrow what you can do the day after tomorrow."*

Why rush?

The next morning, I head down state Route 79 toward St. Louis. But I quickly get sidetracked by inspiration in the form of another passage from *"Tom Sawyer."*

"By and by somebody shouted, 'Who's ready for the cave?' Everybody was."

I'm ready for the cave, too. So I pull off 79, aiming for the labyrinthine cave system that Mark Twain made famous in *"Tom Sawyer."* In real life, it's called Cameron Cave, an appropriately touristy destination in its own right. I park the Wing, pay the $12 entrance fee and wait for the next tour group to enter. To pass the time, I scan the brochure and find another quote from Twain that reveals some of his personal connections to this cave:

"'Injun Joe,' the half-breed, got lost in there once, and would have starved to death if the bats had run short. But there was no chance of that; there were myriads of them. He told me all his story. In the book called 'Tom Sawyer,' I

starved him entirely to death in the cave, but that was in the interest of art; it never happened."

Leading us through the huge cave, with its innumerable passageways snaking off into the darkness, our tour guide tells us true tales of outlaws hiding out down here and, during Twain's boyhood, the body of a young girl being stored in the place. Her father kept her here for two years in a bizarre attempt to petrify her remains. The guide also shows us where the fictional Tom Sawyer and Becky Thatcher got lost. Walking through the narrow passageways, I make sure to keep within sight of the person in front of me. It's easy to see how you could lose your way in here.

After the tour, I'm glad to be out in the bright sunlight again. I ride back to Route 79, heading for St. Louis. It's here that I discover one of the best and

The Bistro in Clarksville, Missouri, is inside a 100-year-old bank building.

most scenic roads of the trip. Route 79 is one of dozens of roads following the Mississippi that have been strung together and designated the Great River Road. Together, those roads let you follow the "Father of Waters" from St. Paul, Minnesota, all the way to New Orleans and the Gulf of Mexico.

At first, 79 is a classic river route, with the Mississippi on my left, and thick forest on the far bank. The water is wide and flat, and the occasional barge reminds you that it's very much a working river. But soon, the road twists inland, offering up long sweepers and rolling hills. The road winds through forest, then past farmland and large pastures, with horses grazing peacefully. This is part of the 30-mile Little Dixie Highway, a state-designated scenic highway. It has a real Southern feel, thanks to plantation-style mansions and the Victorian architecture of towns along the way.

I head for one of those towns: Louisiana, a place with a fair bit of Twain history. It was here that Twain ended his first riverboat trip at the age of 7. He stowed away aboard a boat in Hannibal and was put off in Louisiana when the crew discovered him.

Cruising through town, I soak up the Victorian atmosphere. Then I pick out a spot near the Mississippi and again turn off the bike to contemplate the

The Great River Road

The mighty Mississipp River.

river. Twain returned here for a visit later in life, and he felt the same sense of nostalgia that he had in Hannibal:

"I could not clearly recognize the place. This seemed odd to me, for when I retired from the rebel army in '61, I retired upon Louisiana in good order; at least in good enough order for a person who had not yet learned how to retreat according to the rules of war, and had to trust to native genius. It seemed to me that for a first attempt at a retreat it was not badly done. I had done no advancing in all that campaign that was at all equal to it."

I should be on my way. But again, I consider words of wisdom from Twain: *"Diligence is a good thing, but taking things easy is much more— restful."*

For whatever reason, Twain never seemed to hurry. I decide to follow his advice, settling in for another peaceful half-hour of river-watching.

From his humble origins here, Twain went on to become a riverboat pilot, a newspaper editor in California, and a renowned world traveler who finally settled in Hartford, Connecticut. For Twain, this river was the highway from his Missouri youth to a fascinating and sometimes puzzling world. Ironically, though, the stories the world found most memorable were Twain's tales of adventure set right here, along the Mississippi.

Eventually, I continue down the Great River Road, winding along the Mississippi for a while, then veering through farmland before doubling back to the river town of Clarksville.

Clarksville, with its storefronts and buildings from the 1850s and '60s, is on the National Registry of Historic Places. It's the perfect spot for a coffee break, so I pull in at the Bistro on Artists' Row, which is a converted 100-year-old bank. The coffee is strong and good.

Next stop: St. Louis. The rolling roads and easy pace of the past few days give way to the hustle of a major metropolitan city. Fields become suburban tract homes, then strip malls, then industrial areas as I make my way to the Museum of Transportation, which features more than 300 locomotives, passenger and freight cars, airplanes, automobiles, and more. I study the "Big Boy," claimed to be the world's largest steam locomotive; the Union Pacific "Centennial," the world's largest diesel; and some art deco trains. It's a sharp reminder that the age when the riverboat was king was relatively short-lived—something Twain himself realized by the time he wrote the following in the late 1800s:

"The romance of boating is gone, now. In Hannibal, the steamboatman is no longer a god. The youth don't talk river slang anymore. Their pride is apparently railways—which they take a peculiar vanity in reducing to initials ('C B & Q')—an affection which prevails all over the West. They roll these initials as a sweet morsel under the tongue."

Back on the road, I motor past the factories and warehouses that helped build this river city, and ride into the heart of the downtown riverfront district. There, I catch up with my old friend, the Mississippi Queen. In Hannibal, she seemed larger than life. In St. Louis, the boat's massive presence seems diminished as she sits, tied up in the shadow of downtown. Looking at the stately boat, it's easy to see the irony of its mooring spot. The sternwheeler floats just downstream of the massive Eads Bridge, built in 1847 so trains could cross the Mississippi, linking East and West. At 1,500 feet long, the bridge dwarfs the Mississippi Queen, which is all alone in the dark water, while crowds gather around the newer floating casinos nearby.

No residents or tourists gawk at the boat, and there's no activity on board. In fact, it seems I'm the only person who's interested enough to walk down here. The water flowing under the bridge continues south for another 675 miles, where it empties into the Gulf of Mexico. But in some ways, it's clear that Mark Twain's Mississippi ends here.

16 The Other Ozarks

Text and photos by Grant Parsons

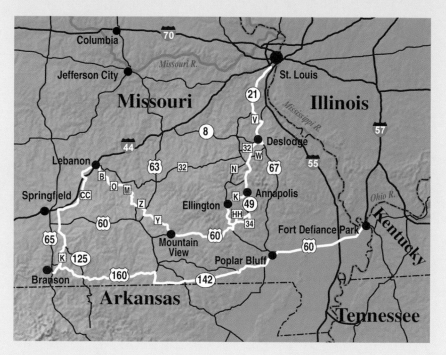

"Where in the heck *is* everybody?"

The thought crosses my mind for perhaps the 20th time this morning as I sweep along smooth backroad pavement in the southeastern Missouri Ozark Mountains. Sure, it's a weekday, so I didn't expect to see a whole lot of people out here clogging up the roads. But I've seen no one—absolutely no one—in a good 10 miles. Not that I'm complaining, of course. I'm perfectly happy to enjoy my own personal ribbons of asphalt through the rolling hills. After a while, though, I can't help wondering where everybody went.

After all, the Ozarks are well-known as a great motorcycle destination. And my first taste of the area's winding roads this morning, savored from the seat of KTM's absolutely thrilling Super Duke, certainly shows why. Already, I've found plenty of rolling terrain, twisty roads, and the kind of rural communities and people that are the perfect antidote to a world where everything seems to look more and more alike. But I'm starting to think that by choosing the Missouri Ozarks—which are perhaps slightly less well known than the same mountains in nearby Arkansas—I may have stumbled onto a

144

Between the twisty backroads and the serene lakes, the Missouri Ozarks are a recreation paradise.

great motorcycling secret, because I get to experience all that without worrying about a lot of slow-moving traffic, all the better. As the miles roll by and a beautiful day warms up, I'm quickly becoming a fan of the Other Ozarks.

For those of us in the eastern half of the U.S., the Mississippi River is an important dividing line between East and West. And after crossing the wide, flowing river at St. Louis, I head straight for the city's equally impressive landmark—the Gateway Arch. This graceful, soaring, stainless-steel monument marks the unofficial start of my tour. That's only fitting, since the 630-foot arch was constructed as a symbolic gateway to the West as part of the larger Jefferson National Expansion Memorial Park. There's plenty of history connected with the structure, finished in 1965, but its oddest chapter may have come in 1980. That's when a parachutist hoping for glory landed briefly atop the arch. Problem is, a gust of wind caught his chute, and he wound up sliding to his death down most of the length of one leg.

I park the Duke and make my own ceremonial journey into the West by walking under the structure. Only problem is I then have to walk back to my bike, ceremoniously re-entering the East. Hmmm. I guess that makes two of us who didn't exactly think through our arch-related endeavors.

Although the Ozarks are calling, if you're a motorcyclist, you can't leave St. Louis without a visit to the impressive Mungenast Museum. So I ride through downtown to Gravois Street, where I discover the cool storefront facility that was enthusiast Dave Mungenast's dream. Sadly, Dave is no longer

The Other Ozarks

Mungenast Classic Motorcycles Museum in St. Louis, Missouri contains the extensive collection of the late Dave Mungenast.

with us. But his enthusiasm lives on in an impressive bike collection that spans the entire history of motorcycling, from the early board-track era to today. It's easy to kill some time here, and I do.

With rush-hour on the way, I hightail it south out of town, where the Ozark foothills start in earnest. I find myself riding through a region that includes towns with evocative names like Leadwood, Mineral Point, Iron Mountain, and Marble Hill. The geologic names are no accident. This area was part of Missouri's "old lead belt," where lead and iron ore were mined. Back in the early 1900s, more than 15 mining companies worked the region, carving thousands of miles of tunnels.

With the city of St. Louis long gone as I begin day two, I point the front wheel of the Super Duke west from Deslodge, into the heart of the Ozarks. Yesterday afternoon's roads were a bit too ordinary for my tastes—interstate and U.S. routes through the occasional Wal-Mart town. So I'm hoping to do better as I pick up Missouri Route 32, then hang a left onto County Route N. It's like flipping a switch. Instantly, the traffic disappears, and I find myself chasing rolling ribbons of asphalt. It's a perfect first taste of the real Ozarks as I thread my way into the St. Francois Mountains toward the morning's first destination: The highest point in Missouri.

I see the turnoff for County Route CC and follow a winding, heavily patched road through dense forest toward the peak of 1,172-foot Taum Sauk Mountain. At the top, I find a parking lot, a ranger's residence, and more of the dense, tall oaks. Luckily, there's an observation tower, too, and I make myself dizzy climbing the spiral stairway to the top. I barely clear the towering trees before I reach a locked door just short of the platform, but the view from the stairs is worth the effort. Down on the ground, it felt like I'm riding through rolling hills. But viewed from here, these are clearly mountains, folded into ridges that lead off into the distance in every direction.

The alphabet, I decide, is definitely your friend in the Ozarks. That's because Missouri's county routes are designated by letters, not numbers. And if my experience is any guide, those ABC routes are where you want to be if you're riding a motorcycle. The road that seals the deal is County Route K from Annapolis to Ellington, a sinuous roller-coaster, deserted of traffic and covered by a canopy of trees. Riding along, relying on the Super Duke's broad torque curve for both acceleration and braking duties, I can't ask for anything better. I'm having such a good time, in fact, that when I reach a numbered state route again, I search the map for a good letter-designated alternate. I find it in Route HH, which ultimately leads over a tall earthen dam holding back Clearwater Lake.

A while later, after changing my route to avoid an oncoming storm, I take my own advice again and string together more than 50 miles of alphabet soup: Y to YY to M to AE to KK

The locals offer a friendly warning.

to O to B. It's a lot of letters, but it still spells fun. I'm headed generally northwest, aiming for the town of Lebanon, which was once a major stop on the famed Route 66. And as the miles roll by, I notice the terrain is changing. What was tight, twisty and technical, is changing to rolling and sweeping, with the occasional farm. The sparse population, and the weathered barns along the way, set a nostalgic tone. With the exception of the nice, modern pavement I'm rolling on, it feels like I'm headed for the Mother Road back in the day.

Of course, when I reach Lebanon, the spell is broken by the usual string of fast food joints and gas stations where I cross Interstate 44. Still, I'm not quite ready to give up on that nostalgic feeling, and thanks to a few tips from the AMA's own Greg Harrison, I don't have to.

Few people know the history of Route 66—and the tricks you need to find the original route these days—more than Greg, who created the AMA's "Raising Route 66" tour along the length of the Mother Road. He notes that more than 85 percent of the old road is still out there, especially near early roadside oasis towns like Lebanon. So I start by heading straight for the center of town, where Route 66 likely would have cut through. Luckily, there's a sign denoting "Historic Route 66"—too easy!

I follow the road northeast toward the edge of town, where Greg has assured me there's a great throwback to the '40s and '50s heyday of Route 66. I find it in the form of the Munger-Moss Motel. It's the kind of old-style motor court that used to serve as way-stations along the road. And it still has its old neon sign right out front. I pull in, throw down the kickstand, and take a moment to soak up the history of the place. Looking back toward town, it's definitely a modern scene. But if I aim my eyes in the other direction, out along the lonesome, straight old road, it feels like I'm looking into the past. Back then, the Munger-Moss' neon sign must have seemed like a lighthouse beacon to travelers heading across the Missouri prairie.

The Other Ozarks

Cop motor, cop shocks, cop suspension, cop tires, and a busted cigarette lighter. Yup, it's the new Bluesmobile on display in Branson.

Of course, now that I've found the old road, I need to ride a bit of it. So I point the Super Duke back through town, and soon I'm cruising through gently rolling farmland toward Springfield. For a while, my route parallels the Interstate, which also follows the railroad tracks. But in time, the modern highway veers west, and I find myself rolling through the tiny towns that Route 66 strung together. The one constant is the railroad. It's pretty easy to see how Route 66's planners chose their route. It's a great departure from a modern world that rushes by, just out of sight, on the interstate.

Branson, Missouri, is the kind of place you either love or hate. This Midwest mecca is home to country-music shows, trinket stores, and the most fudge shops this side of Gatlinburg, Tennessee. Call it what it is: A tourist trap. Not that there's anything wrong with that, at least as far as I'm concerned. But that may be because of the way I come into town.

Having studied the map, I know there's one main four-lane road leading from the interstate in Springfield about 30 miles to Branson. And it's the route that most traffic follows. So I opt for a much longer and twistier course that hooks into Branson from the east. It turns out to be a great set of roads, quickly putting me back into the Ozarks proper, with tight turns and the occasional sweeping view from high up. Ultimately, my route dumps me out at a bridge across a narrow sliver of Lake Taneycomo and directly into downtown Branson.

What I wind up with is all the kitsch, and none of the traffic. And as a bonus, I get to see the old downtown part of Branson first, before I check out the touristy main road that is the Missouri answer to the Las Vegas Strip. With the right frame of mind, it's actually kind of fun. And even if kitsch isn't your thing, Branson likely has something that nearly everyone can appreciate—super-cheap hotel rooms.

I'm on the road early the next morning to check out another feature of the Missouri Ozarks: Lake country. Branson is pretty well hemmed in by water, with Table Rock Lake to the west and Bull Shoals Lake to the east. Both offer up long views of blue water, rocky, mountain shores, and clear skies. I'm headed east, first crossing Bull Shoals in Forsyth, then picking up U.S. Route 160, where I cross the water a few more times. I pick a road heading south at random, and wind my way down to the shore. Parking the bike, I settle in for a cracker-and-Gatorade breakfast, while watching a group of herons feeding in the water. A steady stream of trailer-towing cars arrives, launching a small fleet of bass boats. All in all, it's a relaxing way to spend a morning.

The area's fishing is obviously a major draw, with bait shops, boat dealerships, and signs for marinas dotting the road as I head farther east. A sign at Theodosia proclaims it the "Record Bass Capital of Missouri," which seems a bit odd, since another town about 50 miles away claims to be the "Bass Capital of the World." I waste far too many minutes trying to figure out which slogan trumps the other.

In time, I drop a bit south onto state Route 142, a rolling, winding—and, of course, completely deserted—strip of asphalt that parallel's the state's southern border. With busier routes available to the north and south, I cruise for a good 30 miles seeing only a single car. Soon, though, I reach the town of Poplar Bluff, where my glorious two-lane turns to four, and the terrain turns from mountainous to flat. But I've got one more cool stop to make, about 60 miles ahead, along the Mississippi River.

An hour later, I pull off Interstate 57 in Charleston, and pick up U.S. Route 60 heading for the Mississippi. I'm cruising through low farmland, with a tall levee between me and the water. Then, I round a corner, cross a bridge over the Mississippi, and hang a right into Fort Defiance State Park. I'm on a tiny triangle of land that represents the southern tip of Illinois. On one side of me rolls the mighty Mississippi, separating Illinois and Missouri. On the other side is the Ohio River, and beyond it, Kentucky. Here, at this point, those two major rivers and three states come together. And it's also here, where I've ceremoniously crossed back into the East, that my tour ends.

There sure is a lot of water in these mountains.

THE SOUTHWEST

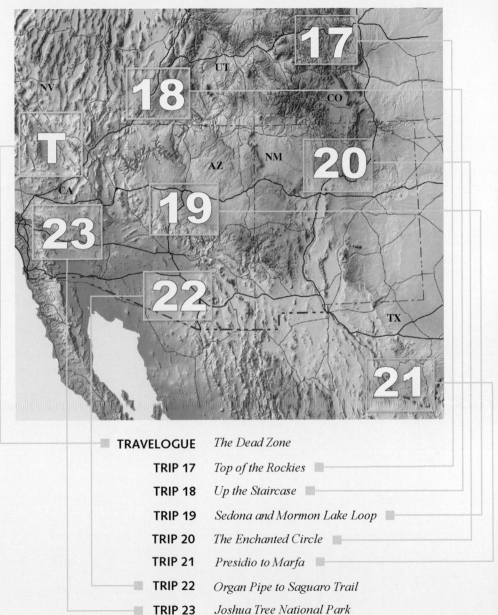

The Dead Zone

Text and photos by Grant Parsons

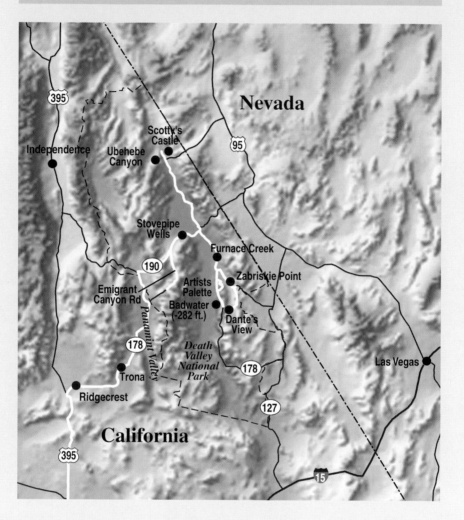

I've been riding all day through Southern California's Mojave Desert, baking under a harsh sun in 90-degree temperatures. So, by the time I crest the Panamint Range in late afternoon, I figure I'm ready for anything. And that's a good thing, because the Kawasaki Vulcan 900 and I are pointed down—way down—into Death Valley.

From the top of the mountains at 4,956 feet along the northwest border of Death Valley National Park, California Route 190 winds through a few good twists, then straightens out and starts dropping. The decline is gradual, and

Death Valley is remote, which is part of the fun.

the scale of the land is so huge that at first, it's hard to tell I'm losing altitude. The giveaway, though, is the temperature. It gets hotter with every mile.

As I descend farther, the view opens up to reveal a vast expanse of sand, knee-high scrub, and shimmering heat waves hemmed in by tall mountains. I allow my eyes to trace the road as it extends across the valley. A dot of reflection captures my attention, and I realize that it must be my destination: Stovepipe Wells Village. But it's still a very long way off. And as the miles roll by, I continue my descent. The heat becomes impossible to ignore, even with my mesh riding gear. I don't need a thermometer to tell me that it's hotter than the 95 degrees I saw on a bank sign a hundred miles ago in the town of Ridgecrest.

Twenty minutes later, I reach the wide spot in the road that is Stovepipe Wells. I park the Vulcan at the gas station and walk through the dry, oven-like heat to the entrance.

There's a thermometer by the door. It says 107. It's in the shade. And it's only April.

Nearby, a plaque commemorates the group of pioneers who gave Death Valley its name. The band became lost in this unmapped valley in 1849 and suffered starvation, dehydration, and disease. Four members of the "Death Valley '49ers" died, and the rest wound up burning their wagons to cook their dying oxen. After three months of hardship, the survivors emerged on foot. These days, of course, Death Valley is a bit more hospitable. At least that's what I'm hoping.

From valley to canyon, Death Valley is full of spectacular scenery.

Few motorcycling destinations are as potentially memorable as Death Valley. It contains the lowest point on the continent (Badwater, 282 feet below sea level). It's the driest place in the U.S. (annual rainfall less than 2 inches). And it's one of the hottest places on Earth (summer temperatures can reach the 130s!). It's also surprisingly accessible. Located on the California side of the California-Nevada border, Death Valley is just 280 miles from Los Angeles and 140 miles from Las Vegas.

The proximity of those major cities, however, belies the fact that Death Valley actually is in the middle of nothing. It's not on the way to anywhere. You don't have to go through it. There are many faster, less intimidating roads that lead around it. In other words, Death Valley isn't a means. It's an end. To go there, you really have to want to go there. And I do.

After picking up the Vulcan in Los Angeles, I point the front wheel northeast through the city's smoggy, traffic-clogged valley. I aim over the San Bernardino Mountains, toward the clear air in Hesperia, on the edge of the Mojave. After a turn onto U.S. Route 395 and a few too many stoplights in this rapidly growing community, I find myself striking out across the desert proper.

The roads out here are long and straight, and I feel more like I'm piloting a boat than a motorcycle. There's no real sense of speed because the scenery never changes and the distant mountains never seem to get any closer. There's not a cloud in the sky, and at the crossroads in Kramer Junction, I realize that's the way it must be here pretty much all the time.

Next to the road are acres and acres of elevated pipes. Running inside trough-shaped parabolic mirrors, the pipes lead to the Kramer Junction Solar Electric Generating Station. Here, sunlight superheats oil, which, in turn, boils water to produce steam for electricity.

Farther north, in the desert town of Ridgecrest, I decide that the sun must make people crazy. In a strip mall on the main road is a sign saying: "Grand Opening: Tanning Salon." What's next? A sauna?

Ah, the march of progress.

The Kawasaki rolls through more faceless desert along California Route 178 northeast of Ridgecrest. The endless sagebrush and painted landscape conjures memories of old Westerns, and I imagine how difficult it must have been to make a living out here back in the day—or even these days, for that matter.

When I roll into the tiny industrial town of Trona a few dozen miles later, I see how at least a few people do it. Sitting on the edge of Searles Dry Lake, Trona is made up of weather-beaten buildings, industrial conveyors, and large, dust-covered dump trucks. The town is a living, working piece of history. Named by John Searles, the dry lake here was found to contain two useful chemicals—borax and potash—in the 1860s. Borax was useful for several industrial processes, but it was also a key ingredient in detergents of that era, and one brand, 20 Mule-team Borax, took its name from the huge numbers of these hardy animals needed to haul heavy wagonloads of the mineral out of the desert. Some say the Trona mines were the first to use the famous 20-mule teams, and many years later, when rival operations over the mountains in Death Valley adopted the 20-mule-team name, the American Trona Company called theirs "Three Elephant Borax." Now that's a tug-of-war I'd love to watch.

I continue north, cresting a line of mountains before dropping into Panamint Valley, a sort-of warm-up for Death Valley. The curves on the downhill run are as twisty as any I've seen since leaving L.A., and it's fun to bank the Vulcan through the heat.

On the valley floor, I kill time playing "how far is it to that next rise over there." The answers vary from seven to 10 miles. Big place, this desert. I'm reminded of the words of Andy Goldfine, the founder of Aerostich. He notes that one of the great things about motorcycles is they tend to make riders feel small and vulnerable, and more connected to the world. As I turn right onto California Route 190 and cross the mountains that ring Death Valley, I understand exactly what he means.

Death Valley is a lot like the parabolic mirrors superheating that oil back in Kramer Junction. With mountains more than a mile high on each side of a wide valley, it's a natural solar oven. And after enjoying a bit of the 107-degree spring warmth on the day I arrive, I'm glad I came prepared. I top off with water, fire up the bike and set off to see what the Valley has to offer.

As a National Park and part of the Mojave and Colorado Deserts Biosphere Reserve, Death Valley's environment remains unspoiled by development, while its history is well-preserved by the dry air. And history is exactly what I find as I retrace my route a few miles up Route 190 and hook a left onto Emigrant Canyon Road. The road begins straight, then rises between narrow canyon walls, offering a few twists that are as refreshing as the cooling air. Continuing to climb for nearly 30 miles, I roll past dirt roads leading to long-abandoned gold and silver mining towns like Skidoo, Eureka, and Harrisburg. Not much is left of them today, but they're reminders that for a brief time, at least, gold and silver deposits spurred rapid growth in the area—followed by rapid bust.

Be prepared and have plenty of water if you are going to cruise Death Valley.

TRAVELOGUE: SOUTHWEST

One early boom helped build Panamint City into what was billed as the toughest, rawest, most hard-boiled hell hole that ever passed for a civilized town. The town sat on the downslope of the dirt cut-off road leading through Wildrose Canyon and back toward Trona. It was home to 2,000 people for three years before the bust, and subsequent flood, wiped it out in 1876.

Like many of the former town sites in Death Valley, Panamint City is best reached by a dual-sport motorcycle. Still, a few interesting sites can be

And this was not the lowest spot.

reached on a cruiser without damaging the paint. One of them comes three miles after the gravel starts at the end of this road.

Up here, where the air is cool at 6,800 feet, a series of 10 beehive-shaped charcoal kilns serve as a reminder of how much work was required to mine precious metals. The kilns were used to reduce pinon and juniper trees to charcoal, which was used to smelt gold ore in the local mines.

Back at Stovepipe Wells, I top off the Vulcan's gas tank, noting that the small service station doesn't even bother to post gas prices, which are 30 cents per gallon higher than most places. After all, where else are you going to go?

I roll past the impressive Death Valley sand dunes, and marvel that people are actually out climbing them in the noontime heat. It's the one place where Death Valley looks worse than it really is. From some angles the view reveals no brush or vegetation of any kind.

Still, the Death Valley moniker is a little misleading. There is life in the desert, but it's specifically adapted to the harsh environment. Some plants on the valley floor have roots that can stretch down 40 feet or more in search of life-giving water. Others have vast shallow root systems to capture moisture from dew. Most animals here are nocturnal, and some, like the kangaroo rat, have evolved so they don't even need to drink water, drawing what little moisture they need from the seeds they eat. Me, I need actual fluids, and I've already drained half of my supply by the time I reach the impressive Ubehebe volcanic field at the park's north end.

In the span of less than a mile, the landscape goes from faceless beige desert to black-sand hills. A tight, one-way loop road climbs right to the lip of Ubehebe Crater. In geologic terms, this crater, half a mile wide and about 800 feet deep, is a recent addition to the landscape. A steam explosion blew

Scotty's Castle, which is actually neither, rises up from the desert.

the volcanic mountain that sat above it across a six-square-mile area a mere 3,000 to 6,000 years ago. What's left now is a pretty impressive hole in the ground ringed with hiking trails that bake in the sun.

Thankfully, relief is available a few miles away at Death Valley's most extravagant landmark, Scotty's Castle. A rich man's massive getaway mansion, the castle is located up the mountainside, well off the valley floor. It sits beside a rare flowing creek, and tall trees shade a picnic area with tables perfect for an afternoon nap. But as I find when I walk though the mansion itself, the place is neither "Scotty's" nor "castle."

The massive Spanish-style villa was commissioned in 1927 by Chicago insurance exec Albert Johnson, who found the desert helped his health problems. But the man on the ground in California who oversaw construction and then served as caretaker, "Death Valley Scotty," told everyone it was his, and the name stuck. As colorful a storyteller and con-man as you'll find anywhere, Scotty wound up in Death Valley after traveling with the famed Buffalo Bill Wild West Show, then conning several Eastern businessmen out of money to fund non-existent mines. Somehow, Scotty and Johnson became lifelong friends, and Scotty actually lived in the villa for long stretches. As far as I'm concerned, that's more evidence that the sun makes you crazy.

The next morning at 4 a.m., I coast the Kawasaki down to the main road, fire the motor and head out. I'm not just trying to beat the heat. I'm looking for the sunrise. I ride south on 190 for 30 miles, enjoying the eerie, pre-dawn desert light and the low-90s temps. The loping thump of the motor is my only companion as I note the elevation changes by the occasional road sign. I drop to sea level as I roll through the sleeping micro-town of Furnace Creek.

On the way to Zabriskie point, I come upon a pair of coyotes, dining on road kill right on the yellow line. I slow, trying to predict which way they'll run. These guys are smarter than the deer I usually see in my headlights, though. They just move a few feet away from their breakfast, lower their heads and bare their teeth. They've played this game before.

At Zabriskie Point, I find a spectacular view of naturally eroded sandstone monuments, and I'm right on time for the sunrise. Then I realize my error. The sun may rising somewhere right now, but it won't clear the wall of mountains here for another hour or so.

Good advice not only for Death Valley, but for anywhere.

I pass the time with another fool who made the same miscalculation, but we soon forget our mistake as the first tips of light breach the mountain wall.

We watch the line of the sun slowly move across Death Valley, dropping from the snow-covered mountains to the valley floor, and finally to the sandstone outcroppings in front of us. Like thousands before me, I ooh and ahh, and snap a few photos before heading back to Furnace Creek in search of breakfast. The town has a couple of food options, a gas station, a museum, several houses and an up-to-$409-a-night resort and spa that includes—you guessed it—the world's most superfluous indoor sauna.

Now this is more like it. My grin is as wide as my helmet as I bank the Vulcan from side to side up the curviest road within a hundred miles. I've already visited one of the park's other great attractions, Artists Palette—a 10-mile loop road made up of first-gear corners through wildly colored rock canyons. But I've been told that the place I'm headed is the one true can't-miss spot of Death Valley—Dante's View.

As I bank the Vulcan side to side, the road only gets better the higher I go, especially beyond the point where tow vehicles are required to drop their trailers if they plan to continue through its tight twists. A road as good as this deserves a payoff, and this one has it in the form of a spectacular overlook. A quirk of tourist timing puts me here at a time when there isn't a single other

The landscape is stunning.

vehicle in sight. I roll my bike right up to the edge for a look. The view—plus the altitude—takes my breath away.

At 5,475 feet, the overlook is more than a mile straight up above the floor of Death Valley. The only sound is the wind. The view is of mountains, sky, and, way down there, mile after mile after mile of dry white salt beds left over from a massive sea that evaporated eons ago. From my eagle's perch, I can look straight down toward Badwater, the lowest place on the continent, a mere 5,757 feet below me. It leaves quite an impression as the Kawasaki's motor cools and ticks atop the edge of the world.

It's getting late, and ahead of me this afternoon is more than 200 miles of desert riding on the way back toward L.A., much of it through the hottest and most imposing parts of Death Valley. By all rights, I should be in a hurry to leave. But I'm not.

Even after taking some photos and enjoying the view for far too long, I still can't seem to pull myself away. Instead, I break out some Gatorade, lean back against the front wheel of the Vulcan and enjoy a solitary moment on a beautiful day. The rest of the world can wait.

Most times, the view from such a great height just makes things far below appear small and insignificant. But somehow, from up here, Death Valley looks even more impressive.

Looking to visit one of the country's most impressive and forbidding national parks? Do it up right:

• Plan your visit: Air temperatures routinely rise into the 120s and beyond during the summer months. Late fall to early spring are prime months.

• The scale of the park, which costs $10 to enter, is huge. Expect a lot of seat time to see the good stuff.

• There are two hotels in Death Valley, both operated by the National Park Service. The motel in Stovepipe Wells offers clean, but basic, accommodations starting at $109, and the Furnace Creek Inn goes upscale from the mid-$200s a night. Camping is also available in several park locations.

• There are three gas stations in the park: at Stovepipe Wells, Scotty's Castle, and Furnace Creek. Fuel, along with everything else, is expensive.

• The road north of Trona to Wildrose canyon looks inviting on a map, but a 10-mile section of it is rough dirt best suited to dual-sport motorcycles. Several mining town sites, cool geological locations and remote views well worth the effort are accessible with a dual-sport motorcycle. Another highlight is the gravel West Side Road, a less-traveled route that follows the Death Valley floor between Furnace Creek and Ashford Mill.

• Flash floods are rare, but they do happen. Check for any road closures before you go at www.nps.gov/deva/.

• With high temperatures, dry air, and long days, Death Valley can be draining, both mentally and physically, especially if you're on a motorcycle. A few things to keep in mind:

• Carry water, and plenty of it. The heat and dry air will dehydrate you more quickly than you realize. A drinking system that straps on your back or fits into a tankbag is ideal, so you can drink while riding.

• Make sure your motorcycle is in top condition. The temperatures are hottest over asphalt roads, making overheating a real concern. Radiator water is available throughout the park, but checking your system before a trip is important.

• Wear gear specifically made for hot weather—perforated leather or mesh textile jackets are necessities, not luxuries, in the desert. Exposed skin will feel warmer than covered skin, especially if you get sunburned.

• It's hot on the valley floor, but temperatures can drop at higher elevations and at night. Carry a range of clothing for varying conditions.

• Sunscreen works. Use it on all exposed skin and your face, even under a full-face helmet.

• Cellphones don't work in Death Valley, so if something goes wrong, you're better off waiting with your vehicle for help.

17 Top of the Rockies

Text and photos by Toby Ballentine

- **DISTANCE** *206 miles (full day)*
- **HIGHLIGHTS** *Eight 10,000 feet passes and five crossings of the Continental Divide all in one day. Old ghost towns and colossal peaks, from which fortunes were made and lost, line the way along the Top of the Rockies. For the adventurous, a gorgeous span of backroad takes you deep into the heart of the Rockies on the Guanella Pass. Elevation change 8,500 to 12,000 feet.*

0 Start in Georgetown. Take Guanella Pass Road (State Route 381) toward Grant.	**110** State Route 91 becomes US Hwy 24.
22 Arrive Grant. Turn right (west) on US Hwy 285.	**111** Arrive Leadville. Then head north on US Hwy 24 to Ski Copper/Camp Hale.
50 Arrive Fairplay. Turn right (north) on State Route 9 toward Breckenridge.	**141** Arrive Minturn. Continue onto I-70.
71 Arrive Breckenridge. Continue on Route 9.	**143** Merge onto I-70 east.
81 Arrive Frisco. Continue on to I-70.	**177** Take Exit 205 State Route 9/US Hwy 6 to Dillon.
82 Merge onto I-70 west.	**178** Arrive Dillon. Continue on US Hwy 6 toward Keystone and Loveland Pass.
87 Take Exit 195 onto State Route 91 to Copper Mountain/Leadville.	**194** Merge onto I-70 East just past the Ike Tunnel.
	206 Take Exit 228 to Georgetown.

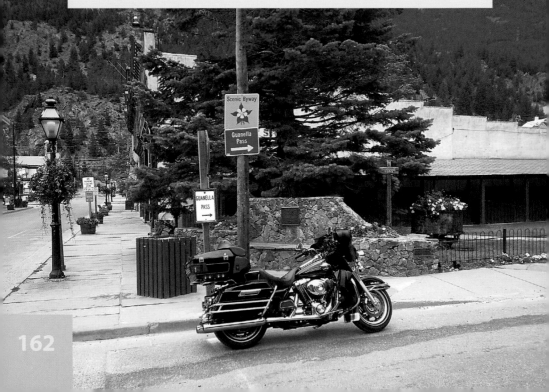

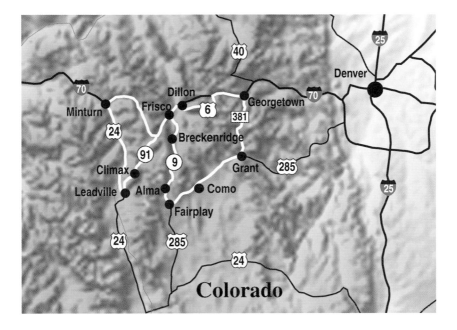

This inverted figure eight loop takes you on two of Colorado's most scenic byways through the heart of the Rocky Mountains. The "Top of the Rockies" was designated a National Scenic Byway in 1999 and rarely drops below 9,000 feet. The old mining town of Leadville lies at the hub of the byway sitting at 10,430 feet between towering fourteeners. The other scenic byway at Guanella Pass links the two mining towns of Georgetown and Grant via an old wagon route built during the 1860s. Both routes combine into an unforgettable journey through pristine natural wonders and rustic, Victorian style mining camps.

One question and one word of caution before we get started: Are you feeling adventurous today? The Guanella Pass Scenic and Historic Byway is twenty-two miles long with about ten miles of pavement or oiled backroad and another twelve miles of well-groomed dirt. The well groomed part can be subject to debate depending on recent weather patterns and road maintenance. The run from Georgetown to the pass summit is usually well maintained, but the backside to Grant can sometimes require navigating through various and sundry potholes. Ask about conditions in Georgetown, and if at all possible try to complete the entire twenty-two miles to Grant as it ties in well with the "Top of the Rockies" loop. If I did it on a Yamaha FZ-1, then no doubt you can do it as well! Otherwise, just head up as far as you can to get a taste for some beautiful backcountry solitude and then return to Georgetown. Connect up with I-70 west to Exit 195 on State Route 91 toward Leadville for a shortened version of this loop.

GEORGETOWN

Located about forty miles west of Denver, **Georgetown,** (www.george towncolorado.com, 800-472-8230) just off I-70, makes an ideal base for exploring the Rockies of North Central Colorado. Nestled at the base of Mt. McClellan, Georgetown was one of the few historic communities not ravaged by fire during the 1800s thanks to the well trained and brave "fire ladies" of Georgetown. The original 100-plus year old Victorian-style architecture gives Georgetown an atmosphere reminiscent of times past and contributes to its local charm.

Old Victorian homes like this one line the streets of Georgetown.

Shops, boutiques, and restaurants now line the center of this once-booming mining town. Old homes meticulously restored surround the small downtown area at 6th and Rose Street. A good place to stay is the reasonably-priced **Georgetown Mountain Inn** (www.georgetown mountain inn.com, 800-884-3201) located on Rose Street. The rooms are large and it is conveniently located in the older part of town. If you prefer camping, head on up Guanella Pass Road (Rose Street) to the Clear Lake Campground (www.fs.fed.us, 303-567-3000).

Georgetown offers several dining establishments from fast food to sit down eateries. My favorite is the **Red Ram Restaurant & Saloon** on 6th Street (303-569-2300). The interior is similar to an old mining town saloon and the meals are great. Another more upscale restaurant is the **New Prague** just past 6th Street on Rose. Or if you just want some ice cream, try "End of the Line" on 6th north of Rose Street. It's a small town, but you definitely won't go hungry.

This historic little mining community is like an Old Western town without the wild action of Gunsmoke or Wyatt Earp. A relatively mild town for the Old West, but a great place to relax after a long day of mountain twisties.

The upscale New Prague in Georgetown, has a great reputation for its food.

Most of the 24 miles to Grant is unpaved.

For you daring souls, start this journey in Georgetown and turn right on Rose Street. This will take you to **Guanella Pass Road** (route 381 on your map) and on to Grant. The road is well marked and paved as you climb toward Clear Lake. Several pullouts line this stretch providing panoramas of Georgetown and South Clear Creek Valley. Have your camera ready as you will be passing numerous lakes and meadows set between mountain peaks. Soon Clear Lake appears on the east side of the road and you will pass the Lower Cabin Creek Reservoir. The road hugs the creek as willows, meadows, and beaver ponds create a rich green blanket framed by snowcapped Gray's and Torrey's Peak in the background. The road snakes up the mountain slopes on to Guanella summit at 11,666 feet.

Descending the backside of the pass requires your full attention as the road may deteriorate. The natural solitude surrounding you, however, seems to rejuvenate and refresh as the road passes Duck Lake and follows another creek toward **Grant.** Just north of Geneva Park Campground, stop at Duck Lake Picnic Area to recharge and enjoy the beauty of this historic backway. The road soon descends (now Route 67) more quickly through a series of switchbacks to Falls Hill and then drops through Geneva Creek Canyon to the town of Grant. The trek may have been challenging, but you will not regret it!

It's a good idea to check the weather conditions on Guanella Pass beforehand, even in the summer

At Grant, turn right on US Hwy 285 toward Como and Fairplay. The road feels heavenly after the washboards on Guanella Pass. Enjoy the smooth pavement as you accelerate to your normal cruising speed. But don't go too fast, because **Kenosha Pass** at 10,000 feet quickly lifts you up and gently sweeps you down in that "I want to do it again" kind of ride. And you *will* do it again on this ride, I promise. About six more times, so just hang on.

The town of **Como** soon approaches. Once housing over 500 people, Como suffered a fire in 1909 and then in 1937 the railroad shut down, leaving little behind. There are a few buildings and just off the road an old railway roundhouse. This roundhouse is now considered a "holy" spot for narrow gauge railroad worshipers and is being restored to its original state.

And then it starts again. Although not excessively high for this journey, about five miles outside of Como you begin another ascent over **Red Hill Pass** at 9,993 feet. Certainly not the most remarkable pass on this trip as the average elevation is around 8,500 feet, but nonetheless a definite kick as you ascend and then descend into the old mining town of **Fairplay.** A nice way to prepare as you approach the switchbacks at Hoosier Pass and the precipice at Loveland Pass.

Soon after Red Hill Pass, turn right on State Route 9 at Fairplay and head toward Alamo and Breckenridge. Although you appear to be in a valley, the elevation is around 9,000 feet! The towering peaks help reinforce the "valley" illusion. Fairplay and Alamo are both old mining towns and still just barely alive. Be sure and drop by the grave of Prunes, the Burro, next to the Hand Hotel in Fairplay. Apparently, this burro worked sixty-two years in the mines and his owner Rupert Sherwood requested they be buried together at this grave site. Like I said, you learn all sorts of interesting tidbits on these motorcycle journeys.

Continue on Route 9 past Alma and you are in store for another treat. Mounts Lincoln, Democrat, and Bross loom ahead as you ascend **Hoosier Pass** toward Breckenridge. The summit at 11,542 feet lies atop the Continental Divide (again) and is about eleven miles from the ski resort. The rolling motion up the pass is fun and can be done at a relatively quick pace.

THE SOUTHWEST

Descending toward Breckenridge is another story. Three miles of switch-backs indulge your every fantasy as creeks run alongside the road with views of mountains in every direction. Scrape the pegs and then continue toward Blue River. As you approach Breckenridge, a small lake with cabins is nestled to the right. If your timing is right (mid-July), the summer flora will add colorful accents to this picture postcard scene. Resist the temptation to race by; slow it down a notch and enjoy the kaleidoscope of colors flowing by.

The road weaves gently through the countryside and follows the Blue River just south of town. This area was once heavily mined in the 1800s and into the 1900s. **Breckenridge** boasted a population of 2,000 by 1882 and secured the depot for the Denver, South Park, and Pacific Railroad. However, by 1945 the population had dwindled to 242 and many historic buildings were demolished. And then "white gold" was discovered in them thar hills! Starting in the 1960s, the Breckenridge Ski Resort was opened and another boomtown was born. The town now boasts a population in excess of 30,000 and vacationers flock to this summer and winter getaway.

Situated at the base of two thirteeners and two twelvers, Breckenridge is indeed picturesque, but also touristy. If you like to people watch and hang out at some eclectic restaurants, this is a convenient place to grab a bite before

Although this part of Guanella is paved, the road deteriorates rapidly.

Don't motorcyclists always travel at their own risk? This sign was posted just before Guanella Pass.

moving on. For more info visit one of their numerous websites such as www.breckenridge.snow.com or call 800-789-SNOW. Personally, I prefer the smaller town of **Frisco** about ten miles north of Breckenridge because all the restaurants are right on Main Street and the town seems to fit more with the biker aura. If you stop in Frisco, try the **Moose Jaw Restaurant** for some reasonably priced burgers and then head over to the **Butterhorn Bakery** for some dessert. Frisco is about one mile from I-70 and makes for a nice break before starting the official "Top of the Rockies" byway.

After lunch, merge onto I-70 heading west. This short stretch of double-wide is gorgeous. The 12,000-foot peaks surrounding the super slab turn the tankers into Tonka Toys and motorcyclists into puny little ants. At Exit 195 turn south on State Route 91 to Copper Mountain and Leadville. For those of you who decided not to take the Guanella Pass route this is where our paths meet (a good meeting place is in Frisco at the Moose Jaw). Now our third crossing of the Continental Divide lies just ahead. As the road winds its way past Copper Mountain Ski Resort dramatic views open up approaching **Fremont Pass.** The scenery unfolds just like that postcard you bought in Denver. If you want to actually touch it and get some dirt on your soles rather then just scuffing your toes, stop at the Mayflower Gulch trailhead about five to six miles from Copper Mountain. An easy two-mile hike leads to the Old Boston Mine with various mining ruins strewn along the way. Good way to work off that high cholesterol burger you ate in Frisco!

Continue up Route 9 past Clinton Reservoir toward the pass. The road carves its way through the granite and weaves uphill to the summit at 11,318 feet. And then nature's beauty shows a smear the size of Rhode Island at the massive mining facility of **Climax.** Probably on a snowy day the scar won't look so bad all covered up, but during the summer it is quite visible. Stop for a quick look, discuss the impact of man's handiwork on nature and then continue on to Leadville. The minimal descent takes you into a valley high in the Rockies. Leadville is the highest incorporated town in North America at 10,400 feet and is surrounded by a host of thirteeners and fourteeners. Mt. Elbert at 14,433 feet is the highest in Colorado.

Looking down at **Leadville** (www.leadville.com, 800-933-3901), the contrasts are markedly visible. The rugged peaks and scenery are blemished with open sores from the mining boom and bust cycles over the last 100 years. The town was home to various mining magnates such as "the invincible" Molly Brown, the Guggenheims, and Horace Tabor. Leadville boasts numerous historic buildings from the 19th century now filled with restaurants and boutiques. The majority of these buildings are located on Harrison Avenue, the city's main street.

So, park your bike by the Silver Dollar Saloon on Harrison Avenue and West 4th Street, grab a drink, hear some stories from the bartender, get some green chile at the "Golden Burro," and then take a walk down Harrison Avenue and the "miner's" version of memory lane. Leadville is a National Historic Landmark District and you could easily spend the whole afternoon visiting the **Tabor Opera House,** the **Annunciation Church,** various museums, and/or just window shopping.

After a short walk, continue north on US Hwy 24 toward **Camp Hale.** Camp Hale was the training site for the 10th Mountain Division during World War II. The camp was finished in 1942 and housed as many as 14,000 troops by 1943. The troops trained in the nearby mountains under harsh winter conditions and many eventually saw action in the Apennine Mountains of Italy. A memorial to our WW II veterans is located at the entrance of Ski Copper and well worth a stop to pay our respects to those who lost their lives in combat.

Now, I want you to guess what is just up the road. You got it! Another pass over the Continental Divide. **Tennessee Pass** (10,424 feet) is located at the headwaters of the Eagle and Arkansas Rivers. Get that bottle of water ready for your half and half routine or just continue on over and enjoy the grand vistas as you wind up and over the divide. About ten miles ahead the old

Even the Interstates in Colorado are spectacular.

mining towns of Red Cliff, Gilman, and Minturn come quickly into view. **Gilman** was active through the 1950s, but was closed by the EPA for pollutants from its zinc and lead operations. There are NO TRESPASSING signs posted around the area, and beware, they apparently are well enforced. **Minturn** is a sleepy little town that has survived the closing of the Gilman mine and now caters to tourists visiting the local ski resorts at Vail and Beaver Creek (and summer motorcyclists riding the Top of the Rockies). Minturn sits on the west bank of the Eagle River and the town is lined with shops and restaurants. From what I understand, it's also a great place to do some fishin'.

US Hwy 24 connects with I-70 about one mile north of town. Merge onto the Interstate and head east on some of the most gorgeous pieces of super slab in the world. I-70 starts by running adjacent to the Vail Ski Resort and then climbs over the 10,666-foot **Vail Pass.** This engineering marvel weaves like an overweight, drunken sailor on top of the Rockies. The billowing white clouds, blue sky, green timbered slopes, and snowcapped peaks make this a rare and unforgettable golden nugget of Interstate.

One slight detour on this return trip takes you over yet another pass across the Continental Divide with views looking down onto I-70. Don't miss this

THE SOUTHWEST

final pass! Instead of taking the Ike Tunnel on I-70, exit to US Hwy 6/State Route 9 Exit 205 to Dillon and then head east on State Route 6 over the 11,990 foot **Loveland Pass** (toward Keystone). This road is a kick and reconnects with I-70 as you descend down the pass. The switchbacks combined with the "Top of the Rockies" vantage point at almost 12,000 feet make this one a doosey. This is well worth the effort as the road takes you up and over with nerve-wracking views looking down on I-70. Hang on!

Heading east once more on I-70, the wide pavement again cuts through more pristine Rocky Mountain scenery. I don't care much for Interstates, but this portion to Georgetown is just as panoramic and makes for an easy, yet scenic ride home. And by the way congratulations! Today you have taken a dirt backroad, driven a full day for the most part above 9,000 feet, conquered eight passes all over 10,000 feet (Red Hill was close enough!) and crossed the Continental Divide five times. No wonder they call this the "Top of the Rockies!"

■ For more trips in this region see *Motorcycle Journeys Through the Rocky Mountains* by Toby Ballentine, available from Whitehorse Press.

18 Up the Staircase

Text and photos by Toby Ballentine

- **DISTANCE** *274 miles (full day)*
- **HIGHLIGHTS** *The ultimate in scenic diversity. Visit Bryce's orange-hued hoodoos, climb up a razor-back staircase, and then visit cool alpine lakes. All in one day! Elevation change 5,500 to 9,200 feet.*

0 Start in Panguitch on US Hwy 89 going south

7 Turn left (east) on State Route 12

20 Turn right (south) on State Route 63 to Bryce

23 Arrive entrance to Bryce Canyon

28 Continue to Inspiration Point, turn around

36 Turn right (east) on Route 12 to Cannonville

48 Arrive Cannonville, turn right on Kodachrome Road

55 Arrive Kodachrome Basin State Park, turn around

62 Turn right (east) on Route 12

95 Hell's Backbone Road Turnoff (for backway detour)

96 Arrive Escalante

124 Arrive Boulder

150 Turn left (north) on State Route 24

151 Arrive Torrey

181 Turn right on State Route 25 to Fish Lake

190 Arrive Fish Lake, turn around

199 Turn right on Route 24

203 Turn left on State Route 62

242 Turn left (south) on US Hwy 89

246 Arrive Circleville

274 Arrive Panguitch

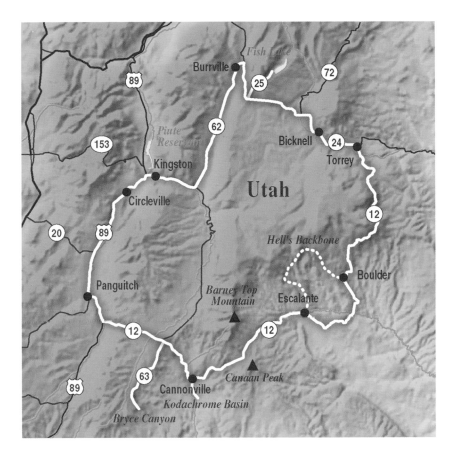

You are about to embark on one of the most enjoyable motorcycle rides of your life. Be prepared for roads that take you through landscape ornate with color and engineered by motorcycle lovers. While driving this loop, you will realize why Highway 12 has been designated a National Scenic Byway and an All American Road by the Federal Highway Administration. This road is indeed a "destination unto itself." And for even further driving pleasure, the route is one of the least traveled in the United States. Most motorists get as far as Bryce National Park and then turn around not realizing that the red canyons only mark the beginning of an unfrequented Scenic Byway. I have made this trip annually for several years over Memorial Day Weekend and am always surprised by the lack of motorists. So listen up and then pack your bags before the word gets out about this little known motorcyclist's dream road.

The trip starts in **Panguitch** and heads south for seven miles on US Hwy 89 to the State Route 12 turnoff. Go east on Route 12 and immediately the fun begins. **Red Canyon State Park** opens in front of you like a miniature Bryce Canyon. The spires and colors are identical to its big brother Bryce,

Panguitch is a stereotypical western town set in the heart of great riding country. As you drive through the Rockies, you will encounter many towns like Panguitch.

except this park is far less visited. Trails and camping are beautifully situated below red-crested towers and a bike path skirts the edge of Route 12, so mountain bikers can also enjoy the surroundings. This seven-mile canyon drive sweeps you through smooth, black-topped asphalt amidst towering spires and overhanging arches. Two miles up the road is a visitors center providing information on camping and hiking trails. If you are up for some morning exercise, both the Bird's Eye Trail and Pink Ledges Trail are short (less than one mile) and end with grand overlooks of the park. For more information on this little jewel, call the **Powell Ranger Station** at 435-676-9300 or visit the website at www.utah.com/nationalsites/redcanyon.htm.

Continuing east on Byway 12, turn right on State Route 63 to **Bryce Canyon National Park** (www.nps.gov/brca, 435-834-5322). This well-known and highly-photographed park is really not a canyon at all. No major river runs through the park, but rather the hoodoos were created by the passage of wind and rain. This, combined with freezing and thawing (and a million or so years), have resulted in an exuberance of colors unlike any place in the world.

The park's entrance is about three miles down Route 63. Bryce Canyon can be extremely congested during the summer, so an earlier arrival is better. To really enjoy the park, you need to spend several days exploring, hiking, and driving. For our purposes, a couple of hours will have to do. In order to do this and get a good feel for the park, drop by the visitors' center about one mile from the park entrance. Watch the movie and get educated and then drive to one or all of the major overlooks just two to five miles away. You can loop around to Sunrise Point, drop by the Historic Lodge for some hot chocolate, and then swing by Sunset and Inspiration Points as well. The roads and paths are well marked and easily accessible. If you arrived really early and the park is uncongested, drive to the southernmost end, but plan on at least another one to two hours as the road is about twenty miles one way (forty miles round trip). The drive is beautiful and the road is windy as it makes its way to Rainbow and Yovimpa Points.

Morning is a good time to see the colors and shades as the light shimmers off hoodoos and slowly changes hues from a rusty gray to brown to yellowish gold. On clear days you can see three states and over 200 miles. Much has been written on Bryce Canyon National Park, so I won't say anymore.

After this unforgettable interlude to Bryce, head back up to Route 63 and head east once more on State Route 12. The Byway passes through the north section of Bryce National Park and then drops into Bryce Valley and the small town of Tropic. Continue on to Cannonville about five miles further down the road. **Cannonville** is the gateway to **Kodachrome Basin State Park.** Turn right at the sign and then drive seven miles south of town. This state park is made up of "sandpipes," or petrified geysers. Named by the

Bryce Canyon National Park can be extremely congested during the summer, so arrive early in the season to enjoy it relatively tourist-free.

Up the Staircase

During the 1930s the Hell's Backbone Road was the only access to Boulder from Escalante.

National Geographic Society, this basin is a photographer's dream. Hiking trails and a small campground with a store are all available at this state park. Well worth the detour if you have time. For further information visit the website (parks.state.ut.us) or drop by the Cannonville visitors center (435-679-8981).

Back on Route 12, **Table Cliffs Plateau** and **Powell Point** rise up ominously as you weave along Route 12 toward Escalante. This road climbs past a rocky area emanating a variety of bluish colors from the clay-covered hills. The colors quickly change to more stark browns as the road enters the upper valley of the **Grand Staircase.** This valley is sandwiched between Barney Top Mountain (elevation 10,571 feet) and Canaan Peak (elevation 9,293 feet). The road runs gently through the valley as if teasing you in preparation for the Haymaker Bench Switchbacks and Hogback Ridge Trapeze just ahead.

The town of **Escalante,** thirty-three miles from Cannonville, is considered the "Heart of Hwy 12." Not only is the town at the midpoint of the Scenic Byway, but is named to honor the Franciscan monk who was the first recorded explorer in this area as he searched for a route from Santa Fe to California.

Drop by the Escalante Interagency visitors center (BLM Information Center) located at 755 West Main or call 435-826-5499 for more information about this remote, yet historically significant area.

One side note at this point: There are several scenic backways (dirt roads) crisscrossing this corridor of Utah that are well worth a visit. Most have historical significance and played a key role in the original settlement of Southern Utah. One particular loop that I enjoy and is convenient to this trip is the "**Posey Lake Scenic Backway**" and the "**Hell's Backbone Road.**" This U loop connects the town of Escalante with Route 12 about three miles west of Boulder. The Backway is not for the faint of heart as it stretches along a road with sheer drops on both sides. Hell's Backbone Bridge, built in 1935, was an engi-

This little building is an old meeting place for the daughters of the pioneers in Bicknell, Utah.

neering feat at the time and is still a marvel. This thirty-eight-mile loop follows the Pine Creek Drainage on the Aquarius Plateau eventually reaching 9,000 feet in elevation. Ultimately, the backroad crossed a huge chasm at Death Hollow and Sand Creek ending up in farmlands about four miles south of Boulder. If you are interested, take the Scenic Byway north (left) at Escalante (Forest Road 153). It is paved for a couple of miles and then veers east just south of Posey Lake to Boulder. It was well-groomed dirt and gravel last time I took it.

Continue on Hwy 12 between Escalante and Boulder on what many refer to as Utah's version of their "million dollar road." For many years, Boulder, Utah, was accessible via Hell's Backbone only and was the last town in the United States to have mail delivered by mules. Parts of this road were only paved in 1971 and now

The Aquarius Inn in Bicknell, Utah is a good spot for lunch.

Colors line the landscape heading toward Fish Lake outside of Torrey on Hwy 24.

provide striking views of the Escalante Basin.

About fifteen miles east of Escalante, Hwy 12 descends to **Calf Creek Recreation Area** (www.americansouthwest.net/utah/grand_staircase_escalante/lower_calf_creek.html). This spot is a perfect area to have a picnic, wade in the creek, or just cool your feet. For you more serious hikers, a six-mile round trip hike takes you to the 126-foot-high Lower Calf Creek Falls. A deep pool with shade trees makes this a great respite away from civilization. A BLM campground and picnic area are available.

After the Calf Creek Recreation Area, Hwy 12 climbs up some glorious switchbacks called **Haymaker Bench** and then crosses the **Hogback Ridge** on to Boulder. The road and scenery intertwine into one natural thread driving atop the pinnacle-like ridge. There are no guard rails and the steep drop-offs on either side make your heart skip a beat while peering down into the ravines and canyons below. Catch your breath at one of the several pullouts along the way and pinch yourself to be sure you aren't dreaming. This stretch of road from here on out defines motorcycle nirvana. A combination of switchbacks, narrow, ridge-like roads, and sweeping curves culminating in an alpine pass at 9,200 feet with sweeping vistas are why this road is a destination "unto itself." Words don't do it justice.

Hwy 12 veers north from Boulder to Torrey and twists through the Dixie National Forest over the 9,000-foot summit. The road was paved for the first time in 1985 and is a motorcyclist's delight. The traffic is minimal, the curves are tight, and the scenery breathtaking. As you scratch your pegs, take time to

The view back toward Fish Lake from Hwy 25 is worth a stop.

pull out at the overlooks and absorb the endless horizons. Views of the Henry Mountains, Capital Reef National Park, and Circle Cliffs are painted like watercolors before you. The hardest part about getting to Torrey is that you will want to turn around and repeat this journey immediately!

Scenic Byway 12 comes to an end upon intersecting State Route 24. The town of **Torrey** is one mile west and is a great stop to tank up and grab a well-deserved bite to eat. Although the town is small (pop. 120), it caters to tourists visiting Capital Reef and Bryce Canyon. For some good food with great views try the **Rim Rock Restaurant** at 2523 E. Hwy 24 (435-425-3388) or **Cafe Diablo** at 559 West Main (435-425-3010). If you spent too much time getting here or want to spend some more time exploring the backways, the lodge at **Red River Ranch** is homey and set amidst a natural backdrop making it a perfect place to unwind (www.redriverranch.com, 800-205-6343).

The return trip from Torrey to Panguitch is about 120 miles and takes you through small town Utah via gently sweeping curves and high mountain passes. I have always enjoyed this run back to Panguitch due to its remoteness and the scenic diversion to Fish Lake Lodge on Route 25 high in the Wasatch Range.

Heading north on State Route 24, you will drive through the towns of Bicknell and Lyman about fourteen miles ahead. Whatever you do, don't blink! The road follows the Fremont River as it meanders alongside the slopes of Thousand Lake Mountain. As you climb toward Fish Lake, the scenery will quickly transition from red rock plateau to wooded alpine valleys. The breeze will cool and suddenly the sculptured sandstone gives way to green forested watercolors.

After approximately thirty miles from Torrey, turn right on State Route 25 through the Fish Lake National Forest toward Fish Lake Lodge. The pavement ascends to 9,000 feet and is gentle and sloping as it slowly climbs to the lake. Be cautious as wildlife is abundant and deer will often dart along the side of the road. Elk and moose are also sighted on this short diversion, so stay attentive and alert.

When you arrive at the lake, the setting is tranquil and quiet. Stop at the historic **Fish Lake Lodge** (www.fishlake.com, 435-638-1000) built between 1928 and 1932 of native spruce logs. Lakeside Resort overlooks the lake and gives you an opportunity to admire its crystal 160-foot deep waters. Some of the west's finest fishing is done here. As the local fishermen say, a Mackinaw Lake trout under ten pounds is just a "pup" and not worth keeping!

After a pleasant break at Fish Lake, backtrack on Route 25 to Route 24, and head north for another four miles until arriving at the Route 62 junction.

Some of the finest fishing in the West is found at Fish Lake, and the Lakeside Resort is often full as a result.

THE SOUTHWEST

This KOA on US 89 has fantastic views of red rock cliffs, and all for a great price.

At 62 go south toward Burrville and then head on down past Otter Creek State Park. The road veers west through Kingston on some nice twisties and then reconnects up with US Hwy 89 about two miles outside of town.

Go south on 89 as the road hugs the Sevier River toward Panguitch. The gentle curves and flowered meadows help ease you back home as your full day of riding ends. There is one more stop, however. For those of you who remember the movie *Butch Cassidy and the Sundance Kid* with Paul Newman and Robert Redford, a diversion to Butch Cassidy's boyhood home just south of Circleville may be in order. The son of Mormon Pioneers, Butch Cassidy turned into one of the most famous outlaws of the Old West. His home is located near the **Butch Cassidy's Hideout Motel** at 339 S. Hwy 89 in Circleville (butch@color-country.net 888-577-2008)

Back on 89, Panguitch is about twenty-eight miles south of Circleville and definitely a pleasant sight after 275 miles of riding. It is time to unwind, reminisce, and wonder how those early pioneers managed to ride these same distances and more on horseback. If anybody deserves an Iron Butt Award, it's the early pioneers!

■ For more trips in this region see *Motorcycle Journeys Through the Rocky Mountains* by Toby Ballentine, available from Whitehorse Press.

19 Sedona and Mormon Lake Loop

Text and photos by Toby Ballentine

- **DISTANCE** *260 miles (full day, including stops)*
- **HIGHLIGHTS** *This trip is a roller coaster of elevation changes. Numerous hairpins coming down canyons and climbing mountains. Sweeping S-curves on the return trip from Camp Verde to Flagstaff. Beautiful backroad detour on Schnebly Hill Road for some unforgettable vistas.*

0 From the I-40/I-17 interchange south of Flagstaff head south on 89A	**63** Turn right back on Main Street and then left on 11th Street
12 Oak Creek Vista Point	**66** Follow 11th Street and then 89A to Jerome
20 Slide Rock State Park	**93** Stay on 89A from Jerome to 69 and Fain Road turnoff—turn left
28 89A and Route 179 intersection in Sedona. Turn left for Schnebly Hill Road (unpaved—optional)	**100** Follow Fain Road and turn left on 69
32 Turn left on Upper Red Rock Loop Road	**103** Take 69 to 169 and turn left
37 Red Rock State Park	**118** Stay on 169 until I-17—go north (left)
41 Continue loop and turn left on 89A	**127** I-17 to the Camp Verde Exit (260)
56 Take 89A to Main Street intersection in Cottonwood—go straight	**163** Take 260 to 87—turn left
59 Tuzigoot National Monument Turnoff	**175** Follow 87 to 487 (Lake Mary Road)—turn left
60 Tuzigoot National Monument	**205** Take 487 to the Mormon Lake Turnoff
61 Turn right back onto Main Street	**209** Roundtrip to Mormon Lake—go back to 487
62 Follow Main to Broadway in Clarkdale to the Verde Railroad	**241** Stay on 487 (Lake Mary Road) back into Flagstaff

The vortex may swallow your motorcycle on this trip through Sedona and Jerome, but don't let that bother you. The only worry you should have is keeping your eyes on the road as you scrub your tires on hairpins through scenery that continues to amaze with each passing mile.

This loop begins in Flagstaff on Hwy 89A and heads south through Oak Creek Canyon to Sedona and then over Mingus Mountain to Jerome and the Upper Prescott Valley. The trip back returns via sweeping turns up Route 260 from Camp Verde to Clints Well and then back past Happy Jack and Mormon Lake to Flagstaff on Route 487.

Over the course of this drive, elevation changes are dramatic, so be prepared for temperature changes, and more importantly, roads that are as varied as the landscape.

A word of advice before this journey begins: be patient as you drive the hair-pinned spine of Oak Creek Canyon. The run from Flagstaff to Jerome is popular and can be busy. Early mornings and mid-week are best, but nonetheless, you will probably be taking it nice and slow as you gaze down at the sandstone monoliths searching for UFOs landing on top of Bell Rock. The trip back from Camp Verde is another story. This backdoor of sweeping curves into Flagstaff is wide open as you climb back up to 8,000 feet and may get the best of you, so be sure to keep a sharp lookout for that State Trooper.

Autumn at Slide Rock showcases a brilliant array of colors.

To begin this trip, follow 89A south from Flagstaff past the Coconino County Fairgrounds and begin your 27-mile, 2,600-foot descent toward **Oak Creek Canyon** and Sedona. The road gently slopes downward for a few miles until you get to the Oak Creek Vista Point. From this vantage point you can visualize the full spectrum of terrain and colors you will be entering. The timberline drops into recesses of orange, greens, and grays with billowing white clouds forming a backdrop. The road below invites you as it twists and turns down the canyon spine. The only problem with stopping is that you will be so anxious to hop back on your bike, you will forget to snap a picture!

184

Continue down 89A, relishing the hairpins as the road winds down Oak Creek Canyon. The vegetation changes from pine and aspen to maple and oak. The road hugs the west bank of the creek for about fourteen miles. Mid-October is a great time of year to enjoy the cooler weather as autumn leaves bring even more color to the diverse landscape.

Various campgrounds line the corridor along Oak Creek Canyon. One of the most picturesque is Cave Springs Forest about four miles from the Vista Point. Sites are secluded and away from the main road. There are even coin showers for the discriminating camper. For more info see www.fs.us/r3/coconino/recreation/red_rock/cavesprings-camp.shtml or call 877-444-6777.

For those of you traveling in the summer months, stop by **Slide Rock State Park** or **Grasshopper Swim Area** to cool your feet and splash some cold water on your face. Slide Rock is composed of natural chutes of flowing water. Nature's version of a water slide. Stop by for a picnic or use that extra pair of jeans to slip down the creek (the ride is a little bumpy). For more information check out (www.pr.state.az.us/parks/parkhtml/sliderock.html) or call 928-282-3034.

After cooling off at Slide Rock, follow 89A for another 8 miles right into downtown **Sedona.** Hwy 89A is lined with shops, restaurants, and malls. Drop by an ice cream shop, wander through town, or just sit on a bench and take a look around. What is truly breathtaking is not the town, but the surrounding landscape. The amber-hued monoliths jutting up around the city create a natural contradiction to the residential and commercial structures clustered at their base.

Sedona is the epitome of an "artsy" town. The resplendent scenery gives the city a charm like few other locales. Although the Oak Creek was one of the original reasons fruit farmers and ranchers originally settled this area, it is the red glow of Sedona that really draws the artists and tourists today.

If you have only a short time to stay, I would suggest a couple of options. Firstly, turn left from 89A to 179 at the stoplight and visit the arts and crafts village of **Tlaquepaque.** This is a delightfully recreated version of Spanish villas and narrow alleys of brick and mortar, which are home to various local art studios. Wander through these shops and get a feel for the essence of this town. Restaurants and often live music add to the charm of this hideaway. Check out the website for a host of information, including a calendar of events and times (www.tlaq.com).

For those of you interested in a scenic dirt back road away from the commercialization, hang a left on route 179 off 89A (first stoplight), go down about half a mile (just past Tlaquepaque), and turn left on Schnebly Hill Road. This route is a six-mile detour, climbing up the side of the surrounding mountains to the Schnebly Vista Point. The first mile is paved and then becomes unpaved for the next five miles. Not an option for street bikes. The

There are great views heading up Schnebly Hill Road, but you will need a GS or dual-sport bike to do it.

road is rocky and, in some spots, sandy, but the views are worth it. The road twists and turns as it slices its way up the side of the mountain and takes about one hour round-trip.

After getting your fill of downtown Sedona, drive back to 89A and continue through the several stoplights until you arrive at the Upper Red Rock Loop Road about four miles south of the 89A and 179 intersection. This detour takes you down to Red Rock State Park for some majestic views of Cathedral Rock. The road winds down the side of the canyon through some residential areas that overlook the park. Be careful, as there are few turnouts and residential traffic uses this as an access road. After about three miles, the road turns into a "primitive" road which sounds scarier then it really is. Take it slow and even street bikes will be fine. The road is well graded fine gravel for just a couple of miles and connects with the other side of the paved loop back out to 89A. Total loop distance is nine miles and the road and scenery are splendid. Try to feel the aura emanating from Cathedral Rock.

At the bottom of the loop is **Red Rock State Park.** Formerly a part of Smoke Trail Ranch, the Oak Creek meanders through this area creating a diverse riparian habitat amidst the red rock. A visitors center with information about the area is available at the entrance. The smoke trail loop is only four tenths of a mile and, if you are lucky, you may even see a wedding ceremony being performed by the infamous "wedding tree." Can

THE SOUTHWEST

"just married" fit on a motorcycle? (www.pr.state.az.us/parks/parkhtml/ redrock.html, 928-292-6907).

The Red Rock Loop connects back onto 89A a few miles south of where you started. Turn left on 89A and follow the signs to Cottonwood. This stretch of road is about fifteen miles and turns into a four-lane highway as it runs through the outskirts of Sedona. Upon entering Cottonwood drive straight on to Main Street. Do not turn left at the posted sign for 89A to Jerome at this point. Main Street leads across a bridge, through old town Cottonwood, and to the Tuzigoot National Monument turnoff. Total miles from the Red Rock Loop to Tuzigoot are about 18.5.

Apple orchards in Slide Rock State Park bear fruit in the fall.

Take a break and cool your feet off in Oak Creek Canyon.

Enjoy this run through small town USA and then turn right at the posted sign to Tuzigoot National Monument. This road is about one mile long and crosses over Oak Creek to the park entrance. The Sinagua Indians built the **Tuzigoot Monument** around 1100 AD (TOO-zee-goot). A two-story pueblo perched on a hilltop once housed over 200 people. A visitors' center and self-guided tours are available to explore these 900-year-old ruins. The views are expansive looking down from the pueblo (www.nps.gov/tuzi).

Another detour in this area (especially for locomotive lovers) is to take a look at the **Verde Canyon Railroad.** To get to the station, return to Main Street, turn right, and go about one mile to Broadway in **Clarkdale.** Veer right to the Verde Canyon Railroad Station. Touted as "Arizona's Longest Running Nature Show," this wilderness train ride takes you into an area not accessible by vehicles. The steep canyon walls of the Verde are home to bald eagles and various other wildlife. The train meanders across old-fashioned trestles and man-made tunnels as it heads to **Perkinsville,** an old ghost town and then back to Clarkdale. Vintage Diesel FP7s pull you in restored Pullmans on this four-hour round trip train ride. If you just want to look, stop by, and have lunch at the cafe/grille, you can save this trip for next time (www.verdecanyon.com, 800-293-7245).

After a visit to the railroad station, head back on Broadway and turn right on Main Street through downtown Clarkdale (short and sweet). About one-quarter mile up the road turn left on 11th Street. The posted sign reads 89A to Jerome. Go straight at the stop sign and you are now back on 89A heading up to Jerome.

This is where the fun really starts. Enough sightseeing, it's time to ride. The next thirty miles of pavement will get your adrenalin pumping. The road twists

The Secret Garden Cafe at Tlaquepaque is a good choice for dinner.

THE SOUTHWEST

The dual-sport option allows you to extend the journey.

and turns through Jerome, climbs up over **Mingus Mountain** at 7,000 feet and then rolls down the backside of the mountain into the Upper Prescott Valley.

The road begins with sweeping S-curves winding up the slopes of Jerome. **Jerome** is built like San Francisco back in the 1800s, except this town hasn't changed since then. The town literally clings to the side of Cleopatra Hill overlooking the Verde Valley and appears to be slipping down the hillside. Once a thriving mining community of 15,000 during the late 1800s and into the 1920s, this "wickedest city" in the west faded from memory during the Great Depression and could barely claim fifty people as residents. Starting in the 1960s, artists, tourists, and retirees slowly put Jerome back on the map. Today, Jerome is a well-know weekend getaway from Phoenix. Driving through the town is like taking a step back in time. The unique setting and early 20th century architecture give Jerome its own character and ambiance. The saloon on the corner at the **Connor Hotel** (established 1898) is a favorite watering hole for motorcyclists. Stop by and listen to a little music before heading up the mountain.

The switchbacks through town last a few miles as you approach Mingus Mountain. The road is carved neatly from the side of the cliffs as it gently climbs upward. About two miles outside of town, a scenic overlook provides

You'll enjoy these sweeping curves as you climb Mingus Mountain toward Jerome.

a grand view looking back to Jerome and the valley below. Stop, take a picture, as this is the only turnout available, and then hop back on 89A and start muscling up the hairpins to 7,000 feet that make this part of the trip a motorcyclist's dream. The road climbs and winds from 5,000 feet up and over the top. The switchbacks are tight, so be careful going around the blind corners. Watch the road for slower traffic and don't get too close to the edge. It is a long way down. But in the meantime, drag your pegs, scrape your boots, and then roll down the backside toward **Prescott**. The miles will pass all too quickly!

The road straightens up about 20 miles outside Jerome on the south side of Mingus Mountain. Look for signs to Route 69 and then turn left at the stoplight on Fain Road. Fain Road is new and may not be shown on your AAA maps. This road bypasses Prescott, and after 12 miles links up with Route 69. Personally, I would avoid Prescott. This area has turned into the closest summer getaway from Phoenix and has more stoplights than I care to count. Fain Road is peaceful and winds around Prescott giving some grand views of the valley and outlying mountains in the process.

At Route 69, turn left and drive about two and a half miles to the Route 169 intersection. As you need to head back north to Flagstaff via Camp Verde, turn left here and go fifteen miles to I-17. This stretch of road is

THE SOUTHWEST

relatively straight and hilly. At I-17, head north (left) for about nine miles to the Camp Verde Exit.

More fun now awaits you. It's time to climb back up the Mogollon Rim toward Flagstaff. Head past the Chevron Station (gas up if you need it) and drive through Camp Verde on Route 260 as it again climbs up some radical elevations. The trip home is high and cool on roads that tempt you along just a little faster (remember . . . self control!). This road is not the rapid-fire switchbacks you encountered in Jerome, but rather gentle sweeping curves that allow the throttle to slip down a few notches. If you can, open your visor and feel the change in temperature while climbing from 4,000 feet to over 7,000 feet on a delightfully long 34 miles. The wide open S-curves tempt you to ratchet it up as you fly toward the clouds. The scenery changes from scrubby desert pine to green pastures with ponderosa pine over the course of this road. Even the smell changes! As most tourists drive up I-17 to Flagstaff, this back way is uncongested and wide open.

When you arrive at the top of the rim, the road ends in a T. Turn left on Route 87, which goes up through Long Valley to Clints Well. The road swerves gently through pine and meadows. The traffic is usually minimal and the scenery green and blue.

Continue on 87 for eleven miles. On the left side of the road is the **Long Valley Cafe,** a grocery store and service station. Tank up, grab a donut, and enjoy the cool crispness in the air. A meadow sways with the breeze east of the road and occasionally elk or deer will wander into view.

About half a mile further up 87, turn left on route 487 (Lake Mary Road) toward Happy Jack and Mormon Lake. This leg to Flagstaff is one of my favorites. Most travelers veer right to Winslow, leaving this stretch of road wide open as it climbs to 8,000 feet and eventually hugs Mormon Lake and Lake Mary into Flagstaff.

There are several lakes in this area, some of which are accessible only via Forest Trail Roads. For you motorcyclist-anglers, staying in this neck of the woods may be worthwhile. Lakes and reservoirs are dotted throughout this region. Blue Ridge Reservoir, Long Lake, Knoll Lake, Stoneman

Hotel Connor in Jerome is a well-known watering hole for bikers.

Lake, Kinnikinnick Lake, and Ashurst Lake are stocked with trout, catfish, bass, yellow perch, and northern pike. From what I hear, an anglers dream!

Campsites are also plentiful and well maintained along this corridor. For more information on this area contact the **Mormon Lake Ranger Station** (928-774-1182) or **Peaks Ranger Station** (928-526-0866). Online access available at www.fs.fed.us/r3/coconino.

Continue winding your way along Route 487 for 26 miles. The road is pleasant, gently curving through the pines on top of Mogollon Rim. Between mile marker 317 and 318, the road intersects with the Mormon Lake turnoff. Turn left for a short rendezvous with the **Mormon Lake Lodge Steakhouse and Saloon** (www.mormonlodge.com, 928-354-2227). This recreational center offers food, outdoor activities, a western-style town, and dinner theater. As you are only 30 miles from Flagstaff, a mesquite grilled steak may be essential to finishing up your trip. If you have the time, chow down and wander around this old western town for a moment.

Returning to Flagstaff via 487 sends you around the north end of **Mormon Lake** and then hugs the upper edges of **Lake Mary.** Various side roads are available for picnic areas and campsites. Anglers can often be seen reeling in their catch of the day or barbecuing some rainbow trout. The scenery is green and calm, with afternoon clouds billowing like white cotton candy in the

The sun setting on the Red Rock Loop just south of Sedona creates amazing colors and shadows.

Wow! You can definitely feel the vortex here!

clear azure sky. After 20 miles the outskirts of Flagstaff are visible, and before you know it, the freeway looms ominously overhead. The sounds of the city are close and imminent. But for some reason, the noise and bustle seem quieter and less bothersome. Maybe the gentleness of the last 70 miles has settled your senses, or maybe that Sedona vortex has quelled your spirit (or maybe you are just flat out tired from a long day of driving and the food in your belly is making you drowsy). Either way, a good night's rest is well deserved!

For more trips in this region see *Motorcycle Journeys Through the Rocky Mountains* by Toby Ballentine, available from Whitehorse Press.

20 The Enchanted Circle

Text and photos by Martin Berke

- **DISTANCE** *162 miles*
- **HIGHLIGHTS** *Smooth two-laners through pristine forested high country, over narrow passes and deep canyons on river roads, and into ski country with or without snow, depending . . .*

0 From Taos take Route 64 east.	**77** Turn right on Route 38
26 Arrive Angel Fire memorial	**93** Arrive Red River
31 Arrive Eagle Nest, continue on Rte. 64 to Cimarron	**104** Arrive Questa, turn left on Route 522 south
54 Arrive Cimarron, retrace route to Eagle Nest	**162** Arrive Taos

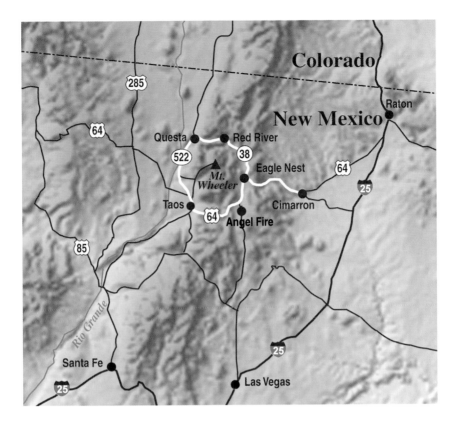

The Enchanted Circle begins and ends at **Taos,** a major spiritual and trade center in ancient times, now an art colony and gateway to major ski areas. Taos, apres-ski season, attracts tourists from all over the country. Its numerous galleries, shops, restaurants, and museums deserve browsing time. It is also home to **Taos Pueblo,** a 900-year-old settlement of the Taos Indians. **Kit Carson,** the famous mountain man and scout, lived in Taos for 25 years and died here. The Kit Carson Home, a 12-room adobe house now a museum, was a wedding gift to his bride Josefa Jaramillo in 1843. A park with his grave and those of his relatives, and Kit Carson Road, Route 64, were named for him.

Heading out of Taos on Kit Carson Road (a.k.a. Route 64), you leave the bustle of tourist town behind and enter a 26-mile ride through Taos Canyon. Cresting the Palo Felchado Pass (9,107 feet), descend into the town of **Angel Fire.** No one is sure how Angel Fire received its name, but one legend has it that Kit Carson described sunlight on the frozen dew at dawn as "angel fire."

Just past the Route 64 Angel Fire turnoff, set on a hillside overlooking the tranquil Moreno Valley, is the **Disabled American Veterans (DAV) Vietnam Veterans National Memorial** (www.angelfirememorial.com, 505-377-

The Disabled American Veterans (DAV) Vietnam Veterans National Memorial, near Angel Fire, New Mexico, has a Memorial Day ride every year.

6900). The monument rises a dramatic 50 feet, with two walls of textured surface nearly meeting at the pinnacle. Built by the family of Dr. Victor Westphall, whose son was killed in a 1968 enemy ambush in Vietnam, the memorial was dedicated as the Vietnam Veterans Peace and Brotherhood Chapel. In 1982 the DAV took full ownership and financial responsibility for the memorial. On Memorial Day, 1983, the chapel was rededicated as the National Memorial.

The road from Angel Fire to **Eagle Nest** straightens and widens. On the left is **Wheeler Peak,** the geologic center of the Enchanted Circle. New Mexico's highest mountain at 13,161 feet, it dominates this mountainous region. The Sangre de Cristo Range, to which Wheeler Peak belongs, is part of the Rocky Mountains and extends into Colorado.

At Eagle Nest, you can sit high and away from civilization. Eagle Nest Lake's majesty comes from the solitude among the peaks at the north end of Moreno Valley.

Route 64 branches away from the Enchanted Circle. Originally part of the Santa Fe Trail, it opened in 1821 and became a major trade route between Missouri's river towns and Santa Fe. Travel over the trail ceased in 1879 but it was where Indian Agent Kit Carson, Apaches, Utes, and countless settlers once trod.

Cutting through Cimarron Canyon/Colin Nebblet Wildlife Area, Route 64 is unrelenting S-turns. The spectacular cliffs are cut by the Cimarron River through igneous rock known as a sill, which was emplaced 40 million years ago by the uplift of the southern Rocky Mountains. It's like riding a rattlesnake's back through high canyon walls of black rock. And you get to do it again. Yaba-daba-doo!

Cimarron, Spanish for wild or unbroken, was one of the legendary spots in the West's exciting history of gunslingers and range wars. Take some investigation time. The Registered National Historic **St. James Hotel** (www.stjamescimarron.com, 866-472-5019) began as a saloon built in 1873 by Henri Lambert, the personal chef to Presidents Lincoln and Grant. In 1880 the hotel was completed and immediately became a hangout for traders, mountain men, and desperadoes. Twenty-six men lost their lives there when one Clay Allison, dancing naked on the bar after having too much to drink, fired 22 bullets into the tin ceiling of what is now the dining room. The holes remain.

Other characters of the Wild West and more recent years also used the St. James as a home base. Train robber **Black Jack Ketchum** hid out there. **Buffalo Bill Cody** met with **Annie Oakley** to plan his Wild West Show. **Zane Grey** wrote "Fighting Caravans." **Lew Wallace** finished a few chapters of "Ben Hur." And **Frederick Remington** painted the nearby hills.

Bullet holes in the ceiling and the ghosts they created live on at St. James Hotel, Cimarron, New Mexico.

The lush green countryside leaves no doubt as to why this is called the Enchanted Circle.

There is even a ghost in Room 18, as highlighted in the TV show Unsolved Mysteries. James Wright won the St. James Hotel in a poker game one night, but when he arrived to collect, he was murdered. There's a kinder ghost in room 17, believed to be Henri Lambert's first wife. Her presence is announced by a flowery perfume you can smell for 10 seconds or so. The third ghost is called the Imp. Breaking glasses, stealing toast, and general prankster stuff is his dominion.

The St. James reopened in 1985 and offers warm, friendly accommodations such as the Bat Masterson Suite, the Jesse James Room, and the Remington Room. Their menu ranges from elegant dining to homemade biscuits for breakfast. If you want to make it a weekend, the Dirty Deeds Afoot Mystery Adventures offers a western mystery where the guests play the roles of Jesse James, Annie Oakley, Wyatt Earp, or another colorful character of the Old West.

Return to the Enchanted Circle via Route 64 west to Route 38, up over Bobcat Pass at 9,820 feet, and into **Red River.** The town, high in the Sangre de Cristo Mountains, is surrounded by 20 alpine lakes, hundreds of miles of hiking trails, and 60 miles of off-road trails. A large ski area, Red River is host every Memorial Day weekend to a large motorcycle rally. The town has all the services, including Carson National Forest Service campgrounds on the west end of town.

This loop offers many off-the-beaten-track diversions. One such unbeaten track is a shrine to **D.H. Lawrence,** built in 1934 on his Kiowa Ranch. It's a pilgrimage off Route 522, up a six-mile dirt road, just past the town of **San Cristobal** and one small stream. The shrine sits on a hillside with a walking path to his ashes and his wife's grave. A visitor register indicates how widely read he is. Aldous Huxley was among the frequent visitors. If you are not a fan, don't bother with the road.

The ride up to Taos Ski Valley is another winding hill climb following a creek created by snow melt, a lovely 30-mile up and down diversion. Another diversion before returning to Taos is the seven-mile ride out Route 64 west, over the **Rio Grande Gorge Bridge.** It is the second highest suspension bridge in the world (the Royal Gorge Bridge over the Arkansas River in Colorado being the highest). Then back into Taos to end the loop and relax at Eske's for a brewsky (www.eskesbrewpub.com, 505-758-1517).

Eske's, a brew pub, serves delicious sandwiches and two types of corn nachos, blue and yellow. Sangre de Cristo Brewing, in the basement of Eske's, turns out fine ales, stouts, and beers. A sampler of all the beers in four-ounce servings is a bargain. The atmosphere ranges from outdoor cafe and long picnic tables to couches and sitting rooms inside. An easy place to walk to, the adobe style building sits behind a parking lot, diagonal to the corner of Kit Carson Road and Paseo del Pueblo Sur (the main drag).

■ For more trips in this region see *Motorcycle Journeys Through the Southewest* by Martin C. Berke available from Whitehorse Press.

Finish up your day at Eske's in Taos, a local brew pub that serves tasty sandwiches, nachos, and a variety of home-brewed ales, stouts, and beers.

21 Presidio to Marfa

Text and photos by Neal Davis

- **DISTANCE** *306 miles*
- **HIGHLIGHTS** *Following the Rio Grande River, you will climb the steepest hill in Texas; desert, rocks, canyons, and vistas of Big Bend National Park, mysterious Marfa lights.*

0 Leave Presidio going east on Hwy. 170

50 Lajitas

67 Study Butte, take Hwy. 118 to park entrance

70 Park entrance

71 Turn right onto Old Maverick Road

84 Turn right to Santa Elena Canyon

85 Santa Elena Canyon, turn around

86 At junction with Old Maverick Road go straight toward Castolon

94 At Castolon continue to Santa Elena Junction

116 Turn right toward Chisos Basin Junction

126 Turn right to Chisos Basin

132 Chisos Basin, return to Chisos Basin Junction

138 Turn right at Chisos Basin Junction

141 Panther Junction, take road to Rio Grande Village

161 Rio Grande Overlook, return to Panther Junction

181 Turn right to eastern entrance

207 Take Hwy 385 to Marathon

249 Turn left on Hwy. 90

306 Arrive Marfa

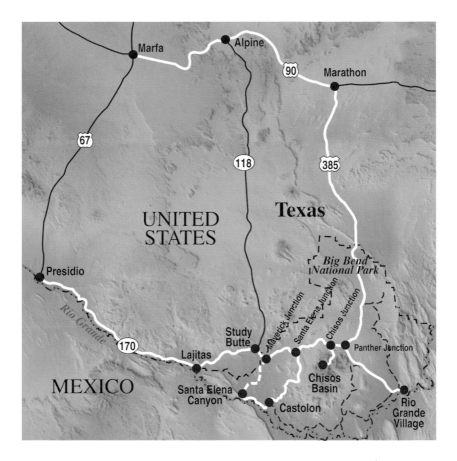

Presidio (pop. 4,000) is known as the hottest town in Texas. Its twin on the Mexico side is Ojinaga and the two towns co-exist as if one. This is the only official border crossing point between El Paso and Del Rio, a 450-mile stretch. The area contains fertile floodplains and is famous for its farming. It is the self-proclaimed **Onion Capitol of the World.**

For places to stay in Presidio, the **Three Palms Hotel** (915-229-3611, $60), located on old Hwy. 67 north, is more than adequate. Next door to the motel is the **Oasis Café,** which is very popular with locals and serves up some good Tex-Mex food. Primitive camping is available only a short distance to the east on Hwy. 170 in the **Big Bend Ranch State Park** near the **Fort Leaton State Historic Site.** The campsite has pit toilets only, but water and showers are available.

Hwy. 170 east from Presidio, known as **El Camino del Rio** (River Road), has been touted as one of the ten best motorcycle roads in the United States. Most motorcyclists would agree with the designation. After 46 miles of delightful riding, you will encounter the hill. At a 16-percent grade, this hill is

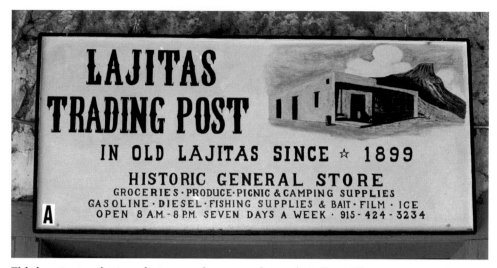

This is not a tourist trap, but a genuine general store in Lajitas. (Photo courtesy of MotoDiscovery)

the steepest in Texas and the road peaks at an altitude of more than 5,000 feet. There is a nice pull-off at the summit and only the hard-core, no-photos-please rider will be able to resist the urge to click away. Walk over the summit and get the view ahead before remounting your bike for the five-mile run to Lajitas.

The small outpost of **Lajitas** was established because it had an easy crossing over the **Rio Grande River,** and over the years it served this purpose well for Indians, traders, and *banditos* alike. In the early 1900s **General Black Jack Pershing** established a U.S. Cavalry post here to deal with **Pancho Villa** and his band.

For years Lajitas was a sleepy little desert town populated by a few seeking solitude. Then in 2000 the entire city including 25,000 surrounding acres was purchased by an Austin multimillionaire who had visions of making it into the ultimate exclusive retreat for the rich and famous. After $100 million were spent in development costs, the whole deal went into bankruptcy and was purchased by another wealthy Texan for only 13.5 million in late 2007. The plan is to take the luxury upgrades originally designed for the upper class and let us regulars in. The jury is still out. You do have to admire these Texans and their dreams though. The resort consists of a period style square containing several stores, hotels, and restaurants. Accommodations range in cost from $200 to $1,000 per night and include apartments and condos. An eighteen-hole golf course is available.

Only one remnant of the real Lajitas exists and continues to do well, Henry Clay III, third generation mayor and goat with living accommodations

THE SOUTHWEST

in the old **Lajitas Trading Post.** Several years back, in a hotly contested mayoral race, the citizens of Lajitas chose a goat named **Henry Clay** as the winner. Henrys main claim to fame, other than being mayor, was his ability to consume vast quantities of beer. Henry died, some say of liver failure, and was succeeded by his son, **Henry, Jr.** Unfortunately, Henry Jr. eventually met the same fate. The grandson, **Henry Clay III** carries on the family tradition today, although a former political opponent, frustrated after losing election after election to a goat, decided to vent his spleen by castrating Henry III in hopes that it would put an end to this political dynasty.

From Lajitas it is only 17 miles to the intersection with Farm Road 118 at **Study Butte** (all services). Turn right and its only a short ride to the **Big Bend National Park** entrance ($15 fee).

After passing the entrance booth into the park, take an immediate right turn onto Old Maverick Road. This is 13 miles of well-maintained dirt that is easily traveled by any bike with competent rider. Take a minute to dismount six or seven miles down this road. The silence will overwhelm most people. Think of the hardships that must have been incurred trying to cross this empty desert land on a horse or wagon.

When you intersect with pavement again, turn right for a mile or so to the dead-end at **Santa Elena Canyon.** A short hike allows you to climb up and

Welcome to Big Bend National Park.

The Rio Grande River created the Santa Elena Canyon which now cuts a dramatic swath on the southern border of the Big Bend National Park. (Photo by Jack Lewis/TxDOT)

into the canyon, which was cut by the **Rio Grande River.** Its sheer cliffs, which reach more than 1,500 feet above the Rio Grande, and narrow passages will amaze you. Plan to spend some time here to explore and enjoy.

Should you not wish to ride this short dirt portion, continue through Maverick Junction on pavement for 13 miles to Santa Elena Junction and make a right turn. It is then 30 paved miles to the Santa Elena Canyon.

After enjoying the wonderful sights and sounds of Santa Elena, take the paved road out and return 30 miles to the main road. This road out of Santa

THE SOUTHWEST

Elena to the main road is an absolute pleasure, with sprinklings of buttes and broad valleys. There are several well-marked pull-offs along this road provided by the park service with informative signs. One of the best is the **Mule Ears viewpoint.**

At the main road turn right and continue about 10 miles to Chisos Mountains Basin Junction where a right turn will take you to the **Chisos Basin.** If the entranceway booth was closed as you entered the park, you will need to proceed straight ahead for another three miles to the **Panther Junction Visitors Center** to get your admission tickets, before continuing back to the **Chisos Lodge** for your overnight accommodations. At the park headquarters at Panther Junction you can obtain brochures, maps, and other information that will make your visit more enjoyable.

If you already have paid the entrance fee, the same information is available at the **Chisos Basin Visitor Center.** The short, six-mile ride into the basin is a beautiful motorcycle road that climbs up over the mountain.

Keep an eye out for these "natives." (Photo by Jack Lewis/TxDOT)

You should be careful when encountering a javelina (wild pig) as they can turn nasty when annoyed. (Photo by Bill Reeves/TxDOT)

Roads in the Big Bend National Park offer frequent pull-offs containing interesting exhibits. (Photo by Jack Binion)

It is quite tight at some places and even has a couple of switchbacks. Other than campsites, the **Chisos Mountains Lodge** (www.chisosmountain lodge.com, 915-477-2291/866-875-8456, $115) is the only available place to overnight in the park and offers a dramatic setting. It has 66 motel-type rooms and six stone cottages ($150) located only a short walk away. Deer, wild pigs, and other wildlife can be seen in the early evenings and mornings as you walk to the basic, but adequate, dining room. At times, most notably during Spring Break, the place can be filled; it is best to call ahead and reserve a room.

Camping is available in Big Bend on a first-come basis at Rio Grande Village, Chisos Basin, and Castolon, at a cost of $14 per night. All formal campsites have showers and water. Chisos Basin offers high-country camping with the lodge located just up the hill with café service. It also has a well-stocked store to meet most of your needs. Rio Grande, as the name implies, is located on the banks of the Rio Grande River, nestled among trees. Backcountry campsites are free, but do require a permit. Before spending the night at a remote campsite, make sure you get current information at the ranger station.

Big Bend National Park is often called **The Last Frontier of Texas** (info 915-477-2251; res. 915-477-2291). Containing more than 800,000 acres, the park is larger than the state of Rhode Island, yet its also one of the least visited parks in the country. Be prepared both for long, remote stretches without amenities, as well as some of the best motorcycling you will have ever encountered. Much of the Big Bend is **Chihuahuan Desert,** but the **Chisos Mountains,** located in the center of the park, rise to more than 7,000 feet in altitude. In the south, the Rio Grande River has cut deep canyons full of cane groves and rich vegetation. Many people spend weeks exploring this area and its natural beauty. The Indians say that when God was finished creating the world, he placed all the leftover rocks in the Big Bend. After your visit, you may be a believer. Note that the rich wildlife of the area is not all friendly toward man: bears, mountain lions, rattlesnakes, huge spiders, and scorpions all call the Big Bend home.

From Chisos Basin, return to the main road and turn right toward Panther Junction. From Panther Junction it is only twenty miles to the village of Rio Grande, which consists of a gas station and snack store. But in addition to the great road in, two things make it worth the trip: the hot springs and the overlook at Baquillas Canyon.

The well-marked right turn to the hot springs will take you down a two-mile side road. The naturally occurring **hot springs** are only a short walk down a well-maintained trail and there are almost always others around enjoying the spot. Bring your bathing suit. After a good soak, you should then continue on the main road through the tunnel to the left turn toward

The hot springs in Big Bend Park offer a refreshing stop. (Photo by Jack Binion)

Baquillas, at the eastern end of **Big Bend National Park.** It is possible to cross the Rio Grande into Mexico via a small boat, but there really is not much on the Mexican side, unless you want a beer. Backtrack to Panther Junction and take Hwy. 385 north toward Marathon.

This road, though flat and straight, leads you through the **Santiago** and **Woods Hollow Mountains** and makes for a great ride. Keep your eye out for low-flying Air Force planes practicing maneuvers.

Marathon (pop. 800) is a typical small, west Texas town in that it has most of the services needed for survival, but little else. The crown jewel in Marathon is the **Gage Hotel,** built in 1927 by Alfred Gage, a rancher who once had a 500,000-acre ranch in the area and needed a place to house his frequent guests and visiting business associates. It was renovated in 1978 and is decorated and furnished in period fashion. Rooms range from basic—bath down the hall, to nice—bath in the room, to wonderful—private suites with fireplaces. It is fairly pricey with rates from $85 to $300, but it is worth stopping just to look around. While all the rooms are in 1920s west Texas ranch décor, they are all different. Consider this a cultural stop.

Fifty-five miles on Hwy. 90 from Marathon will get you to Marfa. About eight miles before arriving in Marfa, note the pull-off area on the left from which you can view the Marfa Lights, as you may wish to return here at night.

As you ride into the town of **Marfa** (pop. 2,500), you will see that the lights are the big attraction here and many of the buildings and souvenir shops sport an alien theme. Recently the town has attempted to become sort

An overnight stay at the Gage Hotel is a treat. (Photo by Jack Binion)

THE SOUTHWEST

of an artists colony and that is attracting a different type of visitor. Marfa also contains a beautiful courthouse constructed from local stone in 1886. Atop the courthouse dome stands a life-sized statue of Lady Justice, though she is missing her scales. A local man who felt that he had not received justice inside, reportedly shot them off upon departing. The movie *Giant* was filmed in Marfa, and the lobby of the **El Paisano Hotel** on 207 N. Highland Avenue (915-729-3145, $100+) displays some of the memorabilia from the film. There are several mom and pop type places along Hwy. 90 in the $ 60/70 range in various states of repair. It is recommended that you check your room and amenities carefully before plunking down your cash; keeping in mind that it is only 21 miles up the road to Fort Davis. There are no campsites available in Marfa or nearby.

No one has ever solved the riddle of the mysterious Marfa lights.

The **Marfa Lights** are an enigma. They are most often referred to as those mysterious Marfa Lights. These bright orbs were first noticed by settlers in the late 1800s. They appear, disappear, separate into multiple lights, change color, and move around throughout the year, but are seen most frequently in the fall. Scientists who have studied them for years still have no explanation for them. Perhaps you can figure it out. The locals love their lights and they are one of west Texas top tourist attractions. Be very careful riding to and from the viewing area, as there is much wildlife along the road at night here.

■ For more trips in this region see *Motorcycle Journeys Through Texas and Northern Mexico* by Neal and Sandy Davis, available from Whitehorse Press.

22 Organ Pipe to Saguaro Trail

Text and photos by Martin Berke

- **DISTANCE** *282 miles*
- **HIGHLIGHTS** *Bonneville Salt Flat-like roads run through the Sonoran Desert, with an occasional dip and a climb to a premier mountain observatory. Up-close desert displays of its plants, animals, and strangely shaped saguaro.*

0.0	Start from Organ Pipe Cactus National Monument take Route 85 north
22.0	In Why take Route 86 east
103.0	Turn right on Route 386 south (sign to Kitt Peak Observatory)
110.7	Arrive at Kitt Peak Observatory, then return to Route 86
118.4	Turn right on Route 86 east
150.2	Turn left on Kinney Road
153.9	Arrive at Tucson Mountain Park, then continue north on Kinney Road
165.5	Turn right on Bajada Loop Road
167.8	Turn left on Golden Gate Road
168.8	Turn right into Signal Hill Picnic Area, then return
169.6	Turn left on Golden Gate Road
174.4	Turn right on Pictured Rock Road
177.3	Turn left on Wade Road
177.9	Turn right on Ina Road
186.9	Turn right on 1st Avenue
189.8	Turn left on River Road
196.0	Turn right on Craycroft Road
199.6	Turn left on East Broadway Boulevard
203.3	Turn right on Old Spanish Trail
208.9	Turn right on Freeman Road (signs to Saguaro National Monument East)
209.1	Enter Saguaro National Monument East
209.3	Turn left on Cactus-Forest Drive
227.4	Return on Cactus-Forest Drive to turn left on Freeman Road (which turns into Old Spanish Trail) and follow signs to Colossal Cave
238.6	Arrive Colossal Cave, return to Old Spanish Trail and take road to Vail
245.9	In Vail take Frontage Road to Interstate 10 west (sorry)
270.6	Exit left onto Speedway Boulevard (turns into Gates Pass Road)
275.6	Continue on Gates Road
280.4	Turn right on Kinney Road
282.0	Return to Tucson Mountain Park

It's a blooming desert at **Organ Pipe Cactus National Monument** (www.nps.gov/orpi, 520-387-6849). Most of the Organ Pipe cactus found in the United States are within the Monument. Ajo Mountain Drive, within the national park, penetrates the desert with 21 miles of hard pack dirt road. Plan on two hours to complete the loop. Pick up the excellent self paced Ajo Mountain Drive brochure at the visitor center. The 22-stop ride is the least expensive course in desert geology and plant life on earth. It will enrich the rest of your Southwest travels. The trail behind the rangers' quarters, beside the campground, identifies plants and their medicinal, tool, or food uses for the early nomadic Native American population.

Just beyond Organ Pipe Cactus National Park is **Why.** Reminiscent of the old Abbott and Costello baseball routine, no one could tell me how Why got its name. Why ask Why? Do all the provisioning, including water, there. The landscape is more moonscape through the Papago Indian Reservation.

The **National Optical Astronomy Observatories** (www.noao.edu/outreach/kpvc/contact.html, 520-318-8726) are located on Kitt Peak. Kitt Peak was selected in 1958 as a site for the national observatory after a three-year

These large cacti are what give Organ Pipe Cactus National Monument its name.

survey of 150 mountain ranges. The observatory is supported by the National Science Foundation and is the site of the world's largest collection of optical telescopes, 15 to be exact. The Mayall 4-meter telescope with a 158-inch fused quartz mirror and mounting weighs 375 tons. So delicately balanced is the telescope that the whole mechanism is driven by a one-half horsepower motor. Try balancing the scooter that well. At 6,875 feet, the 12-mile ride off the desert floor is a good way to cool down everything heated up and to break up the 130 miles from Organ Pipe Cactus National Monument to Tucson.

Gilbert Ray Campgrounds in **Tucson Mountain Park,** six miles north of Route 86 on Kinney Road (www.pima.gov/nrpr/places/parkpgs/tucs_mtpk,

520-883-4200), is home base for the Tucson-based loops. Site C-30 is as secluded as you can get and still be near Tucson. The coyotes howl and yip, letting everybody know whose home is on this range. The best part about going to or from downtown is riding Gates Pass Road.

While registering at the campground I asked an elderly woman waiting for the phone, "What's the best way to Tucson from here?" Scratching her head in a non-committal way, she said, "Well, just down the street is Gates Pass Road, that brings you into the center of town. Or you could go north or south to the Interstates." That was good advice. Gates Pass Road saves 15 miles and lets you ride a good mountain climber, narrow and switchbacked. Take a right onto Kinney Road, left on Gates Pass Road.

Once in **Tucson,** you'll find an endless variety of big city attractions and entertainment. The **Colorado Rockies** baseball team holds spring training here, and the **Pima Air Museum** (www.pimaair.org, 520-618-4800), **International Wildlife Museum** (www.wildlifemuseum.org, 520-629-0100), and the **Reid Park Zoo** (www.tucsonzoo.org, 520-881-4753) offer some unique alternatives.

Saguaro Cactus (sah-war-row) National Park (www.nps.gov/sagu, 520-733-5158) is obviously named for the giant cactus. Famous for its almost human shape, the saguaro cactus begins its life no bigger than the period at the end of this sentence. What it lacks in size it makes up for in numbers. A

The Pima Air Museum in Tucson, Arizona, is home to the "other" crotch rockets.

Organ Pipe to Saguaro Trail

They went thattaway!

The Hohokam pictographs at Signal Hill are examples of an early American writing system.

single cactus produces over forty million seeds in its lifetime of 175 to 200 years. Only one will survive as a mature saguaro. The saguaro cactus plant is a North American original.

Just before entering the westside monument (the difference between a national park and a national monument is the difference between congressional or presidential decree, respectively) is the **Arizona-Sonora Desert Museum** (520-883-2702, www.desertmuseum.org). Rated as a top-ten museum, it houses a hummingbird aviary (wear something flowery for an up close and personal view), the Earth Sciences Complex with its cave formations, and the Riparian (stream-side) habitat where beaver and otter are viewed from an underwater gallery.

The **Saguaro National Monument** itself is divided by **Tucson.** The west side is only a few miles from home base. Take the easy hard-packed dirt Bajada Loop Drive, it's the more scenic. At the T, hang a left and enter the **Signal Hill Picnic Area.** At the top of the rock outcrop, an easy little trail, are pictographs drawn a millennium ago by the Hohokam people. The concentric circles and stick figure drawings have endured 1,000 years of desert harshness and still confound the experts of today. Psst, it's not listed in any literature so take a peek.

After the picnic at Signal Hill (b.y.o. water), retrace Golden Gate Road to Pictured Rocks Road east to Tucson. A few curves at speed will dust off the machine.

THE SOUTHWEST

Old Tucson is where Hollywood meets the Old West.

Follow the direction summary given at the beginning of this trip description for a suggested route through Tucson to Saguaro National Park (East). The **Saguaro Cactus-Forest Drive** is a paved 18-mile loop. There are many hiking trails in both districts. Bring plenty of water.

Out of the monument, continue south (left) on the Old Spanish Trail to **Colossal Cave.** The ride is better than the destination, unless spelunking is a first love. Mama always taught me if you're in a hole, stop digging.

The road south to **Vail** includes a set of dips that will get the scooter airborne without trying. Just before the intersection with Interstate 10, grab Frontage Road east and rejoin Interstate 10 west for home base.

For up to the minute information on where the desert is blooming, call the Desert Botanical Gardens Wildflower 24-hour hotline at 480-481-8134.

■ For more trips in this region see *Motorcycle Journeys Through the Southwest* by Martin C. Berke, available from Whitehorse Press.

23 Joshua Tree National Park

Text and photos by Clement Salvadori

■ **DISTANCE** *150 miles*

■ **HIGHLIGHTS** *This trip goes mainly through open, flattish country, going from low to high desert, and back, with lots of curvy pavement.*

0 From Palm Springs head north on Indian Canyon Drive.

14 Turn right on CA62

33 In Joshua Tree turn right onto Park Blvd.

59 Turn right onto Pinto Basin Road

96 Turn right onto Box Canyon Road

115 Turn right on CA111

125 Turn left onto Avenue 52

133 Turn right onto Washington Avenue

136 Turn left onto CA111

150 Arrive back in Palm Springs at Ramon and Indian Canyon

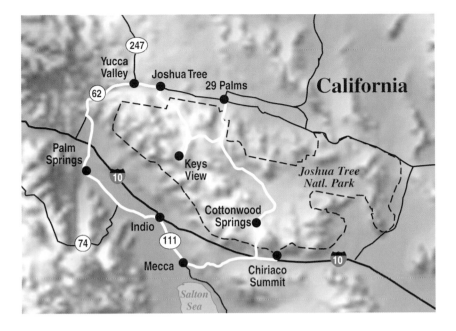

We've all heard of **Palm Springs,** where the rich come to play golf and die, the middle class come to party and leave, and the poor commute to work from **Indio.** Not many people might think of Palm Springs as being the focal point for great riding, but it is.

Nice town, thanks to a phenomenal amount of water deep down in the desert. Through the miracles of modern technology the local authorities pump it out at a great rate and keep 20 some golf courses green and healthy. The place has very much a live-for-today attitude, as nobody really wants to think about the inevitable day when the water gives out. The **Coachella Valley,** which is the long strip running from Palm Springs east to Indio, averages less than three inches of rain a year. But the date farmers use at least ten feet of water on their trees.

"Take the cash and let the credit go, nor heed the rumble of the distant drum." That's a thousand-year-old quote from a poet fellow named Omar Khayyam, which is still suitable.

Downtown Palm Springs is real nice on a quiet Monday afternoon. There are two wide, parallel, one-way streets, Indian Canyon Drive going north, Palm Canyon Drive going south, and the two miles between Alejo Road and Ramon Road is the place to be. There are a multitude of good open-air restaurants, shops and shopping centers, with a few museums thrown in for good measure. **Palm Canyon** is more the strolling side. For post office purposes, everything north of **Tahquitz Canyon** is referred to as north, and south of . . . etc.

For food, if you want Southwest cooking, go to the **Blue Coyote Grill** (445 North Palm Canyon, 760-327-1196). For all-American chow, try the **Burger Factory** (333 South Indian Canyon, 322-7678), where the one-pound "Kong Burger" is good for two people. Breakfast, in this land of food franchises, is best eaten at the **IHOP** (International House of Pancakes, for those who have forgotten) joint (471 South Indian Canyon Drive at Ramon).

Places to sleep are almost infinite, as greater Palm Springs has about 10,000 pillows to offer. Pricing structure is also quasi-infinite, ranging from mid-week low-season to weekend high-season. High scale is the **Hyatt Regency** on Palm Canyon (285 North Palm Canyon Drive), middle is the **Best Western Las Brisas** (222 South Indian Canyon, 325-4372, 800-346-5714). A favorite of the cost-conscious biking crowd is the quasi-omnipresent **Motel 6** chain—of which there are no less than four in Palm Springs; my choice is the one at 595 East Palm Canyon (760-325-6129) which is just a mile away from the action.

For local entertainment there are museums (I like the **Air Museum,** with all the WWII fighter planes), shows (**Liberace** wannabes are popular on the circuit), exertions (like how to learn rock-climbing and tandem sky-diving), and the great American pasttime, shopping. But I prefer to get on the road.

Starting from where Ramon Road crosses between Indian Canyon and Palm Canyon, head north on Indian Canyon Drive. When you cross over I-10, Indian Canyon Drive becomes Indian Ave. About four miles later, Pierson Blvd. crosses Indian Ave.; if you turn to the right you will get to **Desert Hot Springs,** where a dozen spas and resorts are located. This is where the Mafia heavies were reputed to hang out in the '30s, '40s, and '50s, the most famous place being the 56-acre Two Bunch Palms Resort; you need a reservation just to get in the gate—no looky-loos allowed.

At the intersection with CA 62, turn right. You are gaining altitude, going over a hill and dropping into the **Morongo Valley.** By the time you reach the town of **Yucca Valley** (3,256 feet), you have gained even more altitude and are on the edge of the **Mojave Desert.** On the right is **Dick Hutchin's Harley & HYKS** (Honda, Yamaha, Kawasaki, Suzuki) dealership (760-365-6311) and the **Harley Cafe,** open from 7 to 2 every day except Monday. Good food.

At the sign to PIONEERTOWN, pointing left, go straight. John's Place is on your right. Then CA 247 goes off to the left, but you stay straight on CA 62, a/k/a 29 Palms Highway.

In the middle of the small town of **Joshua Tree,** turn right on Park Boulevard, where a sign indicates the way to JOSHUA TREE NATIONAL PARK.

At the **West Entrance Station** to the park, an attendant will take $5 and give you a map. This is high desert you are headed into, and a pretty spectacular place.

These Boy Scouts are getting set for a hike in the Joshua Tree National Park. That's a lot of gear they are carrying.

The park covers some 800,000 acres, and while there are jackrabbits, bobcats, and golden eagles in residence, what you will see most of are cacti, be they Joshua trees, ocotillo, cholla, or whatever. And a lot of very big rocks, often adorned with rock-climbers wearing bright shirts and shorts; geologists say that these rocks are officially known as **monzogranite intrusions**; they do look odd and other-worldly. The road is good, and quite curvy.

If you want to get a fine view of the desert, take the right turn to **Keys View**, (5,185 feet) where the road dead-ends after six-plus miles. Return to the main road, Park Boulevard, and continue to Pinto Basin Road where you will turn right. If you were to continue straight on Park Boulevard, in four miles you would come to the North Entrance Station to the park, and in another five miles to 29 Palms (see sidebar).

Riding along Pinto Basin Road you find yourself dropping down from the high Mojave Desert to the low **Colorado Desert** . . . you can see for miles and miles into the basin. Go gently, as the road is a tad more than twisty, and tourists tend to clutter the narrow asphalt up. And you do not want to impale yourself on a cactus.

After about 23 miles a dirt road, immediately splitting into two dirt roads, goes off to the left. Adventuresome dual-purpose types might find these of interest.

That is General Patton and his dog in front of the Patton Museum.

The ranger station and visitor center at **Cottonwood Springs;** is seven miles further along. The springs and campground are a mile east of the visitor center.

Now you go over **Cottonwood Pass** (2,800 feet) and down **Cottonwood Canyon** on a delightful stretch of road and leave the park boundary.

When you arrive at I-10 you can take an interesting diversion four miles east to the **Chiriaco Summit** (1,705 feet) exit and visit the **General George Patton Museum.** Back in 1940 when President Roosevelt knew that entering the European conflict was inevitable, he had the army set up training bases in the desert in preparation for battling the Germans in North Africa. Every sort of World War II tank is parked outside the museum, and inside is an eclectic display of the equipment used by Patton and his troops.

Afterward, go back the four miles and exit. Cross over the Interstate and turn right on to Box Canyon Road. The road goes through **Shavers Valley** and then drops down into **Box Canyon,** between the **Mecca Hills** and **Orocopia Mountains,** an excellent piece of riding.

Cross over the **Coachella Canal** into a sea of green and you are going below sea level as you enter the southern end of the **Coachella Valley.** This is very fertile land, as long as you have the water to make things grow.

The small town of **Mecca** (Alt. -189 feet), home to several thousand farm workers, is where the American date industry started about 100 years ago. Nobody seems to know precisely how the town got its name, but presumably because many of the date palms were coming from the Middle East.

At the traffic light on CA 111 turn right immediately after crossing over the **Southern Pacific** railroad tracks. If you have a very sweet tooth stop at the **Date Garden Oasis** and have a date shake; an awful lot of sugar is in one of those babies.

Stay on CA 111 through the town of **Thermal** and on into the town of Coachella. Turn left on to Avenue 52, not very romantically named, but

The **Oasis Visitor Center,** and the headquarters of the Joshua Tree National Park, is in the **Oasis of Mara,** in the town of 29 Palms, just a few hundred yards south of CA 62.

The **29 Palms Inn** (760-367-3505), has been offering hospitality since 1928 at 73950 Inn Avenue (don't ask me how they got to 73,000 on a very short street).

The place has more than a dozen separate little residences, either adobe cottages or wood cabins, and a restaurant beside the swimming pool that serves lunch and dinner seven days a week, brunch on Sunday. It is a very nice place to lay back.

29 Palms itself does not have too much to offer, being an old Marine Corps town that has steadily been losing inhabitants, except that it has decided to revamp itself and has taken to calling itself the **City of Murals,** and lots of buildings have their sides painted.

When you are ready, head back south into the park. Your ticket is good for seven days.

useful. Staying on Ave. 52 cross over CA 86 and head straight as the proverbial arrow toward **Indio Mountain.** Major farming here, but specialized, with dates and grapes abounding. Then you enter the new development town called **La Quinta,** with semi-expensive houses all looking just alike. The cross-streets all have presidential names: Van Buren, Jackson, Monroe, Madison, Jefferson. No Clinton, yet, nor Bush. Interestingly, this west end of Ave. 52 has new sidewalks, indicating that a lot of oldies who are buying these houses want places to walk—doctor's orders.

After eight miles turn right (north) on Washington Avenue. Then three more miles to the traffic light at the intersection with CA 111 where you will turn left. This little jog along Avenue 52 has avoided downtown **Indio,** a thoroughly avoidable place.

Where CA 74 goes off to the left, stay straight on CA 111, then stay straight on East Palm Canyon Drive as CA 111 goes right onto Gene Autry Trail. Follow around the curve to arrive back at **Ramon** and **Indian Canyon.**

■ For more trips in this region see *Motorcycle Journeys Through California and Baja* by Clement Salvadori, available from Whitehorse Press.

THE NORTHWEST

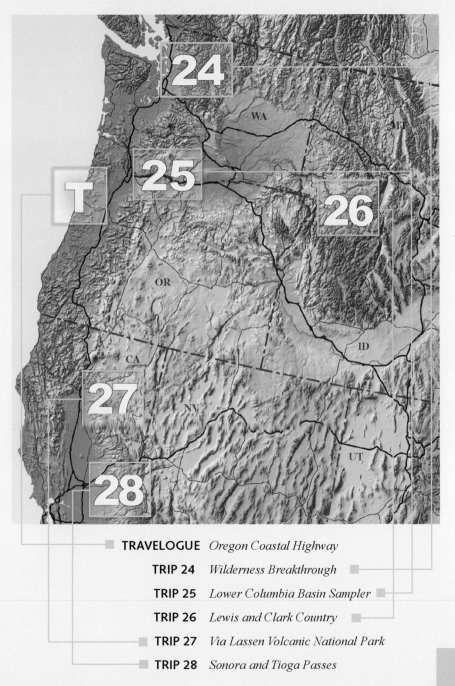

Oregon's Coast Highway

Text and photos by Grant Parsons

This road just shouldn't be here. The asphalt is flawless. The weather is perfect. And I'm riding a Honda Gold Wing through a series of tight, well-banked twisties that feel like they're miles from anywhere. But they're not. In fact, just minutes ago, I turned off a crowded, eight-lane expressway in suburban Portland, Oregon. I followed a line of light traffic up a two-lane road, past several driveways and then a park, where everyone in front of me turned off.

Suddenly, I found myself on a perfect, curvy road that's nearly deserted at 3 p.m. on a workday. As I weave through turns, with the road rising and

Views don't get more spectacular than this.

falling on either side of a long, low ridge, the dense tree cover occasionally clears, offering me a view back at downtown Portland. I can't help but feel like I'm getting away with something.

Welcome to Skyline Boulevard.

Anywhere else, a road like this would have been developed several times over by now. It would be crowded with houses, shops, or apartments. But here, in the shadow of the city, it remains a perfect motorcycle road that only gets better, and more deserted, as the miles roll by. In time, the driveways thin out, and the occasional intersection offers up businesses that have a decidedly country feel. At one crossroads, a small market made of weathered wood looks like it's been there forever.

It's a good omen for this ride, which will only take me farther from civilization. My plan is to follow the Columbia River northwest from Portland about 100 miles to the spot where it empties into the Pacific Ocean. From there, I'll head south down the entire 350-mile length of the Oregon coast to the California line. I'm about 10 miles into that 450-mile trip, and already this place is tossing me surprises.

By the time I weave along the ridge to the quiet intersection that marks the end of Skyline Road, 20-odd miles later, I've passed more motorcycles and bicycles than cars—always a good sign. I click the big Honda into first, hang a right on Rocky Point Road and start weaving down the hill toward the wide Columbia.

Oregon's Coast Highway

If you like your restaurants with a nautical theme, you won't be disappointed.

I think I'm going to like this place.

Traffic is heavy with commuters heading out of Portland when I reach U.S. 30, the major four-lane that parallels the Columbia. I wait for a gap and pull into the fray. The view to the right toward the river is industrial—marinas, loading terminals and houses—interspersed with long stretches of trees. As the miles roll by, I discover one of the great things about the Gold Wing I'm riding: the high-zoot satellite navigation system mounted in the dash. Up ahead, I notice that Route 30 heads away from the river for a while, and I'd rather not. So I pick a right at random, looking for local color, and wind up in the town of St. Helens. It's a working-class town of well-maintained houses with streets that lead right down to a marina on the Columbia.

The view across the river is capped by the towering presence of Mount St. Helens on the Washington side. This, of course, is the volcanic mountain that blew its top spectacularly in 1980, shortening the 9,677-foot mountain by more than 1,300 feet, killing 57 people, and blowing volcanic ash across 11 states. From here, it looks dangerously close to civilization. Not that the St. Helens townsfolk seem to care. As I wind my way back toward U.S. 30, I notice that one pastime for kids here is collecting blackberries by the side of the road. Nice place.

Eventually, the road traffic thins out, while the Columbia gets wider as it approaches the Pacific. I stop for gas and a snack in Rainier, where I discover

TRAVELOGUE: NORTHWEST

one of Oregon's more unusual laws. Years ago, legislators here decided that you couldn't pump your own gas. Some say it's a safety issue, while others say it's designed to preserve the jobs of thousands of gas station attendants. Either way, you're required to have a station employee fill your tank. Motorcycles get an exemption—the attendant can turn on the pump and hand you the nozzle, so you can actually do the fueling. I discover all this as I reach for the filler nozzle at a gas station, only to hear the attendant warn me to leave it alone. He tells me that the penalty for pumping my own gas is $500. But he also says that he can't remember anyone ever being fined.

Astoria, it turns out, is my kind of town. When I roll in before sunset, I discover another elbows-out, working-class place that's short on pretense. Fishing boats share marina space with high-buck cabin cruisers, a boardwalk lines the harbor, and narrow streets snake up the hill from the riverfront, producing a small-town San Francisco kind of feel.

The town's claim to fame is that it's the closest inland port to the ocean on the Columbia. But it's not big enough for the huge trans-Pacific container ships that churn up the river toward Portland, so they pass by, while the fishing boats turn in here. As it turns out, the short trip from the ocean to Astoria is about as treacherous as they come, with a tricky deep-water channel that threads among massive, submerged sandbars at the mouth of the Columbia. A local tells me the channel actually requires ships to turn broadside to the flow of the river, a move requiring a fair amount of precision as captains balance the downstream river current with strong winds and storms pushing upstream. It's dangerous enough to earn the sandbar the nickname "Graveyard of the Pacific." In the past 300 years, this graveyard has claimed nearly 2,000 vessels and 700 lives.

Over a seafood dinner on the wharf—dungeoness crab is the local delicacy—I spend some time gazing at the huge ships passing by, watched by the occasional U.S. Coast Guard helicopter. I'm glad I'm on a motorcycle.

In the morning, I wake to another gorgeous day—clear skies and 70 degrees. Despite rumors of Oregon's rainy weather, the forecast calls for more of the same for the next few days. I wonder if all that talk of rain is just a trick to keep the tourists away.

I celebrate with a quick ride up to the Astoria Column, a historic landmark that sits atop 600-foot Coxcomb Hill just off the downtown. Finding the road to the top normally would be a chore, but I've got the Gold Wing's GPS to guide me along the town's narrow, hillside streets. It's almost like cheating. I'm beginning to really like this bike.

The route threads among expansive historic houses with wide lawns, then enters a park, climbing the whole time. After a few dozen twists and a wide, sweeping lefthand curve clinging to the side of the hill, I reach the top to find a 125-foot spire stretching to the sky. I park the Wing, pay a buck, and climb

You like cliffs? The Oregon coast has plenty of them.

the 164-step spiral staircase. The view is impressive. On a day like today, the scene takes in the entire peninsula, including Youngs Bay, the Pacific, Mount St. Helens, Mount Rainier, the Columbia, and the massive 4.2-mile-long Astoria Bridge across to Washington.

It's pretty nice and all, but I've got a road to ride. So I coast back down the hill, follow the steep streets back to U.S. 30, hang a left, and pick up U.S. Route 101. From here on out, navigation will be simple. I'll be on this road, or just off it, all the way to California.

Look at a map of Oregon, and you'll see that the northern stretch of 101 is the closest spot along the coast for Portland locals. And it seems that most of them are out today. That means the prevailing speed on 101 is about 35 mph. Fortunately, there are plenty of opportunities to hang a right and head a hundred yards over low dunes to the coast to follow a local road. From the seat of the Wing, the view is of modest beach houses, white sand beach, and blue ocean. It's shaping up to be a good day.

At Sunset Beach State Park, I actually have the option of riding on the beach, which is open to motorized traffic. But the 50 yards between the pavement and packed beachfront is a deep, rutted loose sandbox more suited to a dual-sport bike than a Gold Wing, so I pass.

A few miles later, I'm rolling through the town of Seaside, when I see a sign guiding me to the waterfront and almost immediately smell fried dough. Hey, why fight it? I park along an incredibly touristy stretch of main drag near the beach, eating an elephant ear from a street vendor.

South of town the landscape goes from low beaches to the rocky coastline you expect of Oregon. Uninterrupted horizons are replaced by seastacks: 80- and 100-foot-tall rocks sticking straight up a few hundred yards offshore. And, this being Oregon, they're covered with green foliage that makes them seem all the more otherworldly.

Hoping for a better view, I take the turnoff for Ecola State Park. I leave the U.S. route behind and immediately plunge into primeral forest. The new asphalt ribbon weaves among moss-covered conifers and ultimately leads to a parking lot overlooking the ocean. A short walk takes me to the edge of a cliff a good 150 feet above the water, where a lone white lighthouse stands. The 270-degree vista is spectacular, from the deep blue of deep ocean to the stark white of crashing surf to the murky green of endless forest. I breath in fresh ocean air and spend far too many minutes completely zoned out as I gaze toward the horizon. There's a lot to like here.

Back at the bike, I look at the map and count all the Oregon state parks and recreation areas along the coastline. There's at least 37. And that's only on the coast side of the road. I'm beginning to wonder if I've planned enough time for this trip.

I make it maybe 20 miles before I find another reason to stop: the Tillamook cheese factory, home of this world-famous brand. I buy some fresh-made bread and (what else?) cheese, and toss them into the Wing's voluminous tail trunk for a snack on the road later.

Clam chowder, fish 'n chips, oyster stew. Go ahead. Indulge.

It turns out to be a great choice. A lucky detour from Tillamook puts me on what's billed as the "Three Capes Loop." The Wing's nav system shows a broad peninsula with a serpentine road linking together capes Meares, Lookout, and Kiwanda over maybe 40 miles. Sign me up.

This road is a standout, first ringing the west edge of Tillamook Bay maybe 6 inches above the waterline, then diving inland to dodge among trees and dunes. What the asphalt lacks in smoothness—it's built across a giant, tree-covered sand dune, so it requires frequent patching—it makes up for in remoteness. Few cars seem to make the journey. At Cape Kiwanda, I walk down to the Cliffside and eat, a quirk of timing giving me the entire rugged coastline to myself.

If the Oregon Coast has a funky heart—and trust me, it does—it can be found along the wharf on Newport's historic bayfront, especially on a Saturday night. Here, a line of trendy galleries mixes with a working-class fish house and a touristy aquarium. Charter-boat stalls stand next to restaurants and sandwich shops, and the smell is of baked bread and fish scales, espresso and diesel. In a word, this place rocks.

It also appears to be the place where old Volkswagen micro-buses go to die—or more precisely, to retire. I don't think I've seen more of them in one place since I watched "Endless Summer." Of course, a good third of the people jamming the restaurants would fit right into that classic surfer movie, giving the place a very bohemian vibe. I talk to one couple who say they came here from Kansas to visit two years ago and never left. It's easy to see why, and for a while, I contemplate calling my wife and suggesting the same thing.

But morning comes early for a traveling journalist, so I reluctantly tear myself away for the walk back to my hotel to get a good start on the next day. No doubt—I definitely didn't plan enough time for this trip.

Maybe it's because it's a Sunday. Or perhaps it's just that the southern part of the Oregon coast is farther from large population centers than the north. But for whatever reason, when I point the Wing south over the causeway out of Newport the next morning, the traffic and congestion of the day before disappear in my mirrors—and it'll stay that way all day.

Hugging the sheer cliffs that mark this section of coast, the road climbs, and the views out to sea are spectacular. At one turnout, I see waterspouts of surfacing whales. Grey whales are the most common here, and they feed in shallow water near the shore during the summer and fall, migrate south to breed during the winter, then cruise back north in the spring.

This stretch is also home to what may be the single most photographed lighthouse on the Oregon coast. Perched high above the ocean at Haceda Head, this lighthouse has been warning passing ships of the rocky coastline since 1894. Still shining through its original fresnel lens—restored in 2000—it's the most powerful light on the Oregon coast, visible more than 20 miles out to sea. You can take the winding road up to the lighthouse itself, but I enjoy the long-distance view from 101, just south of the park. From a wide pullout, it's easy to kill far too much time watching the lighthouse, the crashing waves, and far below, sea lions lounging on the rocks.

If you get the feeling that it's hard to make miles along this coastline without stopping, you're right.

Remember those great scenes from "On Any Sunday," when Malcom Smith, Steve McQueen, and Mert Lawwill go dirt-riding all over the dunes at Pismo Beach? Well, Oregon has its own beach-riding paradise just down the road, at Oregon Dunes National Recreation Area. Motoring by on 101, I see several shops that rent ATVs by the hour, and a couple of parking lots where empty trailers sit, their owners obviously out enjoying the day.

This 40-mile stretch of sandy hills looks like fun, but it forces Route 101 inland. So by the time I reach Coos Bay at the south end of the dunes, I consult the Wing's GPS and hook a right toward Sunset Bay State Park. Who could resist a name like that?

A few minutes later, I'm back by the ocean, taking in the cool breeze from

The view from Ecola State Park. But almost all of the Oregon coast looks this nice.

the bike as I motor between open vistas and tree-covered lanes. The little road I'm on continues until it dead-ends at Cape Arayo State Park. I kill the motor and hear what sounds like a whole pack of dogs, mildly barking. I look out and see dark shapes on the offshore rocks. A sign tells me that this is a colony of marine mammals—harbor seals, sea lions, and elephant seals. It sounds like the best party on the entire coast.

Realizing there's less of this beautiful country ahead of me the farther south I travel, I engineer a new plan. Any scenic-looking road that loops off of and back to 101 becomes a must-ride. That's how I wind up rolling through a laid-back area of houses in Bandon, where the locals enjoy cliffside views of tall rocks just 30 feet out from shore. And it's how I find a cool working pier farther south in Port Orford, where a funky gift shop shares dock space with deep-sea fishing boats. In between, remote stretches of 101 alternately hug the rugged shoreline and dodge inland.

By the time I reach Brookings, I know I have only a few miles of Oregon left, and the afternoon is nearly gone. I start scanning the roadside, and as I near the California border, I find what I'm looking for and hit my turn signal. I pull over by a lonely stretch of dunes. I park the Wing, and walk the hundred yards or so across low dunes to the beach. Standing there, with the waves brushing the sand, I can look south and see the "Welcome to California" sign up on 101 that marks the official end of this ride.

But the sign can wait. I'm not going anywhere for a while.

Oregon's Coast Highway

24 Wilderness Breakthrough

Text and photos by Bruce Hansen

- **DISTANCE** *276 miles (all day—break this into two rides if it's hot)*
- **HIGHLIGHTS** *From suburban rush to rural scenes in just 10 miles. You must see the striking, remote, and beautiful North Cascades National Park. Bright, sharp granite mountains, silt-green rivers, mellow Methow Valley, and Old West eastern Washington towns. Great pie and fresh peaches.*

From Seattle, go north on Interstate 5 to get to Everett.

- **0** Get on Highway 2 going east
- **2** Take the 204 East exit toward Lake Stevens
- **5** Turn north onto Highway 9
- **49** Turn east onto Highway 20
- **187** About two miles south of Twisp, take 153 going south
- **218** Turn right onto 97 ALT going south toward Chelan
- **227** When you get to Chelan, continue going south on 97 ALT
- **261** At Highway 2, turn west toward Cashmere/Leavenworth
- **276** Arrive in Cashmere

Some folks say this story began in 1814; Alexander Ross and four Indian guides set out to find a shortcut to the Pacific Ocean from the fur-rich valleys in Eastern Washington through the jumble of Cascade Mountains and forests. A fast way to get furs to the market would be worth a great deal. Using a storm that mowed down huge cedar trees "like grass before a scythe," the gods explained to the Indian guides that they were trespassing and should not continue their attempt to cross to the Pacific. Guideless, Ross was forced to turn back.

Four decades later, Henry Custer, working on a government commission, set out to find his way through the Northern Cascades using a western approach. Custer set out from the Pacific heading east into the Cascades. After scaling a tall peak, he saw wall upon wall of peaks and forests extending eastward as far as the eye could see. Although he explored over 1,000 miles of wilderness, he never made it through the Northern Cascades. Nearly 70 years of exploration finally revealed a way through these American Alps.

Men like Ross and Custer did open the mystic and massive Northern Cascades for the gold seekers and loggers to come later. Lucky for modern explorers on two wheels, this special place now has a beautiful highway passing

Fireweed grows near roadsides and open areas. In the background the Northern Cascades seem to jumble together for this photo.

Fireweed will grow wherever a fire has opened up some sky.

all the way through it. This trip will take you though canyons and forests, past grand glacier-clad peaks and into a beautiful, historic valley on the other side. There, you too will find gold, if the peaches are ripe when you pass through.

Start this journey just north of **Seattle** in **Everett.** Coming from Everett, Washington, Interstate 5 is the fastest way to get to this area and begin your own story of your journey through the Northern Cascades. If you have the time, I suggest you parallel the mighty I-5 by riding up Highway 9 just east of the interstate. So near the urban rush of Seattle, this is a pretty, rural highway. As you proceed north, it becomes more intensely rural, rolling and relaxing. Views of farms, tall hills just east of the road, and roadside fruit and corn stands punctuate this Highway 9 ride. Expect your speed to be in the 35 to 45 mph range.

Sedro Woolley makes a fine stop for fuel and supplies before heading up Highway 20 into the wilderness. You might wonder about the name of this gateway town. In 1886, Mortimer Cook built a lumber mill on the **Skagit River** and named it Bug. His wife compelled him change it to the Spanish name for cedar: *cedro*. However Mortimer misspelled the word and the town became Sedro. Three years later a rival mill began operations just a mile away in a town named Woolley after its founder. When a depression hit the logging market, the towns abandoned their intense rivalry and merged.

If you don't pick up any logs or supplies in Sedro Woolley, you may have problems camping in **North Cascades National Park.** Most bikers do not stay overnight in the park. It's a drive-through experience for those of us who do not favor camping. Camp-

Highway 20 starts off in a civilized way, running by pretty farms and cute towns like Concrete.

ers should bring all their food and gear with them, as services tend to be non-existent near most campgrounds. In Sedro Woolley the **Three Rivers Inn and Restaurant** has good beds and a pool (210 Ball St., 360-855-2626).

After loading up with supplies and leaving Sedro Woolley, follow the green Skagit River past peaceful fruit stands, small farms, and mixed forests. If you're hungry, I'd suggest you stop at the town of **Concrete.** At the **Cajun Bar and Grill** you can get a terrific lunch. Concrete gets its name from the limestone mines nearby. The region is still proud of its high quality cement made from local limestone. I like the town for its historical charm and pie.

Once you reach the town of **Marblemount,** you truly feel you are at the last civilized place you'll see for a long time. A sign outside of town warns that there are no services for 69 miles. Originally this town developed to provide the gold and silver miners with supplies. Motels and somewhat seedy RV parks are scattered along the road near Marblemount. Once outside of Marblemount, the road shrugs off its lazy turns and gains energy, as the Skagit River appears even more milky green. Power lines and dams may intrude on your photos along this stretch. Energy-hungry Seattle sucks hydoelectrical power from the green waters of the Skagit.

Wilderness Breakthrough

The green Skagit River flows through some of the most rugged areas I've ever seen.

After a break, it's time to blast through the canyon—keeping an eye out for rocks.

The steep cliffs rising abruptly near the road may make you wonder how these rocks came to be here. Like so much of the Pacific Northwest, it began with volcanic lava. Unlike other volcanic rocks, the lava crystallized into granite, then yielded to deep uplifting forces. As a result of these amazingly unyielding rocks, the mountain peaks loom sharp and freshly cut, crystal cliffs push their chests toward your bike threateningly, and the V-shaped Skagit River canyons resist erosion. When you stop at pullouts, the North Cascades will pull a sigh from your lips. Such power and beauty!

The best glacier views tend to be at the end of hikes, since the road was only completed in 1972. Slides and rock falls keep road repair crews busy throughout the summer. Expect some

THE NORTHWEST

Looking at the Northern Cascades from the east side, they look a bit tame at first.

construction delays when traveling the magnificent Highway 20 through North Cascades National Park.

Stop at the **North Cascades Visitor Center** (206-386-4495) in Newhalem for glacial viewing and tourist information, camping permits, and a chance to stretch your legs. As you motor through this 781 square mile national park, you'll discover some of my favorite parts on the eastern side, as you begin to follow the **Methow River**. If the skies were raining or spitting snow on the west side, it's likely the **Methow River Valley** will be dry—perhaps hot.

Leaving the wild part of North Cascades, **Mazama** stands first in line with services to collect travelers. Afterward, **Winthrop** beckons to tourists with a strong Old West theme. If you come through town on a weekend, it's tough to find a parking spot here. Once you push through the swinging doors of the saloon, no empty bar stools await you. Beautiful custom motorcycles proudly line the curbs. After the loneliness of the mountains, many people find Winthrop a refreshing contrast.

Stay at **Hotel Rio Vista** (800-996-3906). The best food is found at the **Duck Brand Restaurant.**

What I like best about the Methow Valley is the progression of mountains—from sharp granite blades, to more rounded saltshaker peaks, to the high, gentle rolling hills. I can imagine Alexander Ross and his guides

Wilderness Breakthrough

Peaks like this are as common as chrome in a Harley showroom. You just never get used to it.

The Old-West-themed town of Winthrop welcomes bikers as it is the first town with abundant services after blasting through the North Cascades National Park.

s starting here to find the way through the North Cascades, his trail broadened by gold seekers and ranchers who came afterward. As you break off Highway 20 after **Twisp,** you will spot more gentle hills and fruit stands. My advice is to avoid moderation when near these fruit stands. Many have picnic tables and allow you to eat as many peaches as you can buy. Peaches are the true gold of the Methow Valley.

Your goal for the night is **Cashmere,** but stop earlier if the heat, views, or peaches wear you out. One tourist stop I always enjoy is the "hip" town of **Chelan.** Latte anyone? Since the 1880s when miners and tourists flocked to this area, Chelan has been accommodating guests. Offering good food, lodging, and **Lake Chelan**—1,500 feet deep and 50 miles long—this place calls out for a visit. Only Lake Tahoe and Crater Lake are deeper American lakes.

You can get great breakfasts and lunch at **BC MacDonald's** (104 E. Woodin Avenue) and Mexican food at **La Brisa Restaurant** (246 Highway 150 #11).

From Chelan, I'm going to send you down the west side of **Lake Entiat** on Highway 97 ALT toward **Wenatchee.** Watch out for winds, particularly in the late afternoon. When you get to the junction of Highway 2 going west, turn left toward Cashmere. This simple town is where I like to spend the night and enjoy great food. My favorite motel is the **Village Inn Motel** (229 Cottage Ave. 509-782-3522 or 800-793-3522).

A last look back at the wonderland of the Northern Cascades.

Cashmere used to be called Mission, but changed its name in 1904 to its present name after the beautiful Vale of Kashmir in India. The best food in this part of Washington is the **Walnut Café** (reservations recommended—even for lunch) about two blocks from the motel. It's a bit on the gourmet side. If you want simple, downhome food and don't mind a little smoke in your eye, **Barney's Tavern** has great breakfasts and big, simple dinners. Another place with good home cooking is the **Big Y**, located about five miles beyond Cashmere on Route 2 toward Leavenworth on the right just past **Dryden.**

From here you can head south to explore the Mt. Rainier area or the Columbia River basin. You can also make like the explorers Ross and Custer and find your own story, one that ends quite differently than theirs. Thousands of bikers love to take Highway 2 over Stevens Pass back to Everett (120 miles). Too bad our early explorers had so few choices.

For more trips in this region see *Motorcycle Journeys Through the Pacific Northwest* by Bruce Hansen, available from Whitehorse Press.

25 Lower Columbia Basin Sampler

Text and photos by Bruce Hansen

- **DISTANCE** *580 miles (Two long days, or three if it's hot)*
- **HIGHLIGHTS** *Columbia River Gorge, Mt. Adams, perfect biking roads near Condon, Stonehenge replica, Old Columbia River Highway, views of canyons, mountains, plains, and farms*

Day 1

0 Leave Portland going north on Interstate 5 toward Seattle

9 Turn east onto Highway 14 toward Camas

61 Turn north onto 141 toward Trout Lake

69 Turn right toward Glenwood, follow signs

87 At Glenwood, follow signs to Goldendale

111 Look for a fork in the road. Veer right toward the less traveled highway. Turn right on 142.

134 At Lyle, turn east onto 14

162 At Hwy. 97 junction, explore Maryhill Museum and Stonehenge

169 Stay on 97 toward Goldendale. Two miles past Goldendale turn off for viewpoint. If it's clear, you can see four volcanoes. Turn around and go back to the Columbia River and Highway 14

184 Turn east onto 14

264 Turn south onto Interstate 82

277 Turn East toward Pendleton onto Interstate 84

281 Take exit to Highway 207 (Maybe stay in Heppner or Condon)

334 207 turns into 206. You want to be on 206 toward Condon

343 Arrive in Condon

Day 2

0 Leave Condon going south on 19 toward Fossil

21 At Fossil, go south onto 218 toward Antelope

57 Once in Antelope, go north to Shaniko

65 At Shaniko, turn south onto 97

77 Turn north onto 197

107 At Maupin, take a break in the park

142 Turn west on Highway 30 to The Dalles. Go through town staying on 30.

156 Enjoy the Rowena Look Out. Stay on 30 to Mosier.

167 At Mosier, get on Interstate 84 to head back to Portland

237 Arrive in Portland

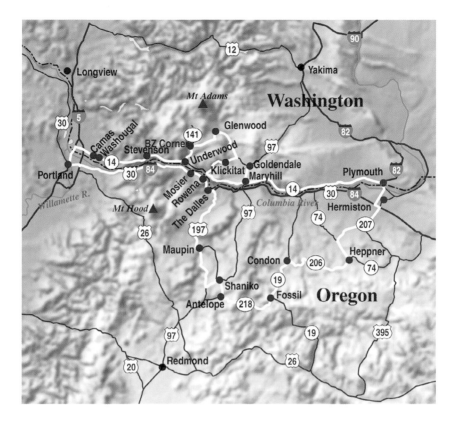

Sometimes you want to be first in line. Sometimes you want all the traffic lights to be green. Sometimes you just don't want to settle for something. You want the best. If you can take only one journey in the Pacific Northwest, the Lower Columbia Basin Ride is the green light, the front of the line, the best.

This is a long, demanding ride. Don't force yourself to keep going if the heat or other factors tire you. Watch for deer and rocks near cliff faces. Watch for tractors lingering around blind turns.

This journey takes you near an interesting volcano, **Mt. Adams,** up bare golden hills bridging the gap between the volcanic matter from Mt. Adams and the amazingly hard basalt slabs that make up most of the Columbia River Basin.

When you ride out of Portland, you are going to head directly for the Columbia River. This great body of water drains an area the size of France and is truly one of the world's prestigious rivers. To explore the whole river basin would take well over a week. I'm giving you this part of the basin in two days.

Begin this journey in **Portland, Oregon**—a hilly, handsome city built

Looking north toward Washington from Rowena Viewpoint. The Columbia River Gorge can be perfect in April.

near the confluence of the **Willamette River** and the **Columbia River.** Head north toward **Seattle.** The two main freeways that will take you there are Interstate 5 (I-5) or Interstate 205. Once you cross the Columbia River, watch for signs indicating Highway 14. Turn north on 14 toward **Camas** and **Washougal.** After passing through these two small towns, you will notice the suburban views becoming more rural. The river on your right, a mixed evergreen/deciduous forest on your left, and the gently winding roads tell you that you've truly begun this journey.

Stevenson rests comfortably just 30 miles from Camas. The town seemed to be dying until a big luxury resort, **Skamania Lodge,** was constructed just west of town. Now its short main street vibrates with life, its veins running rich with tourists' money. When taking this trip, I often stop for food at the **Big River Grill** or the **River's Edge Cafe** in Stevenson. If I have guests, I'll pull into the Skamania Lodge for a terribly expensive breakfast.

From Stevenson, continue east on 14 to **Underwood.** Just past the **Klickitat River,** turn north onto Highway 141 toward **Trout Lake.** Continue on this road past pretty farms, woods, and ever-steeper rolling hills. At **B Z Corner,** (gas and deli food available) barely a town, look for the signs to **Glenwood.** Turn right on B Z Corners/Glenwood Road toward Glenwood. By now you will find that Mt. Adams has become close and perhaps even

THE NORTHWEST

familiar. Mt. Adams is graced by a dozen glaciers and skirted round by miles of pristine forests and gentle farmland. Since northwesterners prize huckleberries, a small, tart blueberry-like fruit, pickers flock to this area in late summer to gather berries and hike the trails around Mt. Adams.

Once you leave Glenwood, you will be riding on a plateau toward **Goldendale.** All around you will be the high brown hills of this part of southern Washington. They go on forever and become more beautiful with

This rider will soon get the best view of Mt. Adams available from any paved road.

each mile. You can't explore them on this trip. Instead, after about 24 miles on the Goldendale Highway, turn right on Highway 142 toward **Klickitat.** This turn is easy to miss and poorly marked. If you find yourself in Goldendale, turn around and go back to Klickitat.

The Klickitat River has cut a sinuous trail through the hard rock of the plateau. Bikers love the pretty views and twisting turns. Part of this highway is one lane, but it's all paved. **The Klickitat Hotel** has blah food, but friendly people. Obey the local speed limits and continue down the highway to the Columbia River and Highway 14. Go east (left). When you get to the junction of Highway 97, turn left and follow the signs to the **Maryhill Museum.**

Besides being a stunning mansion looking out on beautiful views of the

The BZ Corners/Glendale Highway is such a fine road, bikers often spend the whole day riding on it.

These curves near Condon can put a biker into a zone no one but us motorcyclists can understand.

Wheat fields take advantage of the fertile soil near Condon, Oregon.

Columbia River Gorge, it has a nice lawn and shade. About two minutes from the museum is a full-sized replica of Stonehenge.

With your mind refreshed by Maryhill, turn your bike back to Highway 14 and go east. From here, 14 takes you along the edge of the Columbia River with the basalt cliffs on your left. You'll see few other travelers along this route, which is devoid of trees, but rich in geological beauty and golden-stemmed grasses.

Your ride on 14 will end about 90 miles out of Goldendale, but if you love terrific motorcycle roads, the best is yet to come. When you get to Interstate 82, jump on this freeway going south toward **Hermiston.** After about 15 miles on I-82, you will need to merge onto I-84 going toward **Pendleton,** Oregon, for 3.5 miles, then take the Highway 207 exit going south (exit 182).

This gets you to where you want to be: the best motorcycle roads in all the Columbia River Basin. Because of the great Missoula Flood, this area features enormous piles of gravel atop basalt slabs. For bikers this means twisty roads.

Stay on 207 to **Heppner.** Visitors love Heppner for its unspoiled rural character. Have a picnic in the park or just rest on the grass. This pretty town was named after Harry Heppner, a mule freight operator who built a camp here at the confluence of three creeks. You want your mind clear for the ride between Heppner and **Condon.**

Many tourists who visit Heppner go for the fall bird hunting. If it's not hunting season, you can stay in one of the lodges like **Ruggs Ranch** (541-676-5390). Lodging is also available at the **Northwest Motel & RV Park** (541-676-9167). For a great taco salad try Murry's Drug.

From Heppner, though the road below you will not turn to gold, the gold will be in the turns. The roads are so great because of the combination of terrific scenery, quality pavement, and revealed apexes—few blind turns. Watch for deer, especially near dawn or dusk. If you stay on 207, you'll notice it turns into 206 going toward Condon.

The historic **Hotel Condon** was built in 1920 and has been completely remodeled so the 18-room hotel now combines its historic charm with modern amenities (202 S. Main St., 541-384-4624, 800-201-6706, www.hotel-condon.com). For those who prefer a more standard motel, there is the **Condon Motel** on 216 N Washington (N Hwy 19), (541-384-2181). For food, try the **Country Café** (541-384-7000).

At the Antelope Café you'll feel like you are in someone's friendly kitchen.

Between Heppner and Condon, Oregon, this highway is one of the best motorcycling roads in the whole Pacific Northwest.

From Condon, you want to go south toward **Fossil** on Highway 19. Fossil was named for the fossil remains a rancher found on his property. Later, Thomas Condon found the fossilized bones of a saber-toothed tiger here.

At Fossil, head south onto Highway 218 toward **Antelope.** (Stop here for marionberry cobbler.) In Antelope, you can keep the magic going if you head north on 218 toward **Shaniko.** The Old West theme has taken over this tourist town. A local millionaire spent bags and bags of money restoring the old hotel in Shaniko, then a water-rights quarrel with locals shut it down.

At Shaniko, turn south on Highway 97 in order to tour the **Tygh Valley.** Twelve miles from Shaniko, turn north on Highway 197. This turn marks the end of the twisty rural roads, and the beginning of smooth, open, sweeping turns atop enormous smooth mountains of glacial and flood gravel deposits. One of these gravel mounds is several thousand feet high. Now that's gravel! The roads are beautifully paved and well banked.

You'll love the way 197 twists coming into **Maupin,** a major river-rafting center along the **Deschutes River.** The city park is great for a picnic or a shady nap in the grass. Leaving **Maupin,** you'll stay on 197 to see the grandest of the grand gravel hills—usually covered in golden wheat.

As you approach the town of **The Dalles,** make a left on Highway 30. This part of 30 will turn into the **Historic Columbia River Highway.** Stay on 30 toward Rowena. This will run you parallel to Interstate 84 and onto one of the most unreal stretches of highway to be found anywhere.

You've probably heard of the House of Mystery, where strange things happen, or The Vortex, where gravity and perspective go haywire. At the **Rowena Overlook,** you experience slow twisting roads where your floorboards never scrape. It's not magic. In 1922, Engineer Sam Lancaster built this curvaceous highway with a minimum width of 24 feet, grades no steeper than 5 percent, and no curve radii less than 100 feet. Rowena's panoramas of the Columbia River Gorge are among the best views of this whole trip. Don't miss this scenery.

Continue to follow Highway 30 as it winds down the hill to **Mosier.** From Mosier, take I-84 to Portland. From here, the only magic spell for me is the one woven by the knowledge that home is near, and I'll soon sleep in my own bed.

This view from the Rowena Viewpoint west of the Dalles shows the special engineering needed for the underpowered cars of the 1920s.

As you blast down I-84 toward Portland, you can look back at the wonders you experienced. I doubt if anyone could adequately explain the joys of this trip to someone who rides it on four wheels.

Mt. Adams, Stonehenge, the gorge, the perfect rural roads near Condon, the mammoth mounds after Maupin, the stunning roads and views of Rowena: how could strangers understand it all? Maybe if the person you spoke to had walked into a department store to use the restroom and was greeted by a big band, lights, and the owner saying, "Congratulations, you are our millionth customer!" That person might be able to imagine your feelings.

You got the best.

For more trips in this region see *Motorcycle Journeys Through the Pacific Northwest* by Bruce Hansen, available from Whitehorse Press.

26 Lewis and Clark Country

Text and photos by Toby Ballentine

■ **DISTANCE** *756 miles (three days)*

■ **HIGHLIGHTS** *Follow the Payette River to US Highway 12 and on to untouched backcountry explored by Lewis and Clark in 1805. Continue to Salmon for some afternoon whitewater rafting, then head back through the Sawtooth Mountains to Boise but not before a side trip to a couple of ghost towns. Elevation change 1,500 to 8,000 feet.*

Day 1

- **0** Start in Boise, take Hwy 55 north
- **44** Arrive Banks, continue on Hwy 55
- **81** Arrive Cascade, continue on Hwy 55
- **97** Arrive Donnelly, turn right on Roseberry Road to Roseberry
- **99** Arrive Roseberry, turn around
- **101** Arrive Donnelly, turn right on Hwy 55 to McCall
- **114** Arrive McCall, continue on Hwy 55
- **126** Arrive New Meadows, turn right on Hwy 95
- **189** Arrive White Bird, see battle site
- **205** Arrive Grangeville, turn right on Hwy 13
- **231** Arrive Kooskia, turn right on Hwy 12
- **254** Arrive Lowell, spend night if too tired to go on
- **326** Turn right to Powell and the Lochsa Lodge
- **327** Arrive Lochsa Lodge, get a good night's sleep

Day 2

- **327** Start at Lochsa Lodge, head north on Hwy 12 to Lolo or detour to Lolo Motorway
- **373** Arrive Lolo, Montana, turn left on Hwy 93
- **390** Turn left on Hwy 269 (Eastside Highway) to Stevensville
- **413** Arrive Hamilton, re-enter Hwy 93 south to Salmon
- **506** Arrive Salmon, Idaho, go whitewater rafting

Day 3

- **506** Start in Salmon, continue on Hwy 93
- **566** Arrive Challis, veer right on Hwy 75
- **611** Arrive Sunbeam and turn right on optional Backroad to Bonanza (side trip here to Bonanza/Custer on unpaved road).
- **621** Arrive Stanley, turn right on Hwy 21
- **679** Arrive Lowman, turn right on Banks-Lowman Road to Banks
- **712** Arrive Banks, turn left on Hwy 55 to Boise
- **756** Arrive Boise, Whew!

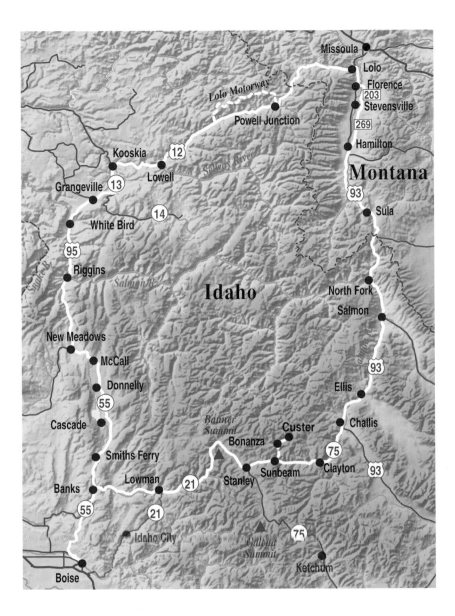

The Selway-Bitterroot Wilderness in north central Idaho and western Montana covers over 1,000,000 acres of a vast wild land. This area straddles the Bitterroot Range and Selway River. Dominated by granite peaks and coniferous forests, the heartland of Selway-Bitterroot is rugged and rarely visited by humans. As a result, little has changed since Lewis and Clark arrived in 1805 searching for a navigable waterway from the Missouri to the Columbia. Confronted with the Bitterroot Range, Lewis and Clark at first veered south to the Salmon River. Soon realizing that was not a viable option, they

headed north and proceeded along an old Indian trail called the **Lolo Trail.**
The Nez Perce had used this route for centuries to hunt bison in Montana. So
with some help from their Shoshone guide, "old Toby" (I sorta like that
name), Lewis and Clark continued west to the Pacific through the Clearwater
National Forest.

Well, it just so happens that one of the world's most magnificent motorcycle rides parallels this journey of Lewis and Clark across the Bitterroot
Range and through Clearwater National Forest on US Highway 12. Their ill-
fated journey south to the Salmon River parallels US Highway 93. And for
those on dual sport mounts, a detour on the unpaved "Lolo Motorway" follows the actual trail used by the expedition in 1805. All of these treks linked
together with the Payette River Scenic Byway (State Route 55), the Ponderosa Scenic Byway (State Route 21) and the Wildlife Canyon Byway (Banks-
Lowman Road) combine to create one grand circle of motorcycling ecstasy.

This journey is approximately 750 miles long and requires two to five
days to fully appreciate the breadth of the history in this area. On the first
day, head north on State Route 55 from Boise along the beautiful Payette
River and then spend the night in the remote "Lochas Lodge" in Powell.

The Payette River flows through forested terrain beside State Route 55 north of Boise.

Sailboats in Idaho? Welcome to McCall.

Spend an extra day here if you want to enjoy the diversion on the dirt "Lolo Motorway." Then continue on the Lewis and Clark Highway (US Hwy 12) to Lolo, Montana. Head south on US Hwy 93 back into Idaho, overnight in Salmon (spend an afternoon or extra day if you want to go whitewater rafting) then hook up with the Ponderosa Scenic Byway (State Route 21) in Stanley heading west and at Lowman catch the Wildlife Canyon Scenic Byway back to Route 55 and home to Boise.

DAY ONE

All right, now that I have gotten you excited about this trip, let's get started. **Boise** is only about 2,200 feet above sea level and can be warm during the summertime. As a result, the landscape heading north of town on State Route 55 is not lush green forested mountains. Rather rolling hills are the norm, covered with green grass in the spring and dry brown splotches in late summer. The road winds lazily through the hillsides as it follows the Payette River to Horseshoe Bend about twenty-three miles north of Boise. At this point the scenery starts to change and Ponderosa Pine begins to cover steep mountain slopes.

At **Banks,** about fourteen miles from Horseshoe Bend, the river splits and the forest becomes even lusher. The elevation is about 3,000 feet. At the confluence of the North and South Forks of the **Payette River,** rafters and

The Salmon River Valley

kayakers are often seen rushing though the whitewater. Continuing north on Route 55, the road hugs the North Fork to **Cascade,** a site well known for recreation about seventy-five miles from Boise. Turn left at the stoplight and at about one mile from the intersection, Cascade Reservoir floods the horizon. A boat ramp and beach area is often crowded with sun worshipers enjoying the warm summer weather. There is a restaurant on the corner if you want to grab a drink.

Back on Route 55, continue north toward McCall. The road sweeps gently beside the river and soon you will arrive in the small town of **Donnelly,** population 138. Don't blink or you will miss the turnoff that takes you to **Roseberry.**

In the 1890s the first Finnish homesteaders arrived and established several communities in Long Valley, Idaho. The primary town was Roseberry located about one mile east of Donnelly. Between 1890 and 1912, Roseberry was a hub of activity boasting a twenty-three-room hotel, various businesses, schools, and even a bowling alley. Then the railroad came to town—but not this town—and by 1959 the last class was held in the local school and the town, in essence, shut down. Starting in 1973, the Long Valley Preservation Society took up the Roseberry Banner and now 15 restored structures line Farm-to-Market and East Roseberry Roads. If you have the time, drop by this quaint, restored town for a glimpse into our "Finnish" past.

Heading north again on Route 55 past Donnelly, you will enter the resort town of **McCall.** This city is everything you could ask in a resort community. A beautiful lake, nearby ski resort, western style storefront veneers, and forest clad mountain slopes surrounding the whole town. To enjoy this scenic interlude a little longer, veer right at the main intersection and head toward the lake. A beautiful park with picnic tables lies adjacent to the lake providing a picture perfect spot to unpack your tuna sandwiches. Or right next to the boat ramp park your bike at the **Mile High Marina** and order a Buffalo Burger on the outside patio. A local guitarist was strumming some old Jim Croce tunes last time I was there. I could have stayed quite a bit longer!

Continuing through McCall, the road doglegs left and after only a few miles at **New Meadows,** turn right on US Highway 95 to **Riggins.** You are now following the Little Salmon River and the road descends relatively quickly through meadows and dry basalt canyons to this small community. Located at the confluence of the Little Salmon and Salmon Rivers, Riggins is often referred to as the whitewater capital of Idaho and numerous outfitters are located here. As you drive alongside the river, don't be surprised to see rafters paddling madly through the rapids set between steep canyon walls.

The elevation continues to drop and at **White Bird** you are only 1,500 feet above sea level. Just after the turnoff to town, the road ascends over a small pass with well marked passing lanes providing a wrist-cracking spurt of speed up the road. Don't go too fast or you will blow right past a turnout for the historic **White Bird Battlefield.** On June 17, 1877, Yellow Wolf of the Nez Perce was fired upon while attempting to make peace with the U.S. Cavalry. This was the opening salvo for the Nez Perce War and the demise of this great Native American tribe. Time permitting, head down the narrow single-laner through the battlefield itself. Interpretive signs are posted with more detailed information along the road. The asphalt runs like a coiled snake through the valley and up the side of the low lying hills. Fun and rarely traveled . . . what more could you ask! For best access, head back to White Bird

Mile High Marina is one of the best spots in McCall to grab a burger, listen to music, and enjoy some breathtaking views.

At historic White Bird Battlefield, Yellow Bird of the Nez Perce was fired upon while attempting to make peace with the U.S. Cavalry.

and turn into town. The road is about fifteen miles long and eventually wiggles itself up past the turnout and reconnects with Hwy 95 just south of the Salmon River outlook.

At **Grangeville,** turn right on State Route 13 to Kooskia. Running through the Camas Prairie, this little winder cuts back and forth through the lowlands and rolling hills before connecting with US Highway 12. Last time I drove it, two crotch rockets blew past me going—I don't know how fast. I can still see their smiles etched permanently in their rear view mirrors.

Soon even more fun beckons you ahead. Be sure your gas tank is full as the next eighty miles will keep you focused on this wild and scenic ride beside the Lochsa River to **Lolo Pass** on US Highway 12. No gas stations are available until Powell and the next fuel stop is about fifty miles miles after that. US Hwy 12 is often referred to as the **Lewis and Clark Highway** or the Northwest Passage Scenic Byway. Various interpretive signs mark the way making this not only an incomparable motorcycle ride, but a trip back in time to one of the most significant events in our nation's history. As you drive this route, little has changed over the past two centuries. The area is still remote, the river still clear, the panoramas still pristine, and the trail still windy. I can see why this stretch of pavement has been voted by many motorcycling magazines as one of the top ten rides in the United States.

You can also opt to spend the night in **Lowell,** about twenty-three miles up Hwy 12, if you're feeling tuckered out. Lowell has a nice resort set right on the Lochsa River called the **Three Rivers Resort** (www.threerivers-resort.com, 208-926-4430). I know 327 miles is a long day to Powell, but the setting at Lochsa Lodge, in my opinion, is also well worth it. Another bonus is that you are right next to a convenient loop excursion on the "Lolo Motorway" in Powell. Just re-member the sun doesn't set until 9:00 in the summer, so you should have more than enough time. A shorter trip

U.S. Highway 12 is also known as the Lewis and Clark Highway or the Northwest Passage Scenic Byway.

to Salmon in the morning may also provide extra time for an afternoon white-water rafting trip down the "River of No Return!" So if you can, keep on truckin'!

Now, if you can force your right wrist to decelerate (I know this will be hard), there are a couple of places worth stopping at along the way. The first is the **Lochsa Historical Ranger Station** built in the 1920s and used by the early forest service to watch for forest fires. Not accessible by road until 1952, this site is a living memorial to the rustic and difficult life rangers lead prior to tourists flocking to our National Parks. Park in the lower lot and walk up the steps to the visitors center. An older couple usually acts as hosts and is more than willing to give you some background into the Ranger's daily routine. The old living quarters and work barn are also open as part of the self guided tour. My appreciation for the Forest Service and the sacrifice made by these dedicated Rangers

The Old Outpost at the Lochsa Historical Ranger Station is well worth a visit.

increased ten fold after walking through this living museum. Don't miss it.

The other stop is **Powell**—definitely worth your time as this is where you will be spending the night! Tucked neatly in a pine-covered glen, Powell is about 14 miles from the Montana border. Turn right on exit 162 into the wooded grove off Hwy 12 and you will find a remote rest stop with a small gas station, food, and lodging. In 1805, Lewis and Clark stopped here totally exhausted and had to kill one of their colts for food. You may feel the same way, but don't do anything drastic—the restaurant serves up plentiful portions to satisfy your gnawing appetite. The blackberry cobbler is particularly scrumptious. The **Lochsa Lodge** was renovated in 2002 and offers both motel rooms and cabins. A restaurant, mini-mart, and campground are also on the premises. This is an ideal spot to relax and spend a quiet evening. You couldn't ask for a better setting. Visit their website at www.lochsalodge.com or call ahead for reservations at 208-942-3405.

DAY TWO

If you do spend the night here and are on a GS or dual sport, consider spending another night. The historic **Lolo Motorway** is just a hop and a skip from Powell. This motorway was built in the 1930s by the CCC to replace the historic trail that once bore the footprints of the Nez Perce. This is the actual trail Lewis and Clark hiked on their trek to the Columbia River. The

The Lolo Trail Crossing was made famous by Lewis and Clark.

Camping just outside of Powell, I'm getting a good night's rest before heading south toward Salmon.

motorway is definitely *not* a motorway, but rather a narrow and rocky dirt single-laner along a mountainous ridgeline. Although the motorway extends quite some distance down to Lowell, I would suggest taking a 15- to 20-mile portion of it. If you are interested, take Parachute Hill Road 569 on the north side of Hwy 12 just before the turnoff to the Powell Ranger Station. Follow this road to Forest Road 500—this is the **Lolo Motorway.** Turn left and get a real taste of Lewis and Clark country from the seat of a motorcycle. Follow the motorway until you arrive at Saddle Camp Road 107 and turn left back to Hwy 12. You are now about 22 miles west of Powell. Total loop is around 60 miles. Plan on four to six hours to do the entire trip. Pack a lunch and stop along the way for a hike to really appreciate the excitement of this fascinating episode in our American history. For more information contact the Powell Ranger Station District, Lolo, Montana, 59847 or call 208-942-3113.

From Powell, continue north on Hwy 12 over Lolo Pass. Stop at the newly rebuilt visitors center for more information of the Lewis and Clark Expedition and the 1877 flight of the Nez Perce. The road then descends into Montana and sweeps past the **Lolo Hot Springs Resort** (stop for some hot chocolate www.lolohotsprings.com, 800-273-2290) and after 46 miles from

Powell enters the town of Lolo, Montana. At Lolo, turn right on US Hwy 93 and just outside of town stop at the **Travelers Rest Historic Site.** Lewis and Clark camped here in 1805 while traveling toward the Pacific as well as on their return journey in 1806. Continue south toward **Florence** and then turn left on State Route 203 (East Side Highway). Follow this through **Stevensville** onto Route 269 and then back to Hwy 93. State Routes 203 and 269 run parallel to and just east of US Hwy 93. I prefer this side road as it is less traveled and, in my opinion, a more enjoyable ride. Before leaving Florence, though, **Glen's Mountain View Cafe** just west of the Highway bakes some awfully good double crusted berry pies. You may want to try one before turning onto the East Side Highway!

Just before Stevensville, the Lee Metcalf National Wildlife Refuge appears on the west side of the road. The highway then cuts through Stevensville toward **Hamilton.** Just north of Hamilton, cottonwoods dot the landscape as you approach the **Daly Mansion.** This Victorian mansion was built in 1890 by Marcus Daly, a copper mining magnate. The 22,000 acre farm surrounding his former home was used to raise some of the greatest racehorses in the country. Called Bitterroot Stock Farm, this area is now a

The Salmon River has been cutting this canyon for some fifteen million years.

Boaters make their way down the Salmon River.

National Historic Site owned by Montana and open from 11 to 4 (www.dalymansion.org, 406-363-6004). Upon his death, these horses were sold for what was considered a fortune in his day.

Continue south past Hamilton, veer back onto Hwy 93 toward Daly and Lost Trail Pass. The Bitterroot Range looms to the west with Trapper Peak at over 10,000 feet as its centerpiece. In the springtime the bitterroot lily blooms with a pinkish hue adding a streak of outlandish color to this rugged wilderness area. The road runs relatively straight as it hugs the East Fork Bitterroot River and then starts to climb toward Lost Trail Pass. This is a steep, four-lane sweeper with historical markers along the way noting the ill-fated detour of Lewis and Clark to the Salmon River. Certainly a pleasant journey today, back in 1805, Lewis and Clark were momentarily lost on this part of the expedition. Their journal records this trek as being one of "the worst" episodes of their entire journey as they struggled over the steep ridges. As your motorcycle zigzags along the mountain crests, try to visualize hiking through this remote wilderness with no map and only a vague notion of what lies ahead.

At **North Fork,** the Salmon River churns wildly along a rock strewn riverbed and hugs the highway pretty much all the way to Stanley. Squeezed by narrow cliffs, the Salmon gushes forward like a hemmed in hose. The Shoshone Indians realizing the savage nature of the river centuries ago named it the "River of No Return." Today, experts have mastered its unruliness and rafting trips are numerous and readily accessible along its shoreline.

The town of **Salmon** (www.salmonidaho.com) nestled within the mountain valley is a convenient spot to overnight before completing this journey back to Boise. Several hotels are located in the small downtown area. Or if you prefer, several historic B&Bs are located just outside of town. Roger and Sharon Solass provide fresh, bountiful breakfasts at an old stagecoach stop in the town of Baker. **Solaas Bed and Breakfast** (www.salmonidaho.com/solaas, 208-756-3903) is located on 3 S. Baker, nine miles east of Salmon. Another B&B is the **Greyhouse Inn Bed & Breakfast** built in 1894 and run by Sharon and David Osgood. The Greyhouse is located twelve miles south of Salmon on US Hwy 93 just across from the 293 marker (www.greyhouseinn.com, 800-348-8097). Rooms and cabins are available. Some local eateries are **Bertram's Brewery** located on Main and Andrew (208-756-3391). For more upscale dining (relatively speaking) try the **Shady Nook** right on Hwy 93 (208-756-4182). If you really want a taste of this community, stay an extra day and indulge in some whitewater rafting down the Salmon. Or, since today's trip was relatively short and you got here by noon (assuming you took my advice and got to Powell last night), take a half-day trip down the river! Just ask anybody in town who the best outfitter is. You'll get an earful.

DAY THREE

In the morning, continue south on US Hwy 93 toward Ellis. The road meanders alongside the Salmon River, scrapes its way through Cronks Canyon, and then slides through low lying hills into **Challis.** Challis is a small town of 1,200 people and was originally founded in 1876 as a supply depot for miners in the surrounding area. Hwy 93 and State Route 75 intersect here. Continue west on Route 75 toward Stanley. About 45 miles from Challis, you will arrive in the small town of **Sunbeam.** If you are interested in visiting two old mining communities turned ghost towns, hang a right on the dirt road to **Bonanza** and **Custer** (backroad to Bonanza). The mother lode was discovered in 1876 and these towns hosted upward of 1,500 inhabitants at one time. Several structures still remain and are now under the management of the U.S. Forestry Service. Some of the buildings are being reconstructed and a self guiding tour is available. A very worthwhile side trip to a couple of well preserved ghost towns. It is best seen on a GS or dual sport type bike.

Fourteen miles further west of Sunbeam on Route 75, the outdoorsmen's mecca of **Stanley** greets you. You are now well into the Sawtooths and some

Enjoy a remote stop in the pines as you follow Lewis and Clark's historic route.

of the most beautiful countryside in Idaho. At Stanley, turn right on State Route 21 and follow the **Ponderosa Scenic Byway** toward Lowman.

The road climbs steeply up toward Banner Summit. Near milepost 126, turn left on **Stanley Lake Road** and continue for about three and a half miles to the **Elk Mountain Overlook.** The pullout is on the right and offers spectacular views of Stanley Lake and the surrounding area. This beautiful alpine lake is nestled between forest-cloaked foothills reminding you more of Switzerland than the Rockies.

After crossing Banner Summit, the road slides through a narrow-walled canyon and then descends into the South Payette Fork river corridor weaving gently through rolling hillsides. As you approach **Lowman** the smells of geothermal heaven will greet you. This area has one of the highest concentrations of hot springs in the United States. Several mineral-rich ponds are publicly accessible and located just off the road with their own National Forest campground. **Kirkland Hot Springs** is one of the most well known and is located about four miles east of Lowman. Although busy at times, during midweek this thermal delight (102 to 118 degrees) may be yours alone for a nice soak.

Now, when you arrive in Lowman, instead of heading south on Route 21

Forest and grasslands cover the landscape. What looks like mist is actually smoke from a forest fire.

THE NORTHWEST

I think I know why they call these mountains the "Sawtooths."

to Boise, turn right on the Banks-Lowman Road to Banks and State Route 55. This thirty-three-mile run is called the **Wildlife Canyon Scenic Byway** and provides some sweet sweepers along the South Fork of the Payette River. The road is a two-laner with no passing lanes, but there are several turnouts for viewing.

As your wrist re-engages for one final lap before returning to Boise, keep a lookout for gravity-defying kayakers leaping through Class IV rapids on the river next to you. Don't be surprised if some of them beat you to the finish line! Keep your other eye focused on the horizon for elk or deer grazing lazily in the meadows (that is until a motorcycle flies by!). Bald eagles flying overhead may also distract you, so do be careful! This short span of byway through another remote and unspoiled part of Idaho is not only a great way to end your three-day adventure through this great state, but is another testimony to the rugged beauty of this entire wilderness area once visited by Lewis and Clark in 1805 and still enjoyed by us today.

▓ For more trips in this region see *Motorcycle Journeys Through the Rocky Mountains* by Toby Ballentine, available from Whitehorse Press.

27 Via Lassen Volcanic National Park

Text and photos by Clement Salvadori

- **DISTANCE** *214 miles*
- **HIGHLIGHTS** *This is an easy loop, easy roads, but the 30 miles you spend inside the park will probably slow you down, as there is much to see and do. Especially if you are a volcanologist.*

0 From Quincy head north on CA 70/89.	**79** Enter Lassen Volcanic National Park.
11 Turn right where CA 70 and 89 split, taking 89 north to Greenville and Lassen.	**85** Bumpass Hell trailhead
	87 Lassen Peak parking area and trailhead
32 Turn right onto CA 147.	**107** Loomis Museum
39 Turn left onto A13.	**108** Exit the park and turn right on CA 44/89 heading northeast.
43 Turn left onto CA 36.	
44 Stop at Lake Almanor Vista Point.	**121** Turn right with CA 44.
49 Cross over the Feather River in Chester.	**150** Turn right on County Road A21.
51 Continue straight as CA 36 meets CA 89, going west together.	**168** Turn right on CA 36.
	171 Turn left onto CA 147.
71 CA 172 goes off to the left for a potential detour.	**182** At Canyon Dam turn left onto CA 89.
	203 Turn left on CA 70/89, toward Quincy.
74 Turn right to stay on CA 89, while CA 36 goes west	**214** Return to Quincy.

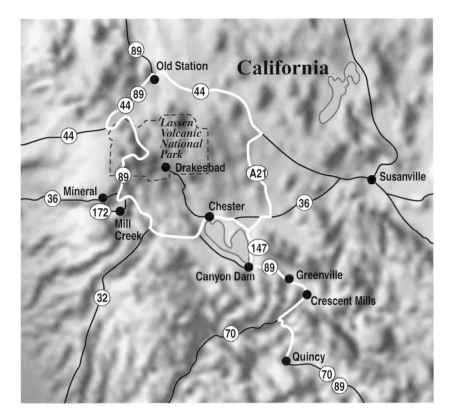

Quincy, the homebase for this trip and the seat of **Plumas County,** gets five feet of snow and four feet of rain every year, mostly in the winter months, and is best known (among motorcyclists) as the site of the annual **49er Rally** put on by the BMW 49er Club at the **Plumas-Sierra County Fairgrounds.** The county itself covers some 2,600 square miles, well over half of which is national forest, and has less than ten bodies per square mile.

Downtown Quincy has two parallel one-way streets (Main going east, Lawrence, west), so a brief jaunt and U-turn gives you the whole place. This is a working town, not a resort place, but has half a dozen places to sleep, like the **Gold Pan Motel** on the north side of town (200 Crescent Street, 530-283-2265) with 56 rooms, or the older, single-story **Spanish Creek Motel** right across Highway 70 (233 Crescent Street, 530-283-1200) with 25 rooms.

The town has more than a dozen places to eat; the best establishment for breakfast or lunch is the celebrated **Morning Thunder** (530-283-1310, 557 Lawrence Street). For dinner try **Moon's** (530-283-0765, 497 Lawrence Street), with a rather good wine list to accentuate your taste in fish, fowl, or dead cow, or **Sweet Lorraine's** (530-283-5300, 384 West Main Street) which offers excellent food and the most sociable bar in town—and some jazz.

If you want a nice place to pick up an Associate of Arts degree, try the **Feather River College.** For the historians among us the **Plumas Museum,** right behind the four-story courthouse (built in 1921, and you cannot miss the Greco-Roman structure), has lots on local Indians, mining, and railroads.

From Quincy head north on CA 70/89, past the airfield. Climb over a small ridge and the road wiggles along through the woods.

Where CA 70 and 89 split, take 89 which heads north to **Greenville** and Lassen. The road takes you along the **Indian River** into **Indian Valley,** with the almost defunct mining and lumbering community of **Crescent Mills.** The route continues on through Greenville to **Canyon Dam,** a village with several stores and a gas station.

Just after Canyon Dam, turn right onto CA 147, which will go up the east side of **Lake Almanor.** Turn left onto A13, which angles northwest toward the town of Chester. At the stop sign at the head of the lake turn left onto CA 36 which crosses over the northernmost arm of Lake Almanor.

Stop at the official **Vista Point,** and admire Lake Almanor. This is a big lake that was created in 1915 after damming the **North Fork Feather River,** and has over 50 miles of shoreline. This all used to be called Big Meadows, a good place to raise cattle in the late 19th Century, and the area became the summer home for wealthy types from the Sacramento Valley.

In another five miles you will cross over the **Feather River** and enter the town of **Chester,** a slightly run-down, but pleasant, touristy town, pop. 2,200, elevation 4,550 feet. One main street, a half dozen motels, a dozen places to eat, and a major tourist season of about three months, minorly touristed the rest of the year. Make the bulk of your money in the summer, and play out the profit through the other nine months.

I'm not much on B&Bs, for good reason. Show up on a rainy day and you can see the lace curtains fall back into place and the owners saying, "Oh no, are those the people that have the reservations; they'll muddy everything up."

But the best B&B in Chester, the **Bidwell House,** is extremely scrumptious, with 14 rooms. The present managers, Eva and Filip Laboda, think that motorcyclists are rather nice people. Though I could imagine some bikers they might not think highly of. John Bidwell built the house in 1901, and it is a lovely sprawling place under large trees. Along with excellent breakfasts, a superb kitchen turns out dinner three nights a week. (530-258-3338, 1 Main Street, at the very east end of town, www.bidwellhouse.com).

If you are into a very rustic setting, 17 miles north of Chester at the end of Warner Valley Road (partially dirt) is the **Drakesbad Guest Ranch** (530-529-1512), with a stunning setting just within the **Lassen National Park** boundaries. Reservations are essential, and I would say a two-night stay is the minimum to get a proper appreciation for the place.

Leaving Chester on CA 36, the road is soon joined by CA 89. In about

Lassen Peak still has snow in July, which shows how late winter lingers at these latitudes and elevations.

eight miles the **Black Forest Lodge** is on your left, an unremarkable building with remarkably good German food, from sauerbrauten to bratwurst, washed down with good beer. (530-258-2939).

The **Childs Meadow Resort** is a further 10 miles down the road on your right, with 20 motel rooms, several chalets/cabins, and a cafe running from 8 to 6 (530-595-3383).

Where CA 172 goes off to the left, you have a decision to make. You can continue on CA 36/89, which goes up over **Morgan Summit** (5,155 feet) and on to Lassen Volcanic National Park, or you can turn left on CA 172 for an entertaining roundabout way of getting to Lassen. This detour takes 14 miles to cover what the direct route covers in three miles. Naturally, I suggest you take the detour.

CA 172 runs along **Mill Creek** into a summer community called, curiously enough, Mill Creek, then climbs up to **Mineral Summit** (5,266 feet), and drops down to intersect with the crossroads community of **Mineral** at the junction with CA 36 (9 miles). **Lassen Mineral Lodge** is at the intersection, with rooms and food (530-595-4422). And gas across the road. Take a right on CA 36 and head back up the mountain, and at 14 miles you intersect with 89 as it heads north into the national park.

Take CA 89 north and enter **Lassen Volcanic National Park** The $5 (per motorcycle) you pay for the privilege is definitely worth it. To the right is **Lassen Chalet,** with souvenirs and some basic food. No grand hotel here in this park, nothing with gorgeous vistas and a fine restaurant; the Chalet is as good as it gets. The fact that the snow closes the park down from November to June might have something to do with that. It is a great 29-mile trip through the park, with the maximum speed allowable being 35 mph. Sort of. The road climbs quickly at the beginning, past the stinky **Sulphur Works,** around **Diamond Peak,** and past **Lake Helen.**

If you want to take a three-mile hike, park at the **Bumpass Hell** lot and head down into this ten-acre Hades. Apparently a fellow named Ken Bumpass (this was back when names were names, and nobody laughed) used to take tourists down into this hellish scene, full of bubbling pits where the water is actually boiling from thermal heat. Nowadays there are boardwalks to stay on, but poor old Bumpass had the misfortune to step on some fragile crust and stuck a leg in; parboiled it was, and had to be amputated.

The pavement is up to 8,512 feet, right south of **Lassen Peak,** highest point the road gets to in the park. If you wish to leave the bike in the parking area and climb the rest of the way to the 10,457 foot peak, be my guest; that's about a five mile round trip, and if your math is any good you appreciate that you are going up 2,000 feet, and then coming down.

The road goes down through the **Dwarf Forest** to **Manzanita Lake.** The **Loomis Museum** (B. F. Loomis documented the whole cycle of eruptions back in the late teens, and was instrumental in having the park established) sits at the lake, and will tell you all you wish to know about the park, and volcanoes.

After exiting the park, turn right at the stop sign where CA 44 joins CA 89. To the west CA 44 goes to Redding, while CA 44/89 goes northeast.

You soon go over **Eskimo Hill Summit,** at 5,933 feet, which must have been named by somebody with a sense of humor.

After crossing over **Hat Creek,** with a store and cafe beside the road, you arrive in **Old Station,** once a stop for the **California Stage Company,** also a military post in the late 1850s, now offering a few tourist services. Here CA 89 splits off to go up to Mt. Shasta, while you turn right to stay with CA 44; a Forest Service information station is at this intersection.

LASSEN VOLCANIC NATIONAL PARK

We might tend to forget we are standing on a volcano, with bubbly bits perking out all over, even though the last major eruption was nearly 70 years ago. It blew its stack over 300 times in the seven years between 1914 and 1921. Mess not with Mother Nature. In the midst of this chaos, it was declared a national park in 1916, thanks to the efforts of Representative John Raker; hence **Raker Peak** in the north of the park.

The road runs around **Reading Peak,** to **Summit Lake** (7,000 feet), through the **Dersch Meadows** and the **Devastated Area** (so named for the lava flow that occurred in 1915), and over **Emigrant Pass;** if you can imagine taking a wagon train through here 150 years ago, think about one Peter Lassen, who did just that. And hence got a small portion of immortality. The **Lassen Emigrant Trail** was active from 1848 to 1851, and as befits a frontiersman, old Pete died in 1859 while prospecting, attacked by Indians who objected to all this white-man's possessiveness.

As the road ascends to the Pacific Crest you get your last view of **Mt. Shasta;** this is officially the **Feather Lake Highway.** Now it is high country, flat and sparsely grassed, as you pass the turn to the right for Butte Lake, the turn to the left for Pittville. A railroad runs just to the north of the road. Long fency lines parallel the road, the important highly stressed corner sections being shored up with rocks.

About five miles beyond the **Bogard Rest Stop** on your right you will turn right at the sign reading WESTWOOD 18, with an arrow pointing to the right on County Road A21. Take it. (If you turn left, a gravel Forest Road will lead you to **Feather Lake** in a mile.) County Road A21 consists of 18 fast miles on a very well-paved, very lightly trafficked cut-off.

Where A21 ends at CA 36, turn right onto CA 36, then in three miles you turn left onto CA 147. You are going to start retracing your steps in a couple of miles.

At the STOP sign in **Canyon Dam,** turn left onto CA 89. Twenty-one miles later CA 70 comes in from the right and you turn left on CA 89/70 to return to Quincy.

■ For more trips in this region see *Motorcycle Journeys Through California and Baja* by Clement Salvadori, available from Whitehorse Press.

28 Sonora and Tioga Passes

Text and photos by Clement Salvadori

- **DISTANCE** *244 miles*
- **HIGHLIGHTS** *This is pass-bagging at its best, two gorgeous High Sierra runs that will take you all darn day. Get an early start.*

0 Take CA 108 Business out of Sonora and turn left where 108 B joins CA 108

9 Turn left for detour along the old road through Twain Harte

16 Sierra Village

19 Long Barn is down off to your right

25 The four-laner becomes a narrow road

29 Summit Ranger Station

31 Cross over the Stanislaus River

46 Donnell Vista

49 The Clark Fork Road heads northeast to a dead end

51 Dardanelle (5,700 feet)

67 Sonora Pass (8,624 feet)

82 Turn right onto US 395 (6,950 feet)

99 Enter Bridgeport

106 CA 270 goes left to Bodie State Park

113 Conway Summit (8,138 feet)

118 CA 167 goes off to the east to Hawthorne, Nevada

126 Enter Lee Vining

126+ Turn right onto CA 120, heading for Tioga Pass and Yosemite National Park

138 Tioga Pass (9,945 feet), Yosemite Natl. Park entrance

184 Crane Flat, turn right following CA 120

192 Hodgdon Meadow and the West Gate of Yosemite

201 Road to Cherry Lake

217 Enter Groveland

226 CA 49 comes in from the left

235 Stay right on CA 49 (CA 120 goes to the left)

238 Stay right as CA 49 merges with CA 108

241 Enter Jamestown

243 Exit right on CA 49 into Sonora

244 Arrive back in downtown Sonora

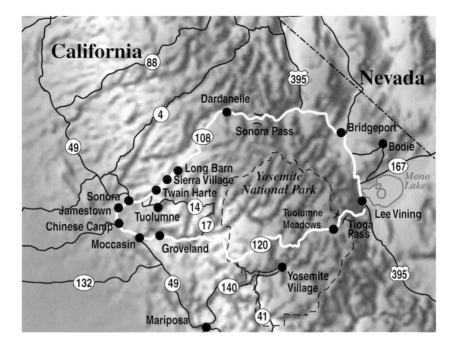

This magnificent loop is based out of **Sonora**—a likeable town. It is the seat of Tuolumne County, steeped in history, and with steep roads to the west going up into the mountains. (What a miserably poor play on words!)

The town sits in the **Sierra Nevada** foothills at about 1,800 feet elevation, with a reasonable year-around climate. It can get hot in July and August, But right behind is the high ridge of the Sierra Nevada, and the temperature drops as you climb. Which also means that when winter comes, these passes will be closed by snow.

Sonora is a tourist destination, more for the Mother Lode and 49er families than the pass-seeking motorcyclists, which means that food and beds are plentiful. It's a smallish place, only 5,000 or so year-round inhabitants, and walkable.

Smack in the middle of town, at the corner of Washington and Stockton streets, is the old **Sonora Inn,** dating from 1896 but extensively redone in 1931; in 1998 it was incorporated into the **Day's Inn** chain, which seems to have done it no real harm. The Sonora Days Inn has 30 rooms, while the two-story motel unit (circa 1960) behind has another 34 (160 South Washington St., 209-532-2400, or 800-329-7466). Outdoor parking is in front of the motel units, but Sonora is a pretty safe place. Up Washington Street a quarter mile is the **Sonora Inn of California,** which used to be the **Sonora Town-house Motel,** a rather bleak, three-storied, asphalted presence with 112 rooms (350 South Washington St., 209-532-3633, 800-251-1538). Back to the old motel concept is the **Sonora Gold Lodge,** on Stockton about half a mile west of the Sonora Inn, with 42 ground-level units (480 Stockton St., 209-532-3952, 800-363-2154).

Food is where you find it. **The Miner's Shack** (157 S. Washington, 209-532-5252) has a goodly array of omelettes in the morning. **Banny's Cafe** (209-553-4709), a block off the main street at 83 South Steward Street, is good, as is the **Diamondback Grill** (209-532-6661), at 110 South Washington. The most elegant fare is, so I've heard, at the **Seven Sisters Restaurant** (209-928-9363) in the **Black Oak Casino,** a few miles out of town.

Head out of town on CA 108 Business, going east toward Twain Harte. Turn left at the traffic light, where 108 B joins CA 108, and heads east over Sonora Pass to meet US 395. The clutter of expanding business boxes along the four-lane road is but the price of progress.

About nine miles out of town a sign points to the left for a detour along the old road through **Twain Harte.**

Twain Harte is named for the 19th Century writers Mark Twain and Bret Harte, who passed this way. The old Route 108, now Twain Harte Drive, curves into town. On the outskirts is the **Gables Cedar Creek Inn,** quite old-fashioned, backing on to a nine-hole golf course, with a number of cabins to rent (209-586-3008). The town announces itself as Twain Harte with

This old lumber-mill on CA 49 is part of the Marshall Gold Discovery State Historic Park, where gold was found in 1848.

a gloriously unattractive framework over the entrance to **Joaquin Gully,** where old 108/Twain Harte Drive veers off to the right. On Joaquin Gully Road is the **Sportsman's Coffeeshop** on the left (209-586-5448), and the **Little Cottage Cafe** on the right (209-586-1402); different menus for different palates. Twain Harte Drive meets CA 108 about a mile further on.

In **Sierra Village,** all the pickup trucks are parked outside **Wens Donuts & Stuff,** which serves breakfast and lunch.

The next village, **Long Barn,** is down off to your right, and you can go through it by paralleling the new 108 for a couple of miles. Having a big four-laner bypass your town is great for the lives of cats, dogs, and children, but less good for business.

Finally the four-laner ends, and you are going back to the narrow road; much more fun.

The **Summit Ranger Station** is about 10 miles beyond Long Barn should you have any enquiries.

After you cross over the **Stanislaus River** the **Strawberry Inn** is on your left, wining, dining, and lodging travelers since 1939 ($75-plus, 965-3662, 800-985-3662).

You will pass a sign that reads: NOT PLOWED; for you Sunbelt folk that means the road is not open in the winter. It can shut and reopen a couple of times in late fall, but once the first big snow comes, that is it for wheeled traffic. Though not for snowmobiles.

Pull off at the **Donnell Vista** and look down on the **Donnell Reservoir,** and northeast to **Dardenelles Cone.** Three miles later the Clark Fork Road heads northeast to a dead end.

The last settlement below the Sonora Pass is **Dardanelle** (Pop. 2). With gas, store, and cabins, the Dardanelle Resort, at 5,700 feet, is the place to stay on this road, in my mind, but bring your own food and be prepared to cook it. Joann Cheney is half of the population, and a permanent resident. A number of summer people have little houses in the area, but none live there. In the winter, when the road is closed, snowmobilers come in. Joann has eight cabins to rent and four motel units (209-965-4355).

Now the road, leaving the valley, starts some serious climbing. Way back in the early 1860s some enterprising types were building a toll road between Mono Lake and Sonora. Now try to imagine going over this in a stagecoach.

Sonora Pass, at 8,624 feet is even more precipitous on the east side.

Down, down, down into **Pichel Meadows,** where that large resort-looking structure on the far mountain turns out to be the headquarters for the **U.S. Marine Corps Mountain Warfare Training Center.**

At the STOP sign turn right onto US 395; the elevation here is 6,950 feet.

The road climbs up over **Devil's Gate Summit** (7,510 feet) and then down into the valley of **Bridgeport Lake.**

Bridgeport is the seat of Mono county, and the courthouse has been dispensing justice for well over a hundred years.

The town of **Bridgeport,** seat of Mono County, consists of one wide street which is awash with motorcycles during the annual "unofficial" motorcycle jamboree every summer. Don't even think of getting a room in town that weekend, as everything is booked solid as soon as the previous one is over. The **Bridgeport Inn,** established in 1877, will welcome you, and they have motel units out behind. The hotel rooms offer genuine 19th Century hospitality (i.e. no phone, TV, or bathroom—that being down the hall); the trick is to get the Mark Twain Suite, which does have a bathroom (760-932-7380). Along Main Street a hundred yards is the more conventional **Best Western Ruby Inn** with 30 rooms (760-932-7241).

Food is found at the **Bridgeport Inn,** the **Hays Street Cafe** (760-932-7141), **Rhino's Bar & Grill** (760-932-7345), or any number of other places. Justice is still meted out in the 1880 courthouse.

About seven miles further south on US 395 Route 270 on the left goes to **Bodie,** probably the most interesting ghost town left, since it has been preserved as a California State Park.

Staying on US 395 you come up to **Conway Summit** (8,138 feet), and after that a great elongated S-curve takes you down to the valley, and **Mono Lake** is spread out in all its geologic grandeur in front of you. Soon CA 167 goes off to the east to Hawthorne, Nevada.

The small town of **Lee Vining** operates off of the tourist trade, and much of that is dependent on whether or not **Tioga Pass** is open. Half a dozen motels cater to the passers-by. The best is the **Yosemite Gateway Motel** (760-647-6467, 800-282-3929), in the middle of town on the lake side of main street—nice balconies overlooking the lake. At the north end of town is **Murphey's Motel,** with 44 units (760-647-6316, 800-334-6316). At the south end is the **Best Western Lake View Lodge** (760-647-6543) with 46 units.

There are several obvious places to eat, but since they cater to the transient

You really should make this trip. Take it, and you will have a proper appreciation for what a ghost town really is. The road out to Bodie is ten miles of pavement, three of graded dirt, maybe a touch washboardy but easy to traverse.

Come up on the rise of a hill, and before you is the remains of Bodie. It looks big, but remember that only five percent of the original town remains. Ghost towns, before they became ghostly, were often quite large, until the precious metals gave out, and then people walked, rode, drove off, leaving the buildings behind. Then scavengers would come along and tear down structures to use the wood elsewhere, or fire would burn everything up, and few ghost towns remain.

Bodie is a State Historic Park and has been left to preserve itself, weathering away at a natural rate. Two bucks will get you past the gate guard. Bodie boomed in the 1870s, with some 10,000 people living here by 1880. Summer temperatures, here at 8,300 feet, were well over 100 degrees, and the winter temps went to 20 below zero. It was a rough place to live, so the boys drank a bit, and shot each other when provoked, and generally carried on. Not your average God-fearing community, although a number of churches tried to remedy that.

The town folded up when the Depression hit, the buildings happily crumbled away, and 30 years later (1962) the state stepped in to prevent the "souvenir hunters" from destroying the place. It's a beaut. Take it in.

When you leave, you can either retrace the entry road, or angle off from the toll-booth on Cottonwood Canyon Road, which runs for 11 mildly rough miles down to Mono Lake and CA 167.

crowd the food is pretty so-so. The best joint is the **Whoa Nelly Deli** (760-647-1088), which is in the Mobil gas station just as you turn west toward Tioga Pass; I kid you not.

Turn right onto CA 120, which goes over Tioga Pass and into Yosemite National Park. A positively grand ride up, climbing 3,000 feet in 11 miles along the walls of the **Lee Vining River,** through the **Inyo National Forest.** Not that there are a lot of trees along the road, as a forest can encompass many different landscapes.

Tioga Pass Resort (209-372-4471) on your right, is the last genuinely free enterprise for the next 60 miles, with gas, food, lodging, and a small store. **Tioga Lake** and **Ansel Adams Wilderness** are to your left.

At the top of **Tioga Pass** (9,945 feet) is the entrance to Yosemite National Park and a motorcycle rider pays $10 to get into the park; the pass is good for seven days.

Although it is a hazy day, Half Dome at the east end of Yosemite Valley, is visible over my front wheel.

The Tioga saddle is a longish one, traveling across the top of the world, and then down a little to **Tuolumne Meadows,** from where many backpackers go hiking off to confront Mother Nature on the terms established by REI and North Face (two of the major purveyors of camping goods).

The scenery is dramatic, with clean granite bluffs all over the horizon. To quote **Charles Frazier,** author of *Cold Mountain,* "Earth has not anything to show more fair. Dull would be the soul who could pass by the sight so touching in its majesty."

And **Tenaya Lake,** also ringed with granite. Now the road gets into heavy fir, and the vistas become tunnels. And down and down and down, past **Porcupine Flat,** all the way to **Crane Flat** (6,200 feet), where gas is available, and a small store with very limited foods.

At the STOP sign—in Crane Flat turn right to continue following CA 120. If you go left, you are on Big Oak Flat Road going into **Yosemite Valley.**

The **West Gate of Yosemite** is at **Hodgdon Meadow.** Show that you have paid your money and then head west on the North Yosemite Highway/ CA 120.

Nine miles beyond the gate on your right is the turn for Cherry Lake, just before crossing the bridge over the **Tuolomne River.** Turn right for an alternate route to Sonora. This is officially U.S. Forest Service Primary Route 17, and provides a great ride, if a trifle bumpy and twisty. At **Cherry Lake,** about 13 miles along, you turn left onto USFS 14 (Cottonwood Road), going west to **Tuolomne,** which is a superb, and completely unused road, built for the convenience of the workers at the **Cherry Valley Dam.** From Tuolomne a run down County Road E17 takes you back to **Sonora.**

CA 120 continues west from the park to **Groveland.** The **Groveland Motel & Indian Village** will allow you to sleep in a cabin or mobile home, a three-bedroom Victorian house, or a pseudo-teepee with communal bathroom (209-962-7865). I prefer going along about half a mile to the

You've paid your $10 to get in, might as well see the rest of it. And it is worth it. I first rode over Tioga in 1965, coming from Massachusetts on my Velocette Venom, and when I got to the valley I was so taken by the beauty that I got a job and stayed for a month. Unfortunately, it is a lot more crowded now.

You descend toward the valley, through two tunnels, with glimpses of **Half Dome** in the distance. Stop at the vista points. Down on the valley floor CA 140 cuts back to go to Mariposa, but you stay with the road going upstream along the **Merced River.** When it crosses over, it becomes one-way going east, passes the CA 41 turn that goes south to Wawona and Oakhurst, and goes all the way into the valley, and is one-way west on the north side of the river . . . a result of much too much traffic.

The valley is a gorgeous, stunning, beautiful, incredible place, if you just lift your eyes above the crowd. Yosemite Valley is full of commercial activity. If you want to stay in the valley, and money is flush, do go to the **Ahwahnee Hotel** (209-252-4848). That phone number will also get you reservations at the **Yosemite Lodge** and **Camp Curry,** which are considerably cheaper. But not nearly as nice.

For food, the Ahwahnee dining room (209-372-1489) will be happy to accommodate you, but the Pavillion Buffet (209-372-8303) is a good deal less expensive.

Groveland Hotel, circa 1849, with a dozen elegant rooms and an excellent restaurant (209-962-4000, 800-273-3314). Just up the street is the **Iron Door Saloon,** dating from 1852, and the **Iron Door Grill** (209-962-6244). Breakfast has got to be taken at **P.J.'s Cafe** (209-962-8638), at the east end of town; the "A.M. Sourdough Sandwich," with sausage, cheese, and egg, is truly tasteful.

At the top of the hill, called **Priest Grade,** six miles past Groveland, the road splits three ways and there is the abandoned Priest Station Motel, which still offers great views of Don Pedro Reservoir should you walk out on the deck. If you take the middle road you will go down the original very steep and very twisty grade. To the right is the new much less steep version of CA 120. To the left is the Priest-Coulterville Road, and if you follow this for 12 miles you will come to Coulterville, CA 49, and the old **Jeffery Hotel**—very much worth a visit. The hotel is a big place, originally built in 1851, and now owned by a motorcycle-friendly couple, Peter and Cherylann Schimmelfennig (209-878-3471, www.HotelJefferyGold.com). They have a couple of dozen rooms, an excellent restaurant, and a very long bar where

The small town of Jamestown attracts a fair number of morbidly in-clined tourists who like to see an effigy hanging from the gibbit on Main Street.

you can order up your sarsaparilla—or something stronger if you are spending the night. If you go north on CA 49 for 11 miles, you will find yourself at the bottom of Priest Grade.

As you cross the bridge at **Moccasin,** CA 49 comes in from the left, and 120/49 continue together alongside **Don Pedro Reservoir.**

At **Chinese Camp,** stay right on CA 49 while CA 120 goes off to the left. There is not much in Chinese Camp except for a few shabby houses and a couple of brick buildings from the Gold Rush days. As CA 49 merges with CA 108, stay right heading east toward Sonora.

Jamestown is just off of CA 49. You go past the Harley-Davidson dealership. If you want a genuine Harley experience, stay at their "motel," a nice studio behind and separate from the shop (209-984-4888). When entering Jamestown, if you take the well-marked turn to the Business District, you will find an interesting street about a half mile long, with lots of food and trinkets available. And the restored **National Hotel** to eat and sleep at (209-984-3446). Also in Jamestown is the **Railtown State Historical Park,** with old steamers chuffing about on a six-mile run.

Since CA 108 bypasses Sonora, exit right taking CA 49 into Sonora.

For more trips in this region see *Motorcycle Journeys Through California and Baja* by Clement Salvadori, available from Whitehorse Press.

Index

About the Contributors

Bill Kresnak is government affairs editor for *American Motorcyclist* magazine. When he's not writing about bike bans and public land closures he enjoys exploring ghost towns and covered bridges, and riding historic routes like that of the Ohio-Erie canal.

Marty Berke is a resident of Volcan, Chiriqui, Panama. He travels throughout the world for both business and pleasure. Part of that pleasure focuses on finding good roads and new ways to share them with you. He is the author of *Motorcycle Journeys Through New England,* and *Motorcycle Journeys Through the Southwest.* He wishes you safe travels on the small squiggly faint grey road map lines.

Dale Coyner's journeys through the Appalachians began out of a curiosity for what was "around the next bend." He came to riding later than some, purchasing his first motorcycle, a Yamaha Radian, after he finished college. He credits the open, freewheeling nature of motorcycling with firing a sense of wonderment about his surroundings that led to rediscovering his native region. He shares his best finds with you in his book, *Motorcycle Journeys Through the Appalachains.*

Grant Parsons has been an enthusiast ever since he bought his first bike—a 13-year-old 1973 Honda CL350. His journey of fun and discovery was punctuated at first by frustrating electrical troubleshooting on the side of various roads, and, many years later, by stops along the same roads, but this time getting paid to do so as the managing editor of *American Motorcyclist* magazine. He recently bought a 1973 Honda CL350 and is once again struggling with frustrating electrical troubleshooting.

Scott Cochran was born and raised in rural Georgia, and learned how to ride a motorcycle without his parents' knowledge or permission. In his *Motorcycle Journeys Through the American South,* he combines his fascination for the history of the American South with his passion for uncovering its best motorcycle highways and byways. Scott and his wife Sylvia publish *USRiderNews.*

James Holter is associate editor for *American Motorcyclist* magazine and responsible for covering motorcycle competition. He enjoys touring the countryside on his Harley-Davidson Electra Glide. He's also an avid dual-sport and off-road rider.

Toby Ballentine's family has lived in the Rocky Mountains for generations and he has relatives in every state in the Rockies. His motorcycling began at age 12 and has never stopped. He spent tens of thousands of miles riding and camping through the Rockies on his GS and a Yamaha FJR (his wife says the FJR is hers). Though he has motorcycled all over the world, his favorite rides are right at home in the Rocky Mountains. Toby is the author of *Motorcycle Journeys Through the Rocky Mountains.*

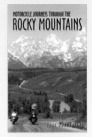

Neal Davis and his wife Sandy have traveled all over the world often by motorcycle. After retiring from a successful career in the oil industry, Neal served in various capacities with organized motorcycle tour operators in Europe and Mexico. Neal and Sandy are currently serving a two-year mission with The Church of Jesus Christ of Latter-Day Saints in South Africa. He is the author of *Motorcycle Journeys Through Texas and Northern Mexico,* and *Motorcycle Journeys Through Southern Mexico.*

Clement Salvadori began riding back when Ike was President and has become one of motorcycling's more erudite observers, having ridden through better than 70 countries on six continents. Over the past 30 years he has written more than a thousand articles for various motorcycle magazines, as well as publishing five books, including *Motorcycle Journeys Through California & Baja* and *101 Road Tales.* He has lived in California since 1980, and uses the town of Atascadero as a base for exploring North American roads, occasionally jetting off to ride the Alps in New Zealand or the Alps in Europe.

Bruce Hansen started motorcycling on a rented 1966 Bridgestone 50 and soon graduated to a Honda 350 scrambler followed by various Harleys, BMWs, and Hondas. He writes about motorcycle travel for *Rider, RoadBike, American Iron, Bagger Magazine, Motorcycle Cruiser Magazine,* and *Motorcycle Escape,* and has written and photographed for *Paddler Magazine* and *Canoe and Kayak.* He lives in Portland, Oregon, and is the author of *Motorcycle Journeys Through the Pacific Northwest.*

Other Books of Interest from Whitehorse Press

Ride Guide to America
The first Ride Guide and companion to Ride Guide to America, Volume 2.
American Motorcyclist Association
ISBN 978-1-884313-51-6 $24.95

The Essential Guide to Motorcycle Travel
How to prepare your bike and yourself for
    extended motorcycle travel.
Dale Coyner
ISBN 978-1-884313-59-2 $24.95

Motorcycle Journeys Through the Alps & Beyond, 4th edition
Indispensable resource for planning your motorcycle tour in Europe.
John Hermann
ISBN 978-1-884313-70-7 $29.95

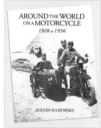

Around the World on a Motorcycle 1928 to 1936
Astute observations of the variety of human culture found
    worldwide in the 1930s from the seat of a Harley-Davidson.
Zoltán Sulkowsky
ISBN 978-1-884313-77-6 $29.95

The Essential Guide to Motorcycle Maintenance
What we all need to know about maintaining
    our motorcycles.
Mark Zimmerman
ISBN 978-1-884313-41-7 $29.95

101 Road Tales
Widsom, musings, and stories from the road by a popular motojournalist.
Clement Salvadori
ISBN 978-1-884313-73-8 $24.95

For more information, please contact:
Customer Service Department,
Whitehorse Press, 107 East Conway Road,
Center Conway, New Hampshire 03813, USA
Phone: 603-356-6556 Fax: 603-356-6590
Email: CustomerService@WhitehorsePress.com

Whitehorse Press
www.WhitehorsePress.com